Qualitative Research Methods in Public Relations and Marketing Communications

Christine Daymon and
Immy Holloway

Routledge
Taylor & Francis Group

LONDON AND NEW YORK

First published 2002
by Routledge
11 New Fetter Lane, London EC4P 4EE

Simultaneously published in the USA and Canada
by Routledge
29 West 35th Stret, New York, NY 10001

Reprinted 2003

Routledge is an imprint of the Taylor & Francis Group

© 2002 Christine Daymon and Immy Holloway

Typeset in Times by Wearset Ltd, Boldon, Tyne and Wear
Printed and bound in Malta by Gutenberg Press Ltd

British Library Cataloguing in Publication Data
A catalogue record for this book is available from the British Library

Library of Congress Cataloging in Publication Data
Daymon, Christine, 1952–
    Qualitative research methods in public relations and marketing
    communications / Christine Daymon & Immy Holloway
        p. cm.
    Includes bibliographical references and index.
    1. Corporations–Public relations–Research–Methodology
    2. Public relations–Research–Methodology. 3. Marketing
    research–Methodology. 4. Qualitative research. I. Holloway, Immy.
    II. Title.
    HD59 .D347 2002
    659.2'07'2–dc21
                                                        2001048321

ISBN 0-415-22273-7 (hbk)
ISBN 0-415-22274-5 (pbk)

Contents

Preface

We have written this book for those studying public relations and marketing communications. Students of advertising, corporate communication, public affairs, communication management, internal communications and marketing are included within our focus. Our chapters are aimed primarily at undergraduate and masters students who are taking courses in research methods or about to embark on dissertation projects. Hopefully, PhD students will use the text as an introduction to the available literature on distinctive qualitative methodologies. Practitioners in the field may find some of the chapters interesting for their alternative approach to the more commonly practised evaluative research with its numbers and statistics.

When writing this text, we had three aims in mind. First, we wanted to help students make an informed judgement about the relevance of qualitative research to current issues in communication management. Second, we wished to provide a tool that would enable them to engage effectively with the 'realities' of managed communication. Third, we hoped to make a contribution towards raising the profile of qualitative methods within public relations and marketing communications research more generally. We have sought to do this by offering practical guidance, together with examples of empirical studies that are based on a qualitative approach. In places, we have presented the views of student researchers about their experiences of researching.

The book is organized into four parts. How to get started is the topic of Part I. This covers the ground between coming to an awareness of the nature of qualitative research and its relevance for contemporary public relations and marketing communications, through to writing a research proposal based on qualitative methods.

Part II is concerned with the design of a research project. It examines different and often co-existing orientations towards research, including case studies, grounded theory, ethnography, discourse analysis and phenomenology. It notes that each of these approaches may encompass a number of specific techniques or methods.

Part III, which discusses the data collection stage, presents a variety of methods for sampling and gathering the data.

Part IV focuses on analysing and interpreting the data and writing them up.

Although the chapters suggest that data collection, analysis and writing are discrete stages, in practice the three often occur simultaneously. The final chapter offers some concluding thoughts about doing research and reflecting upon the process.

The idea for writing this book grew out of our experience of empirical social science as researchers and teachers. We came to the project with diverse interests which converged at the point of qualitative research theory and practice. At one time, one of us worked in industry in public relations and marketing communications, before moving into academe to research, write and teach about the field. One of us is a sociologist, working in the area of health care. She contributes not only an extensive knowledge about the qualitative orientation, but a keen interest in how it can be used to provide insights into social processes, the motivations of human beings and the contexts in which they are situated. These areas concern the depth and diversity of human beings and are highly pertinent to the study of communication management.

We would like to acknowledge the following people for their contributions to this text. First, Matt Holland whose expertise in all things electronic is demonstrated in Chapter 4 and in a section at the end of Chapter 16. The comments of our colleagues Mike Molesworth, Kevin Moloney, Richard Scullion, Les Todres and Stephanie Wheeler helped to clarify our thinking over some of the ideas presented here. Research support from Ai Ling Lai enabled us to finish the book on time. The honest opinions of former students motivated us to write with a 'mindfulness' of the needs and interests of students of the future. Thank you Saori Asakawa, Deliah Cavalli, Kristin Goa, Katrine Jaklin, Joana Machado, Sarah Woodhouse and (especially) Richard Fogg, all now working successfully as practitioners and consultants in public relations and marketing communications.

Christine Daymon and Immy Holloway
Bournemouth, Dorset
Spring 2001

Part I

Getting started

1 The nature of qualitative research and its relevance to public relations and marketing communications

This chapter addresses the distinctiveness of qualitative research and the benefits it holds for exploring contemporary issues in public relations and marketing communications. It notes that:

- two worldviews inform most of the research on managed communication: the interpretive and realist. Qualitative researchers generally, but not always, subscribe to the former.
- different philosophical assumptions are associated with qualitative research.
- qualitative research has distinct features and strengths, including its subjective nature.
- there is an increasing awareness in contemporary public relations and marketing communications of collaborative dialogue. Qualitative research has the potential to enable this to be achieved.

Introduction

Before introducing the distinctive features of qualitative research, we would like to introduce you to the different worldviews behind the research you read about in texts on public relations and marketing communications. By understanding the different stances that researchers deploy to help them conceptualize the world they study, hopefully you will come to appreciate why researchers choose particular methods for their investigations. This, in turn, will help to locate your own perspective as well as inform your knowledge about the cluster of methods that fall within the research approach known as qualitative.

Later in the chapter, we will go on to consider some of the current issues in the field of managed communication, noting how researchers are learning to appreciate the need to engage in collaborative dialogue with all stakeholders. We argue that an important initial means of doing this is by deploying qualitative research methods to understand those who hold or seek to hold a stake in an organization or group. Because qualitative methods tend to be associated with the subjective nature of social reality, as we explain later in the chapter, they are well equipped to provide insights from the perspective of stakeholders, enabling researchers to see things as their informants do.

The research methods that researchers use to help them understand the world of public relations and marketing communications are not neutral techniques but different ways of knowing that world (Bryman 2001). At a simplistic level, qualitative methods tend to be associated with words as the unit of analysis, whereas quantitative methods tend to be linked with numbers. Whether researchers choose to apply qualitative or quantitative methods, each is often linked to a particular worldview related to the nature of knowledge. The two worldviews, or paradigms, which inform most of the research in public relations and marketing communications are the interpretive and the realist (or positivist). Each has different assumptions about the nature of managed communication and how that can be accessed.

Key point

Your orientation to either an *interpretive* or *realist* worldview determines the type of research question you choose for your study and influences the type of investigative methods you select.

The interpretive worldview

Qualitative methods tend to be associated with the *interpretive* worldview. This concerns itself with exploring the way that people 'make sense of their social worlds and how they express these understandings through language, sound, imagery, personal style and social rituals' (Deacon *et al.* 1999: 6). Researchers who adhere to this stance are less interested in studying external forces which may or may not determine people's behaviours, such as the regulations that control advertising standards, or the effect that changing consumer interests have on the types of events that are suitable for sponsorship. Instead they are keen to explore people's intentions, motivations and subjective experiences. They appreciate that people do things based on the meanings they hold, which they attribute to their actions and the actions of others.

Therefore, if you are working within an interpretive stance, you are keen to understand social reality from the point of view of those in it. For example, to study sponsorship, you might investigate a company that has recently been involved in sponsoring an arts event. You might interview people in the company and those involved in running the event, together with some of the audience, to elicit their experiences and thoughts about the sponsorship campaign. You would probably also go to the event to observe how the sponsorship was promoted. This would enable you to see, hear and experience it as a member of the public.

Interpretive researchers challenge the notion that social reality is a given, something 'out there' that shapes people's actions. Instead, they draw on *social constructivism* which is the idea that the 'reality' that we live and work in is built up over time through communication, our interactions with those around us, and our shared history. Reality, therefore, is 'what is shared and taken for granted as to the way the world is to be perceived and understood' (Locke 2001: 9). The reality for those involved in a sponsorship campaign, for example, will differ for different organizations depending on how long people have been working together, the type of people in the team and their experience, the ease with which they are able to communicate with each other, and so on. Therefore, meaning isn't standardized from place to place or person to person. It evolves out of who we are as individuals and the communication interactions we have. Shared meanings are something we accomplish together and they shape our social reality.

Interpretive researchers recognize that in order to understand the world of public relations and marketing communications, they must first actively engage in it before going on to interpret it. Involvement in 'the field' enables them to conceptualize reality from the point of view of those involved in it. By exploring the evidence before coming to an interpretation of it, they embrace the idea that concepts and theories emerge out of the data, that is, they directly relate to a particular, naturally occurring situation. In other words, what you discover in the field isn't determined by the models or theories that you find in the literature before you begin your investigation.

For example, having conducted your sponsorship study, you might come up with a description of the process of being involved in such a campaign. You might find other studies in the literature which have come to similar conclusions. By comparing and contrasting your ideas with theirs, you might provide some informed hunches (working hypotheses) about sponsorship of arts events. Or you might suggest that your findings could be related to other similar organizations.

With such an orientation towards both the nature of the social world and the nature of knowledge about managed communication, it is perhaps unsurprising that interpretive scholars have primarily deployed qualitative methods of research because these allow researchers to get up close to the people they are studying and get involved with them. Qualitative methods, then, are frequently seen to be inseparable from the interpretive, constructivist worldview.

What are the characteristics of qualitative research?

That qualitative methods are informed by an interpretive worldview can be seen in some of its characteristics:

- *Words.* Qualitative research focuses on words rather than numbers, although occasionally numbers are used to indicate the frequency that a theme is found in transcripts or the extent to which a form of action occurs.
- *Researcher involvement.* The main research 'instrument' in qualitative research is the researcher her- or himself who closely engages with the people being studied. This differs from quantitative research where researchers are remote from their informants (because their research is based on methods such as surveys or structured interviews).

- *Participant viewpoints.* A desire to explore and present the various subjective perspectives of participants is associated with qualitative research. Its privileging of subjectivity is also seen in the way that the interpretation of the data is influenced by the researcher's own biography together with their involvement with people in the study.
- *Small-scale studies.* Qualitative researchers are interested in deep exploration in order to provide rich, detailed, holistic description – as well as explanation. Therefore, small samples are the norm.
- *Holistic focus.* Rather than directing their attention to one or two isolated variables, qualitative researchers tend to be oriented to a wide range of interconnected activities, experiences, beliefs and values of people in terms of the context in which they are situated. This provokes qualitative researchers to account for a multiplicity of dimensions and relationships in the context.
- *Flexible.* Although researchers have a topic and an agenda which fuel their research progress, they are usually committed to exploring new and often surprising avenues that emerge as informants reveal their understandings and interests. Research procedures may be unstructured, adaptable and sometimes spontaneous. At times the research process may even be described as rather 'messy' as researchers attempt to unpack the complexities of the social world of public relations and marketing communications. Example 1.1 presents one student's experience of undertaking a project which unfolded in often surprising ways.
- *Processual.* Qualitative research rarely provides static portraits of phenomena. Instead it aims to capture processes that take place over time. The often prolonged engagement of researchers with their research settings means that qualitative research is able to be attuned to change, sequences of events and behaviours, and the transformation of cultures.
- *Natural settings.* On the whole, qualitative investigations are carried out in people's natural environments such as in their offices or where they shop. This enables researchers to observe how they go about their routine activities and interactions. However, this is not always the case as many focus groups involve groups of strangers meeting together in an unfamiliar setting such as a conference room. Even here, however, researchers attempt to engage with participants *about* their natural setting.
- *Inductive then deductive.* Qualitative research tends to start out with inductive reasoning and then, through a sequential process, employs deductive reasoning. This means that you first get ideas from collecting and analysing the data (that is, you move inductively from specific data to more general patterns and commonalities). You then test these ideas out by relating them to the literature and to your further data collection and analysis (deduction). Theory, therefore, emerges primarily out of data collection rather than being generated from the literature and tested out through fieldwork. The literature review at the start of study, therefore, acts to *guide* the study only.

What are the criticisms of qualitative research?

Despite its strengths, qualitative inquiry is not without its limitations, many of which are noted through the course of this book, especially in Chapter 6 where strategies are suggested to address these. Briefly, however, we note four common criticisms as identified by Bryman (2001: 282–3):

Too subjective. Those holding to a quantitative research orientation sometimes accuse qualitative studies of being too impressionistic and subjective. However, subjectivity is the aim of qualitative research, as we noted with regard to 'participant viewpoints' in the previous section. By paying attention to criteria of reliability and validity (or authenticity and trustworthiness) as outlined in Chapter 6, your study will go some way to overcoming this charge.

Difficult to replicate. Because qualitative investigators are the main research instrument, the replicability of a study is practically impossible. But anyway, qualitative researchers are not associated with an interest in replication; their commitment is much more to the integrity of their findings. Careful articulation of the steps taken in the research process helps to clarify the quality of the study and diffuse criticisms of this nature.

Problems of generalization. Qualitative research studies are not supposed to be representative of a larger population, yet a common challenge is that they are too restricted in their conclusions. By providing rich descriptions of what goes on in a particular context, they help to illuminate important issues in a specific case or regarding a particular group of people. Nevertheless, theory-based generalization can be presented, as we explain in Chapter 6.

Lack of transparency. Bryman (2001) argues that qualitative researchers have been remiss in failing to articulate clearly the procedures they followed to select samples, collect the data and analyse them. How data were analysed and interpreted and how a study's conclusions were arrived at are details that are missing from the vast majority of published texts in managed communication. Although the problem is less pronounced in other disciplines, it has not yet been addressed in public relations and marketing communications but needs to be as it relates to the overall quality of investigation. In Chapters 16 and 17, we offer some tips for doing this.

Having discussed the characteristics of qualitative research and noted how they are underpinned by a worldview that is interpretive, we go on to discuss an alternative paradigm that informs knowledge about managed communication.

The realist worldview and quantitative research

The worldview that historically has dominated the field of public relations' and marketing communications' knowledge is the *realist* or positivist. This is concerned to discover universal laws of cause and effect which apply across different times and contexts. Research by Grunig, such as his four models of public relations (Grunig and Hunt 1984, Grunig 1989), falls within the realist framework, as do many of the techniques of campaign evaluation such as Meenaghan's (1991) model of how sponsorship works.

In contrast to the interpretive stance, realism assumes that reality is an objective, observable entity which is independent of those involved in it. Rather than privileging subjectivity, therefore, it emphasizes *objectivity*. If you were to study sponsorship from this perspective, you would start out on the assumption that there are general principles of sponsorship that could be applied to any event or organization. Having read up on these, you would advance some hypotheses (or hunches) about sponsorship that you would test out. A survey of all companies which had engaged recently in sponsoring a variety of events might be a suitable way to start. You could accompany this with another questionnaire to the organizers of sponsored events. The knowledge you derive from your study would take the form of some propositions that would be accepted as facts because they had been checked against reality. What your study would not be able to do would be to provide a rich portrait of the experience and meaning of sponsorship as perceived by the people involved in each sponsorship event, and in their own terms.

The realist worldview usually goes hand-in-hand with quantitative research methods. This is because quantitative techniques seek to distance the researcher from the data, both in the methods of collecting the data (say, by sending out a survey rather than listening to the voices of informants) and also in analysis where numbers and statistics are favoured over words and the organization of language. Other features of quantitative methods are that they tend to be large-scale with a focus on specific factors which are studied in relation to specific other factors. This requires researchers to isolate variables from their natural context in order to study how they work and their effect. You might, for instance, isolate budgets from all the different aspects of sponsorship and test the hypothesis that 'the larger the budget, the more effective the sponsorship programme will be'. A further feature of quantitative studies is that they tend to be structured; procedures and questions are determined before primary research begins. This means that theory is tested out through research rather than emerging from the research. Because quantitative methods are associated with numbers and detachment, they are not well suited to description. This contrasts with qualitative methods, where deep, rich description is one of the latter's key strengths.

A trawl through the literature on public relations and marketing (as well as marketing communications) indicates that most studies are realist in their standpoint and quantitative in their methodological approach. Even where qualitative methods are used, it is not unusual to find a realist stance behind the interpretive façade. This applies to both scholarly and industry research and occurs when researchers apply the methods pragmatically. For example, in the advertising sector, qualitative focus groups are used extensively to test out advertising concepts prior to the development of advertisements or to test campaigns before they go into production. Such research, however, rarely goes beyond sifting the good ads from the bad because the focus too often is on the performance of advertising rather than on what the ad means for research participants. When qualitative methods are used in a purely technical way within a realist framework, their attachment to their interpretive intellectual heritage tends to be ignored and therefore their full potential is not explored.

So, where does this leave us? We have argued that:

- the two main worldviews which inform the knowledge we hold about public relations and marketing communications are generally associated with a particular research approach.
- mainstream research on managed communication is essentially realist in its tenor, appropriating primarily quantitative methods of investigation although sometimes qualitative methods are used pragmatically.
- qualitative research which is connected to an interpretive worldview has great potential for the study of communication from the viewpoint of those involved. Indeed, qualitative studies – or investigations which combine both qualitative and quantitative approaches – appear to be gaining a foothold in the communication, marketing and management literature. This testifies to a growing appreciation of the value of the qualitative approach.

Up to this point, we have written in fairly general terms about the characteristics and advantages of qualitative research. Now we turn our attention to the benefits it is able to provide for our understanding of public relations and marketing communications. First we note some of the current issues in the field and then relate these to the aims of qualitative research.

Current issues in public relations and marketing communications

In our discussions so far we have assumed a connection between public relations and marketing communications. Not everyone would agree with this. Indeed, the disciplines of public relations and marketing communications have developed on parallel courses. At their most simplistic, each has perceived the other as subservient to its own focus. Public relations, for instance, in its concern to build goodwill and mutual understanding between organizations or groups and all their publics, stresses that its remit is broad. Marketing communications activities are considered to be those devoted to one portion only of the range of an organization's publics, that is, the served or to-be-served markets and those who influence them. From a public relations perspective, marketing communications is just one of the many facets of public relations.

On the other hand, as far as a marketing communications stance is concerned, corporate goals are primarily marketing goals. Therefore all managed communications are pressed into the service of informing and persuading customers or potential customers to 'perceive and experience the organization and its offerings as solutions to some of their current and future dilemmas' (Fill 1999: 1). Whether public relations is oriented to brand development and product support, or to the maintenance of corporate goodwill, a marketing communications perspective views it as only one component of the many that make up the marketing communications mix.

Yet not all theorists or practitioners delimit their territories so sharply. Some define public relations and marketing communications as overlapping, complementary practices. Public relations concentrates on developing beneficial relationships internally and in the wider context, thus enhancing the willingness of markets, audiences and publics to think favourably about the organization. This clears the way for marketing communications to go about its business of promoting the organization's products and services. In turn, marketing communications activities contribute to the organization's reputation and image, key items on the public relations agenda.

There are overlaps at a technical level too. The public relations technique of product promotion is used by marketers to improve awareness of new brands, especially in computer-mediated communications where advertising is increasingly less effective. Advertising campaigns are often run specifically to generate publicity at a product or corporate level. This cross-over between the practices reflects similarities between the disciplines in that both are concerned with managing communication.

The notion of managing has been aligned with the concept of control. Traditionally, the literature has tended to emphasize how communicators, in a relatively unfettered way, can rationalize communication systems, manipulate their audiences and achieve success through their so-called 'excellent' but monologic activities. Audiences are *targeted*, messages are *planned*, strategies are created in order to sculpt the images that audiences hold about organizations, and passive consumers are shunted through the various stages of response hierarchy models to their destination at some sort of post-purchase nirvana. In this way, public relations and marketing communications have been seen to be about taking control of information and using it persuasively in order to achieve the goals of the organization.

In recent years, however, a subtle change has taken place in both disciplines and also more widely as modern organizations have shifted their focus from control to *coordination*. In effect, this results in less attachment to formalization – the implementation of explicit regulations, policies and impersonal procedures of control – and a greater commitment to personal, informal mechanisms of coordination such as the building and maintaining of relationships. At the same time, public relations and marketing communications are turning their attention to notions of dialogue and collaboration – communicating *with* people rather than *to* audiences. Creating a collaborative dialogue means negotiating meanings in an interactive manner – in other words finding out what each is about and adjusting to each other. It is not sufficient for organizations or groups to state the identity they desire – or to project the potential benefits of a brand – unless they have first heard, appreciated and taken on board the concerns and opinions of those with whom they are talking.

Heath writes that in public relations, 'publics must be enjoined in dialogue based on who they are rather than merely on who the organizations [. . .] define them to be' (2000: 7). In the same way, the marketing communications scholar, Fill, states that 'good relationships are developed by appreciating the views held by others' and by 'putting oneself in their shoes' (1999: 394). In the early part of the twenty-first century, then, both public relations and marketing communications have a new emphasis on collaborative dialogue.

Key point

Public relations and marketing communications are concerned with managed communication. The two disciplines are increasingly interested in coordinating communication through relationships which are developed and maintained by collaborative dialogue.

While the aim is a worthy one, it is complicated by the increasingly diverse environment in which communicators operate today. The popularity of the Internet has resulted in rapid global communications where communications teams and audiences are spread across the world. No longer can communicators expect their audiences to speak in the same language or to hold similar beliefs and values. Increasingly practitioners and researchers of communication find themselves working not only online with people from different cultures but also – as multicultural workforces become more commonplace – situated in the same physical spaces. Public relations and marketing communicators find themselves servicing clients or operating alongside those who are culturally different, with different cultural assumptions and styles of communication. In order to engage in collaborative dialogue with dissimilar people, public relations and marketing communicators need to be 'mindful' of others' perceptions and evaluations.

Being 'mindful' means a readiness to shift your frame of reference and an openness to new ways of seeing the world. It doesn't mean that you have to agree with someone else's point of view, but it does mean that you have an empathy with them – you know where they're coming from. Companies, for instance, don't just collect information on consumers or lobby groups. They listen to them, seeking to discover their opinions, motivations, expectations and experiences. They try to find out what their stakeholders consider is worthwhile or relevant. They recognize that there is more than one perspective on any issue and that stakeholders will use their own perspectives to interpret company messages.

When companies and others involved in public relations and marketing communications seek to be mindful, they endeavour to get inside the world of stakeholders by first setting aside their own notions of what is appropriate or desirable. This indicates a willingness to appreciate that others may not see things in the same way that they do. It is not until they have reached this point that they can engage successfully in conversations that use the language of stakeholders. Ting-Toomey (1999) suggests that collaborative dialogue involves 'mindful' listening and a respectful attitude regarding the viewpoints, needs and interests of others. Concurrently, it also entails being mindful of your own needs, interests and goals, while thinking reflectively and critically about your communicative encounters.

Key point
Collaborative dialogue involves:

- 'mindful' listening.
- a respectful attitude towards stakeholders' viewpoints, needs and interests.
- recognizing that there is more than one perspective on the world and your interactions with the people in it.
- being 'mindful' of your own needs, interests and goals.
- thinking reflectively and critically about your communicative encounters.

The relevance of qualitative research to public relations and marketing communications

So what value does qualitative research offer to contemporary public relations' and marketing communications' knowledge and practice? The act of being mindful, or putting yourself into the shoes of others, as Fill (1999) recommends, is precisely the goal of most qualitative researchers. Their interest is to understand the world of lived experience from the point of view of those who live and work in it. They are concerned with subjective reality, that is, what events, objects and others mean to other people.

In the past, many scholars and practitioners of public relations and marketing communications have avoided the idea of engaging with and participating in the world of those with whom they wish to communicate. (This is especially notable in public relations' evaluation research.) The dominant worldview has been that numbers talk and that qualitative inquiry is suitable only for early, exploratory research. The latter, however, has failed to utilize the full potential of qualitative methods. Much 'exploratory' research has served merely to add credibility to what the agency already 'knows', to justify the expenditure of a client's budget, or to find out why something has gone wrong (Miglani 1996). That managed communication is a fairly new academic discipline may account for its overriding concern to develop universalistic principles from quantitative studies. There has been little interest by researchers to do research that entails personal involvement with people in natural environments.

Lindlof writes that: 'For too long in the history of communication scholarship, we have focused on what messages refer to, or the effects they have, without examining what messages are or how their articulation creates social realities for speakers and audiences' (1995: 22). We would add that the processes and contexts in which those messages and meanings are created have also been ignored. Instead, quantitative studies have been employed to advocate views of the world that 'do not value the study of situated, emergent and reflexive human phenomena' (ibid.).

From a practitioner perspective, Talmage (1998) writes of his frustrations with the inflexibility of quantitative research where questions are pre-determined and often require a 'tick in the box' response. In noting that quantitative surveys leave no room for informants to say what they really mean or where they're really at, he asks:

> If you seek a mutual relationship with your customer, it makes little sense to ask a bunch of questions – then, insultingly, to make no response [...] Customer feedback that forms an integral part of the relationship between customer and supplier does not fit the market research paradigm of anonymous informants and statistical tables representing collective views. In a context of relationship marketing ... the individual customer's response represents an opportunity to engage in further dialogue [...] If such a dialogue serves to build better relationships, then the opportunity might be offered to all customers, rather than only to some of them. Statistical information about customer perceptions of product and service quality could become merely a valuable by-product.
>
> (1998: 17)

The ambivalence towards qualitative research is diminishing as public relations and marketing communications shift in their focus towards collaborative dialogue. An emerging interest in the micro, the particular and the context – such as, how individuals infuse the advertising of particular companies with meanings and incorporate these into their lifestyles – is beginning to be seen to be as much of interest as the universal. This leads to new types of research questions being asked – such as what is important to individuals rather than how informants respond to what is important to researchers or companies. In this way, there is a willingness to explore the agendas of research participants. Insights and the generation of working hypotheses directly from the data are of interest rather than the measurement of large numbers or the evaluation of pre-determined concepts.

In future, research into managed communication will more conscientiously accommodate different styles of inquiry so that both qualitative and quantitative approaches will co-exist on an equal footing. This may mean the increasing application of multiple strategies in a single research project (such as using document analysis, observation and interviews where one approach complements another), or it may mean looking at the same issue in different ways, using qualitative research for one type of question and quantitative for another. Most interestingly, though, will be the acceptance and deployment of qualitative research as a valid, stand-alone means for understanding patterns and connections in the complex and unexplored, such as how an event or action occurs, how it functions in social contexts, and what it means for participants concerned.

Helpful hint
The research question influences your research methodology. Make sure you have a sound fit between the two. Not all research questions call for a qualitative approach.

Questions that concern qualitative researchers

If you are interested in being mindful of others, of 'walking in their shoes', then your research questions will be those that attempt to unpack the views of people in your study. Lindlof (1995: 6) suggests that questions which animate qualitative inquiry are: What's going on here? What is the communicative action that is being performed? How do they do it? What does it mean to them? How do they interpret what it means to others? How do *we* interpret and document how they act, what they tell us about what they know, and how they justify their actions? What is the relation of us to them, of self to other?

The research question, therefore, drives your methodology. Your worldview determines your research question. Once you have decided on a question that demands a qualitative approach, you can begin to make choices about your research orientation – a case study, grounded theory study, ethnography, discourse analysis or phenomenology – and the various methods you will apply: interviews, focus groups, observation, document research, projective and enabling techniques, or critical incident analysis. These we go on to discuss in the following chapters.

Summary

- The interest in collaborative dialogue by scholars and practitioners of public relations and marketing communications resonates well with the aims of qualitative researchers.
- Qualitative research holds great potential for the study of public relations and marketing communications because of its concern with 'mindfulness'.
- Two worldviews inform most public relations and marketing communications research. The interpretive stance focuses on the constructed nature of social reality as seen by those involved in it. The realist perspective regards reality as an objective, observable entity which is independent of those involved in it.
- Qualitative research tends to be associated with an interpretive worldview. Sometimes, though, researchers use qualitative methods in a pragmatic fashion and pay less heed to their philosophical influences.
- Qualitative methods are depicted as being about words as the unit of analysis rather than numbers. They are associated with small-scale studies, close involvement of the researcher with the context under investigation, flexibility, participant viewpoints, and a holistic focus, amongst other features.

• It is important to ensure a fit between your research approach and your main research question. Questions suitable for qualitative research include how something occurs, how it functions in its context and what it means for participants.

Example 1.1 The process of carrying out a student research project

Joana Machado's (2000) dissertation for a masters degree in corporate communication was entitled *Multiple Identity Traits and Multiple Identifications in a Geographically Dispersed Organization. A Case Study Investigation of the British Council.* The different stages of her research are outlined in Example 8.2. Here she reveals some of her experiences of conducting research that was primarily qualitative.

Selecting a topic
I knew I wanted to explore the more intangible assets of organizations. I first became interested in that area when I undertook a small-scale research project on corporate reputation as part of my coursework earlier in the year. I started looking at topics like cross-cultural management and communication, corporate culture, organizational culture, reputation, corporate personality and identity. These were the topics I most enjoyed studying on the taught part of the masters programme. I had good access to an international organization (the British Council) and knew that I would be able to carry out a case study there. The British Council has offices all around the world and my reading led me to think about the possible difficulties they might be facing with regard to their corporate identity. So I decided to focus on some aspect of that.

Developing a research question
My main research question was more a result than a starting point. It was equally informed by the literature and the data analysis. At first the question was what is the organization's organizational identity? But then I broke it into many others: e.g. is there a consistent identity or does it vary according to factors such as geographical region and the type of people employed? Because my data collection and literature review were done in a cyclical fashion, new questions arose as I read the literature, e.g. is there a connection between identity and identification? At the same time, the data suggested questions that led me back to the literature, e.g. does the type of employment contract that employees have influence their identification with the organization? and does it influence the organizational identity? Throughout my research, I shifted back and forth between the literature and the data that I was collecting. It was only right at the end that I became clear about the main aim of the study.

Selecting a research design
I chose a grounded theory approach by talking to my supervisor and reading about it. I decided to use four different methods based on what I needed and wanted, but also on what I could access and collect. At first I thought of doing mainly interviews but then I realized interviews were hard

to get because people were not always available and because they were geographically dispersed. So I decided to do a few interviews, undertake document analysis (which included website analysis), and use a questionnaire with open-ended questions. Also, at first I didn't plan to use email conversations as a method of data collection but they emerged spontaneously and I realized they were an important source of information. Luckily, I got a very good response rate to the questionnaire.

Problems with the methodology were that:

- I ended up with too many sources of data (questionnaire + interviews + document analysis + informal conversations via email) – and of course far too much data!
- it was hard to get hold of people to interview. Either they were too busy or didn't want to talk to me.
- I had difficulty in accessing internal documents such as communication plans, minutes and manuals. Many of these were confidential and I wasn't given clearance to read them.

Pleasures in carrying out the research were:

- meeting people and listening to their different experiences and opinions.
- receiving words of encouragement from many anonymous respondents participating in the survey.
- a sense of global reach when coordinating a questionnaire to twenty-seven countries
- seeing the findings emerge and make sense.

Developing theoretical concepts
I found the theories very, very gradually, by discussing with my supervisor, collecting and analysing the data, going back to things I had read before. I read around the topic, looking at the public relations, marketing, management and organization studies literature, and then wrote about the main definitions and elements related to my topic. Then I started some fieldwork and from there, new aspects were brought into my thinking. This led me to a new round of reading, which helped me to shape the next stages in the data collection. The process was cyclical all the way through and this ensured that the debates in the literature review corresponded to those in the analysis of the findings. Therefore, my literature review chapter was not ready until I had finished writing the analysis chapter.

Until I completed the dissertation, I was not very clear about what I was going to find out and conclude. I found the whole process very exciting. It was like trying to solve a puzzle.

Relating to the supervisor
Writing a dissertation is a very solitary work. I was going so in-depth in my thoughts and dilemmas, and the issues were so specific, so complex or even so insignificant, that no one else would listen to me. At the same time, I was becoming obsessed with the dissertation and I would some-

times think or dream of nothing else. In that sense, I really needed to talk about it and my supervisor was 'the only person on earth' who could understand me. I found tutorials very stimulating: each was like a boost of energy and ideas. The same for written feedback on my drafts. Communication via email was very useful too, although I'm very glad I was not doing my dissertation away from the university and relying only on email to relate to my supervisor. In my case email was good to schedule tutorials, ask straightforward questions and other simple things.

Feedback from my supervisor was crucial for me. On the one hand, it helped me to maintain a sense of the big picture and develop my thinking. On the other hand, it called attention to detail and forced me to do better. Even better than what I thought my best was.

Afterwards

After I had finished the dissertation, I approached the British Council and spoke informally about my findings with one of the senior managers there. It was interesting to see that his opinions and experience corroborated most of my findings. That gave me confidence to do a more formal presentation to the organization. They said that some of my findings were surprising, others were like looking into a mirror. This was a rare opportunity to share my views. Giving and getting feedback in this way was very rewarding because I never expected my dissertation to be of use to anyone other than myself.

2 Selecting a topic and relating to your supervisor

This chapter aims to get you started on the road to undertaking research. It deals with:

- how to go about selecting an appropriate research topic.
- ways of triggering your ideas and developing a central research question.
- two key characteristics of research: originality and feasibility.
- the personal value of the research topic.
- relating to your research supervisor.

Coming up with the initial idea

Finding an interesting and feasible research topic is rarely a straightforward, logical process because good ideas originate in a mix of theory, experience and prior findings. 'What am I most interested in?' is the first question to ask yourself. Unless a topic relates to something you have a genuine interest in – whether intellectually, politically, culturally or just because you've always wanted to find out more about it – it is unlikely that you will enjoy doing your research project, or even do it well.

Helpful hint
Sources to trigger your ideas about a general area to research:

- the academic and professional literature.
- your own experiences and interests.
- experts.
- the priorities of research funders.
- your academic supervisor.

Read the literature

The professional literature draws attention to the companies and people involved in current industry issues (in the UK, trade journals include *Campaign, PR Week, Marketing Week* and *Marketing*). It helps to generate ideas for research topics as well as highlighting potential informants and case study organizations. The academic literature points to the topics that have already been researched, where there are gaps in the literature, or where research needs to be extended or developed. You might consider carrying out research on a similar topic to one that has been investigated elsewhere, using the same methods but conducting your investigation in a different context, such as a different culture or commercial sector or type of organization. For example, much public relations research stems from the United States of America and similar research could usefully be undertaken in other geographical regions in order to confirm, add to or challenge its findings.

An important point to keep in mind, however, is that qualitative studies, unlike quantitative studies, cannot be truly replicated for a number of reasons. First, the researcher him- or herself is the research tool, that is, data are collected through direct interaction between the researcher and informants. Each researcher, therefore, sees the world through the unique lens of his or her own background, personality and understanding of the subject. Second, the in-depth exploration of a phenomenon or topic differs from one research project to another. Each project follows a different path because of the inductive nature of qualitative research. Third, qualitative research is flexible; the sequence of interview questions or the focus of observation varies between studies. Therefore, while the use of other researchers' ideas and methods is helpful, you will not be able to completely replicate an earlier study in another context.

Example 2.1 Applying the ideas of previous research to a different cultural context

Betteke Van Ruler (1997) used both qualitative and quantitative methods to study public relations practitioners in the Netherlands. She applied David Dozier's (1984, 1992) ideas, which were based on the North American public relations sector, to help her identify the roles of Dutch practitioners. However, she extended his role categories to take account of the different Dutch context.

Instead of investigating a similar topic in a different context, you might think about applying the ideas of previous research to a different sample. This will, of course, depend upon your own interests and the particular gap in the literature that you have identified.

Example 2.2 Applying the ideas of previous research to a different sample

Denise DeLorme and Leonard Reid (1999) developed an earlier study of American moviegoers' perceptions of product placement in films. The original study in 1994 involved an homogeneous sample of frequent moviegoers who were students aged between 18–21. The 1999 investigation had a heterogeneous sample of both frequent and infrequent moviegoers in two different age groups, 18–21 and 35–48. Their findings indicated that different age groups held disparate meanings about brands in films.

Useful sources are journal articles and books (at the end of these, you will usually find suggestions and implications for further research), unpublished theses and dissertations, conference proceedings and reports, reports from government-sponsored bodies and research institutions, reviews of the field of study, e.g. *Handbook of Public Relations* edited by Heath (2000) and *Marketing Communications* by Fill (1999), as well as the media (such as the dedicated media and marketing sections in some newspapers).

Example 2.3 Finding a research idea from a newspaper article

A study by Judy Motion (2000) of the personal promotion strategies of women politicians in New Zealand was sparked by a media article on the female leader of the New Zealand opposition party. The article included a photo captioned 'leadership passion' where the party leader and her husband were portrayed as lovers. Motion recognized that this positioning of a woman as a lover instead of a politician is a media trend that focuses on women politicians as gendered subjects. She wondered, therefore, how public relations techniques might be used by women politicians to construct their identities as politicians rather than allow themselves to be constituted as gendered subjects. This led her to design a study which involved interviewing women members of parliament, women mayors and public relations practitioners who work with New Zealand women politicians.

Relate it to your own experiences and concerns

Your own experiences and concerns can provide a rich source of ideas for research. Situations or activities at work may spark an initial thought or question which, on reflection, provides the basis for an interesting research project. For example, Sarah Woodhouse, an undergraduate public relations student, spent a year on work placement in a large London company. She discovered that only the most basic publicity techniques were practised in the PR department. This she found surprising because her more senior colleagues in the company actively espoused the need to practise 'excellent' public relations. In order to uncover reasons for the discrepancy, Sarah decided to focus her final year dissertation on this topic, specifically aiming to explore if communication practices are influenced by organizational culture. Because Sarah was already known to the organization, she was able to gain good access for interviews and questionnaires.

Another opportunity for research could be provided by the voluntary organization where you help out, such as enabling you to examine the effects of cause-related marketing, for instance. Similarly, suppose you are involved in sport or drama; it is possible that you already have a good list of potential informants for a study into the effectiveness of sponsorship activities.

Consider your gender, age or ethnic background; you may have access or insights into issues that are unavailable to others. However, be cautious about drawing on your own experiences. On the basis of these, you may have acquired particular biases or made prior assumptions. Therefore, it is advisable to enter the research arena with an open and flexible mind, suspending some of the ideas you already have about the research phenomenon so that you are unprejudiced about it.

Example 2.4 Drawing on one's own background to find a research topic

Beatrice Bergner trained as a classical actress and performed on the stage for many years in Germany and also on television before deciding to study for a masters degree in corporate communication. For her dissertation, she wanted to bring together her interests in drama and management communication. Therefore, she chose to investigate if theatre-based rehearsal techniques could be helpful in developing managers' communication skills. Her unique background enabled her to draw on both German and English scholarship in the fields of drama, management, public relations and marketing communications. Her primary research consisted of interviews with managers, management trainers and a director of the Royal Shakespeare Company. She also carried out observations of communication training workshops where she was able to apply her specialist knowledge to help her understand the suitability of the techniques being taught to managers.

Talk to experts

Conferences are useful for stimulating novel research topics for a number of reasons. First, they provide the opportunity to hear some of the most up-to-date thinking. Whereas the papers published in academic journals may have been written one to two years previously (because of long lead times), conferences allow researchers to present and debate their working ideas. Second, conferences are useful for making contacts and networking. A casual conversation over coffee with an expert in your area may generate a whole new set of possible research topics.

Find out the priorities of research funders

Grant-awarding and funding agencies regularly publish details of their current research priorities, inviting researchers to apply for financial support. While it is not wise to be driven by someone else's agenda, new research ideas may be triggered by a funder's call for applications and proposals.

If you are being sponsored to undertake a course of study, say by your employer, you might have little say in the selection of a research topic which is determined by the priorities of your employing organization. Ideally, though, your employer will act as a sounding board, allowing you to test out ideas that may have both educational and commercial value. It is worth bearing in mind that the expectations of sponsoring organizations and educational institutions differ, and it is not uncommon for employers to try to influence the research design and dissemination of results. If this is the case, it is essential that you endeavour to uphold the academic aims and standards of your course.

Talk to your academic supervisor

Because your supervisor is likely to be experienced at guiding students through the research process, he or she is an ideal person to bounce ideas off. Aside from offering advice about how to brainstorm your way to a topic, or how feasible your research ideas are likely to be, your supervisor will have suggestions for topics, perhaps in areas he or she is currently researching. We discuss the student–supervisor relationship later in this chapter.

If you are a postgraduate research student, you should expect to cover more than one of the above in order to establish that their work is original and adds to current knowledge.

Identifying a topic and a central research question

Having trawled through the literature, talked about your ideas and reflected upon them, it is probable that you have now identified a fairly general area that you would like to research. At this stage, it might be something as broad as consumer behaviour amongst youth. However, this is too wide a topic to be achievable, so the next stage is to narrow down your ideas.

Wolcott (1990) uses the analogy of a zoom lens on a camera to identify a focus for research. In photography, if photographers zoom in on one small image, they gain considerably in detail. They zoom back out again in order to see the broader context in which the narrow image is situated. In research, you apply the same concept. Taking the broad area of interest, you zoom in on a more manageable aspect of it. Is there something missing from existing studies in this area? Is there something related to the topic that you are particularly concerned about? Eventually, you will be able to identify a number of researchable topics in your chosen area.

For instance, the area of youth and consumer behaviour could be refined to a study of youth culture and the meaning of consumption, or communication with youth markets, or influences on university students' purchasing habits, and so on. Eventually, you will zoom back out again in order to set your research into its broader setting, associating the topic with relevant literature, and relating it to previous empirical studies as well as a conceptual framework.

However, what you are trying to do at this early stage is to come up with a topic that is researchable and manageable, and for which you can go on to develop a single, overarching research question that will guide the research. Qualitative research usually starts out with a *how* or a *what* question. Although *why* questions are sometimes found in qualitative studies, they are more likely to occur in quantitative studies because the latter is more interested in studying cause and effect (although this is not necessarily excluded in qualitative research).

Qualitative research seeks to identify how people interact with their world (what they do), and how they experience and understand their world. So, for instance, if you were to conduct a qualitative investigation on the topic of university students' purchasing habits, you might ask the question, 'What factors influence university students' intentions to buy?' Further sub-questions emerge once you get into the process of reading the literature and commencing the fieldwork.

Example 2.5 Start generally then focus down

General area of interest:
Relationship marketing in the retail sector.

Research topic:
Relationship marketing strategies targeted at retail customers.

Central research question:
Which aspect of marketing communications campaigns is most conducive to building long-term relationships with customers?

Aim:
To investigate which aspect of marketing communications campaigns is most conducive to building long-term relationships with customers.

Unlike quantitative research where a research plan and objectives are strictly defined from the outset, qualitative research usually evolves during the research process. This is because the rich data that are collected in qualitative research provide an opportunity to change focus as guided by the ongoing analysis. Such changes of direction do not 'come out of the blue but reflect the subtle interplay between theory, concepts and data' (Silverman 2000: 63). This is discussed again later in the chapter but, in the meantime, we return to the subject of the initial selection of the topic and the central research question.

In qualitative research, topics are selected because they are either a problem for which you seek an answer, or because they are a mystery that you wish to solve.

An interesting problem

When the central focus of research is a communication-related problem, the study typically aims to assess the nature of the problem in order to find an answer. The problem might be a situation, a context or an issue that you find intrinsically interesting, perhaps one from your own job-related experience or from reading the scholarly or professional literature.

Having identified an interesting problem, you need to establish that it is a worthwhile topic to study. Creswell (1998) suggests asking, 'Why is this study needed?' because this will start you thinking about the 'source' of the problem and the literature that relates to the topic. The rationale for the study of a particular problem might be to fill a void in existing literature, to establish a new line of thinking, to assess an issue with an understudied group or population, or because the study heightens

> awareness for experience which has been forgotten and overlooked. By heightening awareness and creating dialogue, it is hoped research can lead to better understanding of the way things appear to someone else and through that insight lead to improvements in practice.
>
> (Barritt 1986: 20)

Motion's (2000) study of New Zealand women politicians (which is outlined in Example 2.3 earlier in the chapter) started out with a problem: how could women politicians use public relations techniques to construct their identity as politicians instead of gendered subjects?

A mystery

Taking a slightly different approach, Alvesson and Sköldberg (2000) suggest that because the research process is all about solving a mystery, it can be compared to a detective novel. Two central components are involved: formulating the mystery and then solving it. To get started, the researcher asks 'What *puzzle* or *mystery* am I trying to solve?' According to Silverman (2000), there are three kinds of puzzle:

- How or why did X develop?
- How does X work?
- What influence does X have on Y?

Therefore, if your interest is in relationship marketing in the retail sector, you might find you are interested in one of the following questions:

- How or why do hotels build relationships with their customers?
- How do marketing communications strategies that aim to maintain relationships with customers differ from those designed to develop awareness in customers?

• Which aspect of marketing communications campaigns is most conducive to building long-term relationships with customers?

Having decided on a central research question, this can be restated as the aim of your research.

In quantitative research, researchers go on to develop a set of objectives or hypotheses which determine in advance a tightly structured line of inquiry. Hypotheses are like a set of predictions about what you expect to find in the collected data. They act, therefore, as a 'recipe' or formula for how the study should be conducted. In contrast, qualitative research is more adaptable, unfolding as it goes along. It is not uncommon for qualitative researchers to spend some time in fieldwork before deciding what aspects of their topic are important to investigate in depth. This is because qualitative researchers are primarily interested in understanding communication from the perspective of their informants. Initially at least, they usually work inductively, trying to generate theories that will help them understand their data. This is in contrast to much quantitative research which, on the whole, deductively tests hypotheses with the collected data. We discuss the inductive process further in Chapter 16.

However, just because qualitative research is flexible, there is no excuse not to come up with a clear sense of purpose from the outset, argues Silverman (2000). In making this statement, he ignores a key principle of grounded theory (a qualitative approach which we discuss in Chapter 8) which requires you to begin *without* a hypothesis. The idea in grounded theory is that your research focus develops from the data you collect. In this way you generate ideas and theory that are directly relevant to the context you are studying. In general, however, it is worth developing a central research question or research aim from the outset because this guides everything you do.

Over the course of the research process, your central research question leads you towards the literature that is relevant for your project. As you read,

Central Research Question

Literature <----> Fieldwork

Sub-Questions

What data to collect

How to collect the data

How to analyse the data

How to answer the central research question from findings

How to develop theory that relates to the central research question

Figure 2.1 The Central Research Question Guides the Research Project.

subsequent research questions take shape. These, in turn, indicate the type of data you need to gather, and the most appropriate means of collecting and analysing them. Your central research question, therefore, focuses your whole study. Eventually, you link the results of your analysis back to your main question, providing an answer and also, hopefully, developing some theoretical principles from the study.

Originality and feasibility

There is little point in undertaking qualitative research projects unless your research can be shown to be original and feasible. If it is not original, then knowledge will not advance. If it is not feasible, then it is unlikely that the research methods will produce findings that solve the research problem or mystery. The characteristics of originality and feasibility are now outlined.

Originality

Although research should make an original contribution to the body of knowledge, in reality it is very difficult to be completely original. Instead, researchers aim to add to already existing knowledge in order to help further understanding about managed communication.

Silverman (2000) suggests that one way to achieve the latter is to follow a published study that mirrors your own research interests. From the wealth of previous studies in public relations and marketing communications, it is possible that someone has already conducted an investigation on your topic. If this is the case, you could follow the lines of the previous study in its entirety or, if time and resources prevent this, use it to guide your research approach. An earlier work, for instance, may lend support for your choice of research methods. On the other hand, if you consider that it is defective in its sample, method, analysis or interpretation, you could offer your adapted methodology as an attempt to redress the limitations of the previous investigation. Other research on the same topic encourages you to reflect on your own approach and conclusions in an informed way. Following others, therefore, is not rote imitation but should involve creatively challenging a previously conducted study (Locke, Spirduso and Silverman 2000).

Obviously, the extent of 'originality' required for a research project will differ between undergraduate and postgraduate levels. MPhil or PhD theses are required to make a significant, original contribution. Whichever level you are working at, your study should aim to fulfil the criteria for originality by:

- discovering new insights, and/or
- providing evidence of independent, critical thought (Silverman 2000).

Building on the ideas of Phillips and Pugh (2000), we suggest that original research can be characterized in three ways:

- it is a novel development of an existing idea or issue.
- it is a novel application because it cross-fertilizes concepts, techniques or methodologies in new ways.
- it is a novel interpretation of previous work or ideas.

Originality: novel developments

Studies of this nature achieve one or more of the following. They:

- *Set down a major piece of new information in writing for the first time.* Elsbach and Sutton (1992) carried out a longitudinal study of how organizations use publicity to gain legitimacy for controversial and possibly unlawful actions. They showed that publicists in two social movement organizations applied impression management tactics to transform events from identity-threatening into events that ultimately protected and possibly even enhanced organizational image. The work of Elsbach and Sutton leads us to question the ethics of some public relations practices.
- *Continue someone else's idea or develop further their methodology.* In 1997, Johnson explored communicators' use of computer-mediated communications. Newland Hill and White (2000) built on her work by studying practitioners' perceptions of how computer-mediated communications fitted into existing communications strategies.
- *Bring new evidence to bear on an old issue.* Although the topic of creativity as it applies to the execution and outcome of projects and campaigns has been explored in some depth, there are few investigations into how creativity is organized and managed at an organizational level within the public relations consultancy sector. With this in mind, Daymon (2000) investigated the experiences of public relations consultants, and presented evidence to illustrate how creativity is stimulated or stifled within consultancies.
- *Carry out empirical work that has not been done before.* Moloney (1996) identified a significant knowledge gap about commercial lobbyists in relation to their 'for hire' role. For the first time, he conducted research on this topic, interviewing in depth the clients of lobbyists and also the decision-makers about their attitudes and relationships with lobbyists.

Originality: novel applications

Studies of this nature achieve one or more of the following. They:

- *Apply a concept from research in one country/culture to another.* The results of a study in Belgium by De Pelsmacker and Geuens (1996) indicated that different communication effects result from different emotional stimuli: warmth, eroticism and humour. In 1998, the same researchers used a similar mixed-method research design to study the same phenomena in

Poland in order to understand if consumer responses are affected by differences in cultures and also marketing and advertising traditions.

- *Apply techniques, concepts or methodologies normally associated with one discipline to another.* Studies which employ a discourse analysis methodology are scarce in marketing communications although they are more common in psychology and sociology. By following this critical approach, Hackley (2000) was able to bring to the surface the underlying issues of power and tacit control in a London advertising agency.

Originality: novel interpretations

Studies of this nature achieve one or more of the following. They:

- *Make a synthesis that has not been done before.* Dall'Olmo Riley and de Chernatony (2000) explored the views of senior consultants in corporate and marketing communications agencies. They uncovered theoretical and conceptual similarities between the notions of 'the brand' and relationship marketing and put forward the idea of relationship marketing as a further step in the branding process.
- *Use already known material but with a new interpretation.* There are various ways of undertaking a secondary analysis of other researchers' material. You might, for example, read published reports or documents in the light of a new perspective or different research question from that engaged in the first inquiries. Or you might reuse an existing dataset (such as all the transcripts from someone else's research project) and derive interpretations, conclusions, or knowledge additional to, or different from those presented in the first report.
- *Use the author's own voice and perspective in writing.* Katsutoshi Fushimi speaks both Japanese and English fluently, is a native of Japan, has lived in the United States for some time and is an expert judoist (McAlexander, Fushimi and Schouten 2000). His personal judo interests and his academic field, the sociology of sport, enabled him to offer a novel interpretation of how the symbols of a subculture of consumption (judo) are transferred from their original host culture (Japan) into a very different host culture (North America). In planning your own research and writing, you should reflect upon who you are as an individual and how that will distinguish your access, analysis and interpretation from anyone else working on the same topic. Articulate this in your writing. This is discussed again in Chapters 9 and 17.

Feasibility

You will need to ensure that you have chosen a topic which is achievable within the constraints of time, resources and other commitments such as a full-time job (if you are studying part-time). In addition, you should take account of your own technical abilities.

Helpful hint
Make a list and check your research is feasible at each point:

*   time.
*   resources.
*   your technical abilities.
*   other commitments.
*   access.

Most qualitative research methods require you to have excellent interpersonal communication skills. If the thought of entering a large organization in order to conduct depth interviews with senior and junior employees fills you with dread, it might be worth considering a topic that does not require close interactions with unfamiliar informants but which lends itself to less personal methods. Listening skills, too, are of major importance if you wish to really explore the insider's perspective.

What is the duration of your research period and can your proposed topic be completed within this time? A key skill is the ability to pick a topic that can be achieved within the research period. It is unlikely, for instance, that a longitudinal study of the development of a communications campaign could be completed within the one term that is usually available for research in a taught post-graduate programme. Remember to allow enough time to read the literature, design the research, collect the data, analyse the results, and complete the writing of your report.

The issue of time relates not only to the duration of research, but also to the management of time on a day-to-day basis. What else will you be involved with while undertaking research? Qualitative research methods can be very time consuming. Before finalizing your research topic, it is worth considering how to juggle any other activities you are committed to, such as a part-time job, holidays, or attendance at lectures and seminars. Choose a topic that will fit into the time available.

What is the cost involved in carrying out your proposed research, and can you afford it? Not only are travel costs to the offices of informants often very expensive, but the cost of recording and transcribing interviews can be prohibitive. For interviews and focus groups, you will need a tape recorder, microphone, tapes and, ideally, a transcribing machine. Without the latter, it will take up to ten hours to type up a one-hour interview. With it, you or a good typist could take between five and seven hours. This means that if you cannot afford to pay a typist or wish to type up the transcripts yourself in order to relate more closely with your material, you should plan to spend several weeks in front of a computer putting your informants' comments onto the page.

Are you sure that you can gain access to your sample? The prospect of conducting an in-depth exploration of how advertising campaigns are devised in a major London agency may be exciting and original. But your study will not be feasible unless you can be assured of good access to the company and its employees. Ensure, therefore, that you can gain entry to a company before you decide to make it the focus of your research. Chapter 5 sets out more on gaining access to the field.

Personal value of the research topic

When deciding upon a topic to study, it is worth noting that, aside from its educational value, the right choice of research project can be useful in terms of enhancing your career. If you choose a topic that is aligned to your career aims, your project will enable you to develop a specialist understanding of a particular field. That knowledge is likely to be attractive to future employers. For instance, say you want eventually to work in the IT sector; as a topic of study, you might decide to explore the implications of digital technology on the practice of public relations planning within the IT sector. This would allow you to develop your thinking about two key areas: the IT sector and the impact of new media on public relations. A further benefit of research to your career is through the contacts you make when carrying out interviews or observations. It is not uncommon for research students to end up with jobs in the companies where their fieldwork took place.

We have already noted briefly the contribution that the research supervisor can make to your decision-making about a research topic. Now we move on to consider the role of the supervisor and the importance of this relationship through the course of your research project.

Relating to your supervisor

Supervisors are not there to tell you what to do. Their role is to guide and advise rather than direct (unless you have acted contrary to ethical and research guidelines). This means that, in most cases, you are expected to work with a measure of independence. However, both you and your supervisor have a common aim, that is to achieve a study of a high standard which will be completed on time. To accomplish the goal, both of you should be committed to the contract of respectively doing and supporting your research.

Your relationship will only be effective if you are able to trust each other. As a researcher, you have a duty to the public relations and marketing communications discipline to report data truthfully, accurately and as completely as possible. This applies not only to the content of the dissertation, but also to conversations within the student–supervisor relationship. The ethical rules of fidelity and veracity are very important in establishing a trusting relationship. In this context, truth telling is essential. There is an obvious duty for both researcher and supervisor to recognize the need to share all aspects of the study phases, be they positive or negative.

We would argue that supervision is an essential component of research work and a very important aspect of establishing rigour and trustworthiness in your study. The supervisor who is best able to provide a positive learning structure is flexible and approachable, draws out your ideas, and creates an open learning climate where you feel confident enough to challenge and pursue new avenues. Even if you lack this type of supervisor, you can still go on learning. Supervision is based on a framework of ground rules which Sharp and Howard (1996) suggest should be negotiated by student and supervisor at the outset. They advise that you should:

- *Attempt to ascertain the supervisor's own views of the staff–student relationship.* Knowing your supervisor's views on how the supervisory relationship will work helps you to adapt to his or her expectations.
- *Agree with the supervisor the routine aspects of the relationship (and take responsibility for their implementation).* It is useful to agree upon the frequency of contact with your supervisor. This varies according to your needs and the stage in the research process. At the beginning when you are working up your ideas, you may need to meet on a weekly basis. However, this schedule can be revised as the work progresses. It is most unwise to allow regular contact to breakdown because regular meetings help to motivate you and keep you focused. There should be a systematic and structured programme of work which forms the basis for the student–supervisor relationship, but the instigation for both the programme and for contacting supervisors has to come from you.
- *Produce written lists of queries prior to meetings with the supervisor.* By putting any questions or problems down on paper in advance of meetings, you are forced to define and confront any areas of your work about which you may feel uneasy. This in itself is a useful exercise. However, the list also helps to set the agenda for the meeting, saving precious time for both you and your supervisor.
- *Keep written notes of meetings with the supervisor.* It is up to you to take the responsibility for documenting the deliberations, decisions and action taken with your supervisor. At each supervision meeting, something positive should have been achieved, such as feedback on your initial ideas, questions answered, or suggestions and ideas to follow. Often it is difficult to remember all the points discussed. Notes taken during the meeting and summarized afterwards help to clarify the next stage of your progress.
- *Agree with the supervisor the nature and timing of written material to be submitted.* Find out if your supervisor requires you to submit a monthly progress report. The discipline of recording your progress succinctly, and relating it to your aims and research plan is an excellent preparation for the writing up phase of your study.

It is often difficult to make a start on writing, particularly when a great deal of data have been collected that may initially seem overwhelming. Indeed, many

Example 2.6 Student voices

Here are some voices of public relations and marketing communications students as they look back on their research relationship with their supervisor. Note also the student comments at the end of Chapter 1.

I felt that my supervisor pointed me in the right direction without setting limitations for my ideas. I believe it is important to maintain 'ownership' of the project. I have never enjoyed letting other people read my drafts and 'unfinished' work, but sometimes it is necessary to get an 'objective' opinion on what one is writing, as it is easy to get too absorbed and detail-oriented and spend one whole day working on a single paragraph. Apart from asking critical questions and giving me another viewpoint on the subject, the supervisor also encouraged me to finish my draft chapters within the timescales that were set, and therefore helped by providing a bit of structure to the progress of the project.

Katrine Jaklin

I was mentally exhausted (perhaps a slight overstatement) after my first meeting with my supervisor. I had never thought so quickly or deeply in such a short space of time. I must admit – I was fairly unsure of myself. I mean, a dissertation is a mammoth piece of work. Perhaps the first thing my tutor enabled me to do was to gain some 'intellectual self-confidence', as he might say. The guy seemed to talk in riddles at times. This was really frustrating to start with, and made our relationship a little rocky from my perspective. However, after a while, I adjusted and actually started to like it. I, too, started to think in questions – and this really helped me research and write. I've ended up respecting my tutor. He's not made writing my dissertation 'easy' – but he's given me some great advice and really helped me to think.

Richard Fogg

I had a good experience with my supervisor. I know I'm structured [in thinking and planning] – and I was working with a supervisor who also is structured. I think it was important for me to have a supervisor who could challenge me with new ideas, without getting the topic totally off the track [. . .] I kind of think of the dissertation as a co-operation with the supervisor, not a self-made piece only.

Kristin Goa

students delay writing up in the belief that much of the research is 'in their head'. In our experience this is a fallacy, as it is essential to start writing early. Indeed, supervisors *expect* students to start writing from an early stage. Your supervisor will ask for chapters on background, literature review and methodology, depending on the type of research (see Chapters 3 and 17). This ensures that you not only understand the process but also produce some ideas which generate fresh motivation and interest, even though sections of the writing might have to be changed at a later stage. In this way, you become immersed in the methodology, and some of the problems and pitfalls of the research become obvious. This allows you to resolve them at an early stage.

It is essential, therefore, that you agree a timetable for the submission of your draft chapters. Supervisors are busy people, involved in other activities such as teaching, academic management, research and writing for publication and often do not have particularly flexible schedules. Therefore, it is a good idea to agree mutually convenient dates for when you expect to be able to submit your written work, and have it returned to you with constructive comments.

Unfortunately, supervisors are not always gentle and diplomatic in their comments and criticism. Some students are easily hurt by it, but their advice is best taken without seeing it as a personal attack, instead of as an academic argument. In any case, the relationship you hold with your supervisor develops over time, as you each learn about the other's character and interests, and subsequently negotiate the relationship. Ideally, mutual respect should develop. Cryer (1996) stresses that, as a research student, it is in your own interest to develop and nurture this relationship. She points out that there are two aspects to the relationship. One is professional, and the other is interpersonal. The latter involves treating your supervisor 'as a human being, who has strengths and weaknesses, personal satisfactions and disappointment, good days and bad days, just like everyone else' (p. 59). If you are interested in reading more deeply on this topic, we recommend that you refer to Cryer (1996) and Phillips and Pugh (2000).

As supervisors ourselves, we would agree with Sharp and Howard's (1996) advice to students not to be diffident about 'managing' the student–supervisor relationship. We, like most supervisors, welcome our students taking the initiative in this respect; indeed, this encourages us to respond more effectively and enthusiastically in our supervision.

Summary

- Supervision is an essential component of research work and a means of establishing rigour in research.
- Ideally, the student–supervisor relationship is based on trust and mutual respect.
- The process of doing research begins when you decide upon a broad area that interests you. Ideas emerge from your reading, your experiences or from conversations and conferences.
- Hone down your general ideas into a specific topic so that your research is manageable. Do this by formulating a central research question about a problem or mystery that you would like to solve in your broad area of interest.
- The central research question drives the type of research that needs to be done in order to provide an answer.

- A good research topic is original. Originality means that research is (a) a novel development of an existing idea or issue, or (b) it is a novel application of current concepts, techniques or methodologies, or (c) it is a novel interpretation of previous work or ideas.
- A good research topic is feasible. Feasibility concerns whether or not your project is achievable and manageable, taking into consideration such constraints as time and resources.

Considerations such as these will influence your choice of topic. The next stage in the research process is to review the literature and write your research proposal. This we discuss in the following chapter.

3   Reviewing the literature and writing the research proposal

A literature review is a description, critical analysis and evaluation of relevant texts – both current and seminal – that relate to your research question or topic. On the basis of your literature review, you develop a coherent argument for your own research. The literature review in qualitative research is not completed at an early stage but continues to be updated through the entire period of your data collection, analysis and writing up of the final document.

In this chapter, we outline:

*   reasons for carrying out a literature review.
*   reading strategies.
*   stages in the process of reviewing the literature.
*   recording and referencing.
*   writing a research proposal.

Why carry out a literature review?

The purpose of carrying out a literature review is to establish a rationale for your study and show why your research question is important. As Hart states, the literature review differentiates 'what has been done from what needs to be done' (1998: 27). We draw on her ideas to suggest that the goals of undertaking a literature review in public relations and marketing communications include the following:

*   to identify the main writers and researchers and their particular perspectives on your topic area.
*   to develop an understanding of the nature and structure of your topic area.
*   to position your research in its historical or cultural context.
*   to establish a new perspective on the topic.
*   to relate theoretical concepts and ideas to professional practice.
*   to acquire and develop the language and terminology linked to the topic.
*   to trace and describe the main methodologies and research procedures used by other researchers in relation to the topic.

Most importantly, you need to show the significance of your research question and relate it to its context, signalling at the same time why the study needs to be done.

Familiarity with the literature prevents you from repeating the flaws and weaknesses of other research studies. As you review the literature over the course of your research, you should examine the arguments of other writers and researchers which confirm or contradict your ideas on the topic. Consider these conflicts and discuss them. This enables you to develop a debate which, in turn, becomes the structure for your eventual written review of the literature. Don't be tempted just to describe the work of other researchers – you need to evaluate it critically as well.

Reading strategies

How do you know where to begin reading for a literature review? Your previous studies may have given you an indication of a book or an article that you could start with. This reading might lead you to the works of related writers. A search through the indices of abstracts can point you to interesting research. However, it's best to begin with a systematic search of the online databases and relevant websites. In the next chapter, you will find a step-by-step procedure for doing this, together with a list of some of the most important databases in the field of public relations and marketing communications. Once you have identified key texts, bear in mind that if these are not stocked in your local library, it may take time for them to be ordered and arrive. Allow plenty of time for this.

There are a number of strategies for reading. It is useful to start by previewing: this involves skimming and sampling. Skimming entails quickly 'skipping' through the text, leaving out chunks that do not seem relevant initially. Sampling involves reading the first and last paragraphs of a chapter or article and the first and last sentences of each paragraph. Previewing is a way of gaining an overall sense of the text as a preliminary to reading more intensively. It helps you to distinguish major concepts from those of little importance for your own particular study. Through further reading, you can go on to look at how these concepts have been defined and used by other researchers and writers.

Once you have an overview of the text, you can read more purposefully. One way of doing this is to read slowly and thoroughly, with specific questions in mind, especially those concerning what is being argued by an author and whether or not that argument is sound. Crème and Lea (1997: 70–1) suggest that the following questions are helpful:

- What specifically is the author trying to communicate?
- What is the central thesis or idea of the chapter, book or article?
- What sort of evidence does the author use to support the argument?
- What methods are used in research?
- Does the argument seem logical?
- How does the material relate to other sources on the subject?

- What related arguments or theories does this reading make me think of?
- How could I use this in conjunction with the ideas I already have on this subject?

Be discriminating in your reading. It is not necessary to read (and write about) every text that might have a tentative connection to your topic. Choose those that have a strong link to your research question. Remember to summarize and make notes on each text that you read.

Stages of the literature review

In some cases, the literature review starts even before you have identified a research topic. In all cases, it continues throughout the whole period of your research. Undertaking qualitative research entails a continuous interplay between reading and reviewing the literature, collecting the data, analysing the data, and writing the final research report. Your review of the literature does not stop until you have put the final full stop on your written report or dissertation. Having said that, there are several identifiable stages in reviewing the literature. They are:

1   The preliminary review which is presented in your research proposal.
2   The main review.
3   The ongoing update of the main review.
4   The review of the literature linked to emerging categories and themes.
5   The final update.

Preliminary review

The preliminary review of the literature should be carried out during your preparation of the research proposal (see page 43 for how to write the proposal). The main purpose of the preliminary review is to demonstrate the gap in knowledge that you intend to fill. Golden-Biddle and Locke (1997) suggest that this might be by identifying that:

- the existing literature is incomplete.
- the literature has overlooked alternative ways of looking at a phenomenon.
- the literature is 'wrong, misguided or incorrect'.
- existing knowledge could be represented and organized differently (such as by putting together work that is considered unrelated). Example 3.2 later in this chapter illustrates this approach.

In the preliminary review, you attempt to identify and summarize the work of expert writers and key researchers in the area of your research, together with the work of writers on the methods you propose to use.

Your review will be complete when you have provided an overview of the main debates and most significant research studies that relate to your topic, together with the methodology and procedures that other researchers have used to explore the area. You should attempt to be critical in your approach to the literature.

The preliminary review provides an early indication of the significance of your study because it locates your research within the tradition of research in public relations and marketing communications. More importantly, it provides a clear rationale for why your research is original and why you should undertake it. (Turn back to Chapter 2 to see some examples of original research.)

Example 3.1 Locating research within the wider body of relevant literature

In order to improve companies' understanding of what makes brands successful, Leslie de Chernatony, Francesca Dall'Olmo Riley and Fiona Harris argued that it was important to identify criteria that were appropriate for measuring brand success. They provided a rationale for their study as follows:

> The academic and trade press refer to the 'success' of brands or 'successful brands'. This literature infrequently defines the criteria used to measure a brand's success and among the studies which do there is disagreement regarding suitable measures, e.g. business-based criteria such as market share (Buzzell and Gale 1987) versus consumer-based criteria such as brand awareness (e.g. Pitta and Katsanis 1995). Furthermore, there is confusion between what constitutes brand success and the *strategies* that should be used to achieve it. As a result, many studies (e.g. McBurnie and Clutterbuck 1988) have talked about suitable strategies to achieve brand success, without having clearly defined the criteria upon which success should be judged (e.g. financial performance or brand awareness, or a composite measure). Finally, previous studies have failed to identify success criteria that would stand the test of time (e.g. Pascale 1990) even though writers such as Hansen *et al.* (1990) have argued that excellence should have some duration and should be measured in such a way as to forecast the future.
>   It was apparent after a literature review that, while a large body of literature exists on the measures of marketing success, no definitive source emerged that specially focused on brand, rather than marketing success. [...] Thus the main aim of this paper is to consider appropriate criteria to measure brand success.

(1998: 765–6)

Don't worry if you can't find a great deal of literature that directly relates to your topic area. If you are convinced that you have conducted an extensive trawl of the public relations and marketing communications texts (using the various online search techniques described in Chapter 4), and have also considered the literature in related disciplines (such as management, sociology, psychology, organization studies, or other fields which might have a possible connection to your topic) but still haven't discovered much published research on your topic, then maybe there simply isn't any! Qualitative research, because of its exploratory nature, is demonstrably most useful when there has been little written about the topic area.

At the end of the initial review, you should feel familiar with the existing literature which relates to your own research topic. The reader of your research proposal should be left in no doubt that your proposed study is appropriate to meet the research aim or to provide an answer for your main research question.

The main review

The literature review does not end with the initial search and critique, but it continues throughout your study, parallel to data collection and analysis. After your proposal has been accepted by your supervisor or research committee, you should make an immediate start on reviewing the literature. What you are endeavouring to do is to locate the work in its wider context and provide a critical review of the subject area and existing research in the field.

The literature review which you compile at this stage is not as extensive as that for a traditional, quantitative study where you are interested in reviewing all of the literature in the field prior to commencing your data collection. Instead, in qualitative research, the main purpose of reviewing the literature is to find out about previous research and the methods adopted by other researchers in order to demonstrate the need for your own research. In effect, you are building upon the work you did in the preliminary review stage. Although the literature provides guidance for your research, you should resist being impelled in a certain direction just because everyone else has followed that route. Don't forget that your own data should decide the direction and design of your study; they have priority over the work of others.

There are some major tenets in relation to the literature review:

- *the main literature should be reasonably comprehensive but cannot be all-inclusive.* After you have searched through the relevant literature and summarized the main ideas from the studies, you need to show how this work relates to your own research. Ensure that you critically appraise the findings and methodologies of other studies. Not all of the material you identify will be relevant for the literature review. If you end up with an unmanageable amount of concepts or studies in the literature, your research topic may be too broad and will have to be refined. It is important, therefore, for the literature to be representative rather than all-inclusive.
- *the literature review should be up-to-date.* Ensure that you keep up-to-date with the literature, reading the professional and academic journals as they are published. Don't forget to carry out regular online searches.
- *the literature should include the main classical and foundational work.* By

considering the classic or seminal texts that underpin current thinking, you are able to position your study within its historical context. In some cases, you may wish to build upon the ideas of the main theorists, or indicate how their research is directly connected to your topic.

• *the review must be systematic*. This means being methodical, purposeful and focused on your research question throughout your reading and critical evaluation of the literature.

Reviewing new areas of literature and updating the rest

As your research proceeds, you are likely to uncover new areas which will necessitate further literature searches. In addition, new research and concepts will be introduced into the academic arena through the publications of other researchers; this applies especially if you are carrying out lengthy postgraduate work. Many novice researchers find staying abreast of the literature an over-whelming task at this stage. However, by updating the literature review as you go along, your own theories and ideas will become more focused and linked in various ways to the work of those who have undertaken and published research before you.

Reviewing literature that relates to your emerging categories and themes

The continued search for related ideas and themes is particularly important for qualitative researchers. After you have collected your data and begun to analyse them, you will discover significant categories and themes in the data which will help you to identify its meaning (see Chapter 16 for more on analysis). The link between your findings and the research literature becomes very important at this stage because other researchers' findings may confirm or contradict your own data and your initial interpretation of them. Throughout the process of analysis, then, you are engaged in a continuous debate with the ideas and findings in the work of other researchers.

The final update

The final update takes place when you write up your research report. It includes the introduction of any new texts which may have been published since you began your study. Occasionally you might find, right at the end of your study, that another researcher has carried out a similar project. You will then have to show how your research differs and attempt to critique the other author's work without prejudice.

Example 3.2 Developing an argument and rationale for research

In a North American study, Kimberly Elsbach and Robert Sutton (1992) showed how company spokespeople can transform events that seem to be identity-threatening into events that ultimately protect and perhaps enhance organizational image. Over seven paragraphs, their literature review on the topic developed an argument which pointed to a gap in the literature that their study aimed to fill. The following traces their argument and main points, each of which is a synthesis of the ideas of other writers and researchers.

1   Organizations are rewarded for having a legitimate reputation.
    BUT
2   Maintaining legitimacy is difficult because the expectations of different stakeholders about what legitimacy means are conflicting, vague and changeable.
    SO what do organizations do about this?
3   Institutional theory suggests that organizations facing conflicting demands can adopt structures and practices which distract attention from what stakeholders consider unacceptable. This gives the impression that they are legitimate.
    BUT
4   Institutional theory provides an incomplete view. It doesn't take account of the impression management tactics that organizational publicists use. Therefore, a blend of institutional theory with impression management theory might be helpful for understanding how organizations protect legitimacy.
5   One particular study has used both approaches separately. Findings of this study are noted. This implies that an integration of both approaches might be useful.
    BUT
6   There are no studies that have interwoven the two perspectives together.
    THEREFORE
7   Elsbach and Sutton's longitudinal study of two radical social movements combines both perspectives, using them to provide insights into how company publicity can lead key stakeholders to endorse and support potentially controversial and possibly unlawful activities.

The literature review in this article continues with a discussion of the study's research methods. It is important to note that Elsbach and Sutton's final version of the literature review was written after they had completed their research and, therefore, they are able to note in paragraph 7 that they arrived at this model 'inductively'. This means that they discovered which theories would be most useful to them only after data collection had begun. Their argument in the literature review was not finalized until they had analysed the data.

If you were writing the above for a proposal, you would only be able to indicate in paragraph 7 that this is what you *intended* to do, bearing in mind that your literature review would develop over the course of your project.

Recording and referencing

A bibliographic reference is a set of data or elements describing a document, or part of a document. It is sufficiently precise and detailed to enable a potential reader to identify and locate the document. When you are reviewing the literature, it is easy to lose and mislay references over the course of time. Therefore, from the start, set up a system for systematically recording of all your reference material.

For each text you read, you will need to note the following:

- author's surname and initials (all surnames and initials if there are several authors).
- date of publication.
- title of article/book/chapter.
- unabbreviated journal title, volume, issue number and page numbers.
- full book title, chapter title, author(s) for chapters in an edited book.
- name and location of publisher.
- page number from which you took direct quotations.
- the library or other source from which the book was obtained (so that you can retrieve it at a later date).

(Adapted from Holloway and Walker 2000)

As you read, record your references in any way that suits you best. Many researchers develop a card system, others a computer file or bibliographic database such as those referred to in Chapter 4. Against each reference, record a summary of the published study, the methods used and any quotes that you find useful (don't forget the page numbers for these). Most of us learn to our cost that we have not recorded references adequately and must search for them at a later stage. This sometimes means re-reading a whole book. Therefore, keep thorough records and don't be caught out in this way.

As soon as you start writing you can establish two lists of references. One is active and contains all the references you have collected. The other is a list of all references which are likely to be used or which you have ordered from the library. When the copies arrive, you can transfer these to the 'active' list. At the beginning you might not see the relevance of a certain text even though it is connected to your field. Keep a photocopy, however, just in case. This saves having to reorder an article or book from an external library at a later stage.

In the text of your proposal, and later in the body of your research report, you

Helpful hint
References need to be cited in two different places. First, at the point at which a document is referred to in the text of your proposal or subsequent written report; second, in a list at the end of the work. The latter is referred to as a reference list or a bibliography.

will need to cite the bibliographical references of all documents you have used or to which you have referred. It is very important to be consistent and accurate when citing references because the references may need to be traced at a later date by someone else who reads your work.

Check with your institution for the system of referencing that they follow and then conform to that in all your writing. Many universities follow the Harvard System of referencing. We provide an illustration of this in Example 4.9. For a useful online guide to how one university uses this, both for citing within a text and also in the bibliography at the end of a report, go to:

www.bournemouth.ac.uk/using_the_library/html/harvard_system.html

For a guide to citing Internet sources, go to:

www.bournemouth.ac.uk/using_ the_library/html/guide_to_citing_internet_sourc.html

In summary, carrying out a literature review is a necessary research skill and, when done well, demonstrates that you:

- know about your topic and related areas.
- have understood theoretical and methodological issues related to your study.
- know how to acknowledge and integrate the work of others without stealing their ideas.
- are able modify and adapt your own study in the light of what you have read.

We move on now to consider the research proposal which you first read about earlier in the chapter in relation to the preliminary literature review stage.

Writing the proposal

Whether you are designing a piece of research which aims to obtain funding from an external research council, or whether you are a research student planning your dissertation, you will be expected to write a proposal. This acts as a plan for action, as well as a means of communicating your intentions to those who either allocate research funds or give consent for you to go ahead with your research. Two comprehensive guides to writing proposals are Punch (2000) and Locke, Spirduso and Silverman (2000). We draw on these as we offer our own thoughts on developing an effective proposal.

The proposal sets out the exact nature of the project, and how it is to be investigated. Initially, you come up with a short, general outline of your proposed research. This might be only two or three pages long and is intended to give your supervisor, academic institution or company an idea of the area on which you are intending to focus. You then develop this with a supervisor into a more formal document of around 3,000 words (the exact length will depend on the requirements of your institution). Working up a proposal can take about one month for an undergraduate proposal, to twelve months for a PhD proposal. Research councils require very detailed proposals before they allocate money to individuals or research teams. Whether you are writing a proposal to be read by a potential supervisor, members of a proposal review committee, or a funding body, your proposal should contain the elements shown in Table 3.1. Because qualitative research is flexible, the following outline is indicative only; you may choose to structure your proposal differently, depending on the aims of your research.

Readers of proposals will be concerned to make judgements about, first, the overall viability of the proposed study as a research project, second, your ability to carry out the research, third, technical issues such as the appropriateness of the design, or quality issues concerning data collection and analysis (Punch 2000). Readers will be seeking answers to the following key questions:

- Is the proposed research feasible and 'do-able'?
- Is the research worth doing?
- Can the candidate do it?
- If done, will it produce a successful dissertation at the degree level involved?

(Punch 2000: 12)

Make sure that you have provided your readers with sufficient information to address these issues. When writing your proposal, it is helpful to imagine that you are a consultant pitching for a piece of new business through the medium of the research proposal; you will need to demonstrate to your readers your competence to undertake such a piece of work. Do this by clearly articulating what it is that you want to find out, why it is worth doing, how you intend to do it and the broader context in which your research will take place. Even if your research is intended to be of the emergent kind (where questions evolve through a cyclical process of fieldwork, reading and analysis rather than being pre-planned), you still need to demonstrate that you are able to take a thorough, disciplined approach to research.

Punch (2000) points out that the proposal is a stand-alone document and should not need your presence to interpret what is being said. Therefore, nothing should be implied; your proposal should make sense to a reader who does not know you, has not discussed the work with you, and may not be an expert in the field in which you propose to research. At this stage, it may be helpful to read the discussion about carrying out an 'audit trail' in Chapter 6.

Issues of quality and ethics

Even at the earliest stages of your research, you need to be able to show that you have taken heed of the quality benchmarks which enable others to evaluate it. We discuss how qualitative research can be judged in Chapter 6 by reference to notions of reliability and validity. Ensure that you are thoroughly conversant with these terms, and can demonstrate in your proposal how your project is reliable and valid.

Table 3.1 Indicative outline for a research proposal

Working title	Provide a title (and subtitle) that describes the depth and breadth of the topic and indicates the methodology to be used.
Background and focus	State the focus, the background and context of the research, the scope, and the main question/s to be investigated. In some cases, it may be appropriate to refer to professional journals in order to highlight a problem or key issue confronting the public relations or marketing communications industry. Outlining the professional context in this way helps to position your work in its business context. Some academic work on the topic area should be *briefly* introduced here in order to present a rationale for your study (i.e. is there a particular gap in knowledge that your study will address?). You will develop this aspect more comprehensively in the literature review section. In this section of the proposal, you should state your research aim or main question.
Literature review	What is the significance of the project to our knowledge of public relations and marketing communication? That is, why does the problem or question need to be studied (and why now)? Use references to explain how the study relates to, builds on or differs from previous work in managed communication. Introduce key concepts, theories and research approaches that relate to your research question. Indicate the key debates in the field, continuously relating your discussion to the research problem or issue. State how this review of the literature has shaped and contributed to the project's evolution. If relevant, explain the proposed practical value of the research. In some cases, you will be ready to identify further research questions at this point. These should be clear, researchable and related to each other.
Proposed methodology	Discuss the methodological approach you intend to take and provide a rationale for it. Provide a concise justification for your qualitative research approach, or combination approach, presenting references to support your case (refer to Part II of this book).
	Discuss how entry and exit to the field will be accomplished (see Chapter 5 in this book).
	Describe how and what data will be collected and why you have selected specific methods (see Part III of this book).
	Indicate how people will be approached for information, how observation visits will be scheduled, the social contexts of observing and interviewing, the use of audio-visual equipment, and so on.
	Note your intended sample and rationale (see Chapter 11 in this book).
	Outline how you propose to analyse your data and how your interpretation will relate back to the initial questions posed (see Chapter 16 of this book).
Ethical issues	Explain how issues of access, informed consent, privacy and other ethical issues will be dealt with (see Chapter 5 of this book).
Potential problems	Indicate any possible difficulties you foresee and how you will endeavour to overcome them.
Timings	Outline a provisional work schedule of the tasks that you need to complete and when.
Resources	List the resources you are likely to need, such as equipment and costs.
References/ appendices	List all texts cited in your proposal. Follow this with any appendices.

With regard to ethical considerations, there are three key issues which need to be addressed in your proposal. These concern the protection of people involved as participants in your study and involve issues of access, informed consent and privacy. They should be considered within the design of any research project. Turn to Chapter 5 to read about ethics and how they relate to this stage of your research project.

Summary

- In its final form, the literature review is a coherent argument that leads to the description of your proposed study (Rudestam and Newton 2001).
- Reviewing the literature is a continuous process that begins when you prepare your research proposal and finishes when you complete the research report.
- There are different reading strategies ranging from a quick overview to more purposeful, intensive reading where you critically engage with the literature.
- It is important to systematically record all your reference material as you go along.
- References are cited in the text and also in the bibliography at the end. The Harvard System of referencing is commonly used.
- The research proposal is a plan for action as well as a means of communicating your intent to carry out research that is significant, reliable and valid, and which conforms to ethical principles.

4 Tools and techniques for locating, retrieving and storing electronic text

Matt Holland

This chapter describes the techniques needed for using electronic databases to locate and retrieve references to, and full text of, articles in journals, conference papers and chapters in books. It also outlines tips for recording and storing references electronically.

This chapter details how to:

- use language that databases can understand so that you can navigate quickly and effectively through them.
- carry out searches for keywords, phrases or strings of words.
- search for references that relate to your topic which have been cited by other authors.
- narrow your search down to within a particular field.
- record and reference your material by using bibliographic software packages.

At the end of the chapter, a list is provided of bibliographic and full text databases that relate to public relations and marketing communications.

Introduction

Researchers in public relations and marketing communications have access to an extensive literature in electronic form. A generic term to describe these electronic resources is databases. The databases discussed here are text databases that contain references to journal articles, conference papers and, sometimes, chapters in books. As these databases contain exclusively bibliographic information, they are usually referred to as Bibliographic Databases. Databases are searched by entering either a keyword or an author's name to find relevant references. They are divided into three types: Indexes, Abstracts and Full Text databases.

- Indexes provide brief citations containing sufficient information to enable you to locate a reference.
- Abstracts provide brief citations, and in addition, abstracts or short summaries to help you decide if a reference is relevant before you try to find it.

•   Full Text Databases provide citations, abstracts and full text of the reference with pictures and diagrams.

Using Full Text Databases means that when you have found a relevant reference, for example a journal article, you can display, save or print the full text of the article from your computer. You no longer need to go to the library and find the print version on the shelves. In the public relations and marketing communications area, Full Text Databases are well developed, providing you with a significant degree of full text access to journal articles. See Table 4.2 for a complete list of all databases relevant to public relations and marketing communications.

Advances in technology are changing the way databases are accessed. In the past the most common form of access for researchers was by using a CD-ROM. Generally, CD-ROMs were physically held in a university or college library, and researchers had to visit the library to use them. Increasingly the usual means of database access is over the Internet, remote from university or college campuses. Now you can expect to access databases from wherever you can get to an Internet connection. It could be in the library or the computer centre, but might also be from your home, your office or Internet café. This chapter does not cover the technical aspects of database access. Access will be determined by local conditions at your sponsoring university, college or institution.

Given that appropriate databases are available and that you have access to them, you also need a methodology to guide you through the process of database searching. This consists of a number of discrete activities:

Step 1   Writing a statement describing what it is you are searching for.
Step 2   Choosing a database likely to contain relevant information.
Step 3   Preparing a search plan (identifying concepts, key words and contingency plans).
Step 4   Implementing your search in your chosen database (perhaps using the database field structure).
Step 5   Critically reviewing the results of your search.
Step 6   Revising your search plan in the light of Step 5.
Step 7   Implementing your revised search plan.

The search process is not linear, however. It is possible that in getting to Step 3 you may want to revisit Step 1, to revise your research statement or, in getting to Step 4, you may want to return to Step 2 in order to choose a new database. Searching databases requires you to reflect on both the process (what you have done and how you have done it), and on the outcomes (the information you retrieve). To be able to change your search in the light of your reflections, you need to understand and be able to implement the tools and techniques described in the next section.

Using databases inevitably means you will retrieve data in an electronic format. You need to be able to store and manage these data, which you can do by using word processor and database packages. You might also consider using a specialist software package designed to handle references. The generic name for these packages is Personal Bibliographic Software (PBS). This is discussed later in the section on Recording and Saving Electronic Information.

To summarize, as a researcher you need to:

- have a knowledge of relevant electronic databases.
- be able to access databases.
- be familiar with the database structures.
- be able to search systematically.
- be skilled in managing the output of the search process.

Searching bibliographic and full text databases

Database structure

Whenever you use printed information, you have an understanding of the likely structure of that information. For example, a textbook will have a table of contents, chapters, page numbers and an index. Knowing that makes it easy to navigate quickly through the text and locate the information. Databases also have a structure, and knowledge of this similarly enables you to locate and extract information quickly.

A database is a computer file comprising a number of records. To give you an idea of the size of bibliographic databases, the number of records may vary from 100,000 to over 1,000,000. A record is equivalent to a journal article, a newspaper article, a conference paper or a chapter in a book. Each record is divided into fields that contain the individual units of data that make up a record. Typically there are fields for author, article title, journal title, volume number, issue number, date, abstract and keywords.

Fields are normally identified by field labels or field names, for example, the field label *AU* for author and *TI* for title. Field labels and field names vary from one database to another. The number of fields also varies. Basic fields such as author and title are always present. Complex databases have additional fields that are particular to certain subjects. For example, PsycINFO (Psychological Abstracts) has a field for populations *PO* (see Example 4.1) to distinguish between experiments on human and animal populations.

Approaches to searching

Broadly, three approaches are available to you:

- simple keyword searches.
- in-field searching.
- citation searching.

Example 4.1 Sample record from PsycINFO (Psychological Abstracts)

AN: 1997–38903–002
MT: Print-Paper
DT: Journal-Article
TI: Assessing the use and impact of humor on advertising effectiveness: A contingency approach.
AU: Spotts,-Harlan-E; Weinberger,-Marc-G; Parsons,-Amy-L
AF: U Wisconsin, Parkside, WI, US
SO: Journal-of-Advertising. 1997 Fal; Vol 26(3): 17–32.
JN: Journal-of-Advertising;
PB: US: CtC Press/JOA.
IS: 0091–3367
PY: 1997
LA: English
AB: Examined humor effectiveness in magazine advertising by using a conceptual framework adapted from P.S. Speck (1991) along with a product-contingent focus. Magazine advertisements were collected by 3 co-researchers who sequentially searched the targeted product category files of Starch/INRA/Hooper. The resulting approach affords a clearer understanding of the appropriate use of humor through the examination of (1) the humor mechanisms employed, (2) the intentional relatedness of humor to the ad or product, and (3) the type of product advertised. Descriptive results of the study indicate that current practice for many advertisers is to employ incongruity-based humor in a humor-dominant context. That practice is contrasted with others to examine the influence of humor on the effectiveness of print advertisements for different product groups. Study results indicate that current advertising practices may not be the most effective in terms of advertisement performance. (PsycINFO Database Record (c) 2000 APA, all rights reserved)
KP: product-contingent approach to examination of humor effectiveness in magazine advertising, adults
MJ: *Advertising-; *Humor-; *Magazines-
CC: 3940-Marketing-and-Advertising; 3940; 39
AG: Adulthood
PO: Human
PT: Empirical-Study
SF: References
UD: 19980401

Simple searches are where you type in keywords that represent your search e.g. advertising and humour.

In-field searching combines keywords with commands to search only in specific fields, for example searching for an author's name in the author field (see Example 4.2.)

Example 4.2 Searching by author's name

Marc G. Weinberger has written several scholarly articles on the topic of humour and advertising over a period of time. A search for *Marc G Weinberger* as author in a major business and management database like ABI Inform retrieves seven substantial articles on the subject.

Citation searching uses a key reference you have found in your own reading to locate other references. Essentially it asks the question 'Which other authors have cited in their own bibliographies the article I am interested in, and therefore might be writing on a similar topic?' How to implement this powerful technique is described in the section on Citation Searching.

It is quite likely that you might employ all these strategies over the life cycle of a single project, beginning with a simple keyword search, refining it using in-field searches and finally using a retrieved citation as a basis for a citation search.

Search interfaces and searching

Each database has a search screen where you are invited to type in your search. The design of this screen controls what you can enter and the functions you will be offered, although some databases offer one screen for all types of searching. Most databases, however, offer more than one search screen directed at users of different abilities. A Basic mode for inexperienced users is generally offered first with options to go to Advanced or Expert modes. The Basic mode is appropriate for simple keyword searches, while the Advanced and Expert modes offer the enhanced capabilities which we go on to discuss through the rest of this chapter.

- Basic Search for new users – a single text-box for you to type in keywords.
- Advanced Search for experienced users – designed to guide you through advanced searching, helping you to use the enhanced search capabilities.
- Expert Search for experienced users – a single window that assumes you have knowledge of database commands and can type them in without help.

It may be that as you become familiar with the databases you will develop a personal preference for one or other mode of searching.

Planning your search: concepts

Before searching begins, be clear about your own information need and the objectives of your search. It helps to view the process as a problem-solving exercise. The first step is to understand the problem. The process of articulating a problem using language is helpful in clarifying your own ideas and is essential if you want to communicate ideas to others (people) and to databases (machines).

Example 4.3 Research questions

- Find recent research on the use of humour in advertising.
- Find recent research on the use of fear as a means of persuasion.
- Find recent research on the use by companies of public relations agencies involved in crisis management.

Normally a research problem is expressed as a single statement or question (see Example 4.3).

Once you have identified a problem and expressed it as a single statement, the next step is to break it down into its component concepts. Concepts are the ideas that comprise the research question. For example, the comment *Find recent research on the use of humour in advertising* can be divided into three concepts: Concept 1 recent; Concept 2 humour; Concept 3 advertising. It is helpful to think of these in the form of a table.

Concept 1	Concept 2	Concept 3
Recent	Humour	Advertising

At this point it is possible to make some assessment of the viability of a research question. A statement that contains two concepts might be too broad. The literature on *humour* and *advertising* could be extensive, in which case it is advisable to think of ways to contain your search. For example, you may wish to look only for recent articles or look at a specific form of advertising such as *television advertising*. Even if you choose not to modify your approach, thinking of these alternatives provides you with contingency plans, that is, ways of increasing or reducing the number of records your search retrieves. Adding a concept reduces the number of records you find. Even if you do not start out looking at *television,* it helps to know that if you retrieve too many articles using just *humour* and *advertising* you have considered this possibility and are prepared to look at *television, humour* and *advertising*.

Planning your search: selecting keywords

Having identified concepts, you now need to identify keywords to describe your concepts. You would normally choose keywords from natural language, the language you use in everyday speaking and writing. This raises the problem of selecting single keywords that represent the whole concept you want to find. Often this is not possible and you have to choose a selection of keywords that have the same meaning or nearly the same meaning, that is, synonyms. Take for example the concept of the *humour*. It is possible to write articles about the *humour* that don't use the word *humour*. Authors may use different words such as *joke, comedy, wit* or *irony* or *satire* or *parody*. So a search that looked at *advertising* and *humour* might equally include these words too. The database software does not understand the meaning of the word H U M O U R. It only checks to see if that word is present in the database. Therefore you need to key in other words or synonyms to help locate the maximum number of articles on your topic.

However, some keywords find too many articles, either because they are words commonly used in natural language or commonly used in the database you are searching. For example, using the word *communication* in ComAbstracts, a communication database, finds large numbers of articles – possibly the whole database! Similar examples are if you search for the word *management* in ABI Inform or *psychology* in PsycINFO (Psychological Abstracts). These words are said to have excessive recall, because they find too many articles for them to be useful.

Helpful hint: strategies for coping with excessive recall

The term *advertising* can have excessive recall in some business and marketing databases. There are some tactics you can use to get around this:

- Search for the word *advertising* in a specific field, for example the title field or abstract field (see the earlier section on in-field searching).
- Search for the word *advertising* as a thesaural term (see the later section on using controlled indexing languages).
- Search for the word *advertising* as part of a phrase (see the later section on phrases and proximity).

Spelling is critical not only because it needs to be correct, but also because of the differences between US and UK spelling. Major databases relevant to public relations and marketing communications are produced by North American companies or professional or academic organizations and the records they contain are written by academics working in North American universities. This means that you should prefer US spellings when using keywords. Typical examples are 'our/or' endings and 'ise/ize' endings. Using the example of humour and advertising, searching for *humour* instead of *humor* makes a significant difference in the number of articles retrieved. To give you an idea of how significant the difference in recall might be, *humor* is likely to find 80 per cent more articles than *humour* in a database such as ABI Inform.

Inevitably when searching in a large database, you will retrieve irrelevant articles that still contain the keywords you have typed in but have no relation to the topic for you have are searching for. This is caused by ambiguity in the keywords you have selected. It might be in the meaning of the word where one word can mean more than one thing (semantic ambiguity). *Holland* is the name of an author as well as the name of a country. It might also occur in the context in which the word is used (contextual ambiguity). For example, a search for the occurrence of the words *advertising* and *humour* in a single document does not guarantee that the subject of the articles is going to be about *humorous advertising* (see Example 4.4).

Example 4.4 Not all articles that contain your keywords will be relevant

A search using keywords *advertising* and *humour* retrieved the following articles which contain the keywords used but are not directly about the subject humorous advertisements:

- an interview with an advertising executive described as a Rottweiler with a sense of humour.
- an article in which studio executives complain about a lack of humorous writers, while advertising executives are said to be cynical about TV comedy programming.

If you discover that the majority of the records you have retrieved are irrelevant then you need to go back to your search plan and revise it.

If you apply some of the techniques in this chapter to finding recent research on the use of humour in advertising you will be able to write a fuller search plan using concepts and keywords. It helps if you create a search plan as a table, listing concepts first and under them the keywords which describe them.

Concept 1	Concept 2	Concept 3
Recent	Humor	Advertising
Keywords	*Keywords*	*Keywords*
1995–2001	Humor or humour or joke or comedy or wit or irony or satire or parody	Advertising

Boolean logic

George Boole (1815–64) was a logician working in Queen's College County Cork, Ireland in the 1850s. His enduring legacy was to develop a system of logic that now powers modern computers. Boole's system of logical operators, called Boolean Logic, enables you to retrieve information from computers by express-

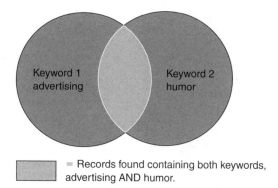

= Records found containing both keywords,
advertising AND humor.

Figure 4.1 Boolean AND.

ing the relationship between words and phrases in a way that the database software can interpret. Boolean Logic has three components, or Boolean operators:
AND, OR and NOT.

Boolean AND

AND links concepts together and asks the database software to locate all the
records that contain Keyword 1 and all the records that contain Keyword 2, then
to compare both sets of records and display only records that contain both terms.

This can be represented in a Venn diagram (Figure 4.1). Each circle represents the sets that contain the words *advertising* and *humor*. The area in the
centre, where the circles overlap, represents the records that contain both terms.
These are the records, which are displayed as results.

Boolean OR

OR links keywords together and asks the database software to locate all the
records that contain Keyword 1 and all the records that contain Keyword 2, then
to combine both sets of records into a single set (see Figure 4.2).

Each circle in Figure 4.2 represents the sets that contain the words *humor* and
comedy. Using OR displays all the records that contain one or both words. This
is represented by the total area of both circles.

Boolean NOT

NOT excludes keywords and asks the database software to locate all the records
that contain Keyword 1 and all the records that contain Keyword 2, then exclude
all records that contain Keyword 2 even if they contain Keyword 1 (see Figure
4.3).

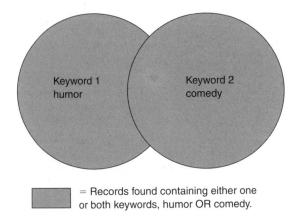

= Records found containing either one
or both keywords, humor OR comedy.

Figure 4.2 Boolean OR.

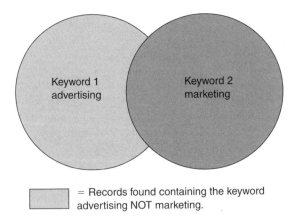

= Records found containing the keyword
advertising NOT marketing.

Figure 4.3 Boolean NOT.

Each circle of the Figure 4.3 represents the sets that contain the words *advertising* and *marketing*. Using NOT, only displays records that contain the word *advertising*.

Combining different Boolean operators in a single search

Now that you have understood the function of Boolean Logic you need to go one step further and understand what happens when you use more than one Boolean Logical operator (AND/OR/NOT) in a single search. Take for example the search:

advertising OR *marketing* AND *humor*

How will the database software implement this search? All the articles that contain the word *advertising* will be retrieved and all the articles that contain the words *marketing* and *humor* will be retrieved. Both sets of articles will end up being added together and displayed as results. In a large database like the Social Science Citation Index this could exceed 5,000 articles. The huge number is because the majority of records in this index contain the word *advertising*. However, this may not be what you were looking for. What you really wanted was for the database software to locate all the articles with either *advertising* or *marketing* in them, and then to see which of these articles also contained the word *humor*. In other words, you wanted the database software to implement OR before implementing AND. There is another step you have to take to make this happen which is described in the next section.

The way to do this depends on the search interface, that is the way in which the database software organizes the screens for you to type keywords into. Some databases such as ComAbstracts provide a single text box for you to type in your entire search. In this case, if you want to search for *advertising* OR *marketing* AND *humor* you have to add some structure to the keywords in order to ensure that the OR terms are treated first. This is done using parentheses ( ). The terms in parentheses are treated first:

(advertising OR *marketing)* AND *humor*

This solves the problem posed at the beginning of this section.

Advanced Search windows usually offer a series of text boxes combined with pull down windows for you to select various Boolean operators. Figure 4.4 is from the ProQuest UMI search interface for ABI Inform. The keywords are typed into the text boxes in the centre, and the Boolean operators have been selected from the pull down menus on the left of the screen.

It's worth pausing a minute to think how you could use an interface like this. With complex searches it's a good idea to think of each concept as a discrete unit of information. In the ProQuest UMI ABI Inform example in Figure 4.4, one concept is allocated to each text box. This means that within each text box you can use Boolean OR to link as many keywords as you like to describe that concept. In effect you are putting in the concepts working from the top to the bottom of the screen and the keywords on each line moving from left to right. Note one further point. The In ProQuest UMI ABI Inform interface has changed the Boolean operator NOT to AND NOT.

Finally, it is worth reviewing search interfaces which allocate numbers to keywords. These interfaces have a single text box to enter your search, but display the number of records retrieved by each keyword in a display window. Each keyword is also allocated a number automatically by the database software beginning S (meaning Set). In the example, advertising becomes S1. Next, the number of records containing the word advertising are listed (1,800), then the keyword itself (*advertising*). Once you have entered a keyword into the database software you need only refer to it by its set number S1, saving a great deal of effort in typing.

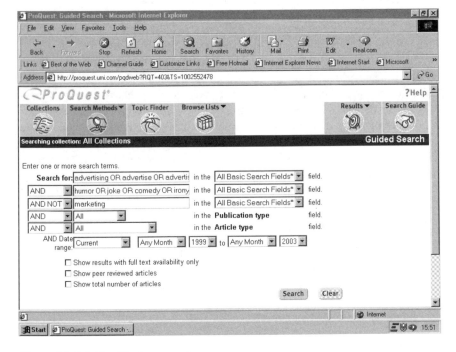

Figure 4.4 Selecting Boolean operators.

Source: The screen shot displayed here is published with permission of Bell & Howell Information
and Learning Company. Further reproduction is prohibited without permission.

Search
S1 and S4

Results
S1   1800 advertising
S2   2000 humor
S3   300 satire
S4   2300 humor OR satire

Just as in the example of the Advanced Search interface, it's a good idea to
create each concept as a discrete set. As this type of interface has only one text
box to type into, this means keying in each concept and its associated keywords
separately using OR, then adding the sets you create together at the end using
AND/NOT. You will probably see that this saves typing in very long searches
and if you make a mistake in typing you only have to retype the concept where
you made the error. Using AND to join concepts together at the end is easy
because you need only refer to them by their set numbers.

Search
S4 AND S10 NOT S11

Results

S1	...
S4	2500 advertising OR advertise OR advertisements
S5	...
S10	2700 humor OR joke OR comedy OR wit OR irony OR parody
S11	300 marketing
S12	120 S4 AND S10 NOT S11

You can also treat concepts as discrete blocks because it is good practice to think this way. It's much easier to plan and implement a search that has individual concepts, than to try to conceive a search as a whole. However you do it, whether you group concepts and their associated keywords using parentheses, type in each concept on a separate line, or create each concept as a separate set, this technique is good practice when searching.

Truncation and wildcards

Many words in English have more than one ending. Database software only retrieves an exact match of the words you type in, therefore all examples of each keyword need to be present in each search. The word *advertising*, for example, has a number of possible variations:

*advert*ising
*advert*s
*advert*isement
*advert*isements
*advert*isers
*advert*ise

All of these are relevant to the concept of advertising. If you were to retrieve all the relevant records in a database on the subject of advertising, all these words would have to be present in the search you type in. However, they share a common stem, *advert*. A search for all the words that begin with *advert* would solve the problem of having to key them all in separately. This process is called truncation, that is, shortening words with a truncation character, usually a '*' or '?'. So entering *advert?* as a keyword retrieves all the words that begin with *advert*. This saves you a great deal of time and relieves you of the bother of having to think of all the possible endings which, even with a simple keyword like *advertising*, are numerous.

Some words, however, present problems because individual letters within them can change. Cris*i*s becomes cris*e*s when used as a plural. Organi*s*ation becomes organi*z*ation in the transition from UK to US spelling. Therefore, in order to ensure you retrieve all versions of these words, a useful technique is to substitute a wildcard character, normally a '*', to search for any letter in the missing space. For example, *cris*s* finds cris*i*s or cris*e*s.

Using phrases and proximity commands

Some keywords are better expressed as phrases or strings of words together. If you were interested in the topic of *public relations,* you would expect these words to occur together in any relevant article, i.e. the word *public* followed by a space and then the word *relations.* As the likelihood of words occurring together is less than the likelihood of words occurring separately in a record, phrases tend to retrieve fewer articles. Where phrases represent technical terms occurring in the literature (see Example 4.5) they are useful tools for increasing the number of relevant articles.

Example 4.5 Technical terms containing three or more words

The following examples are technical terms containing three or more words, taken from the area of public relations and marketing communications: *integrated marketing communications, point of sale advertising, marketing information systems, internal public relations, word of mouth advertising.*

To be able to enter phrases, you need to be able to specify how words will relate to one another, or the proximity between words. Proximity is the term that describes this technique. There are, in fact, two ways of using proximity in a search:

- specify the order in which your keywords occur, e.g. if you want to search for *integrated marketing communication,* you want *integrated* to occur immediately before *marketing* and marketing to occur immediately before *communication* in articles you retrieve.
- specify the number of words you will accept between the keywords you have chosen. You might be prepared to accept them in no particular order in the same sentence. For example, if you were searching for *magazines* and *advertising* you would accept finding an article that contained this sentence: 'Advertising provides the principle income for *magazines*; money from sales contributes only 20% of income.'

Both these techniques use what are called *proximity indicators.* Different databases implement proximity commands in different ways. Usually, but not always, they use the terms WITH or NEAR. To take the first example, if you wanted to find the words *integrated marketing communications* as a phrase, the phrase with its commands would look something like this:

integrated WITH *marketing* WITH *communications*

WITH is the usual command for asking for one word to occur next to another in the order that you have typed them. The second example, *magazines* in the same sentence as *advertising,* might look something like this:

magazines 5NEAR *advertising*

NEAR is the usual command and the number 5 is the number of words you will accept between each keyword.

In some database software, if you type in more than one word the software will assume that you meant to use a phrase. It's best to consult the Help pages to see how they are implemented in the database you are using.

In-field searching

At the start of this chapter, in Example 4.2, you saw an example of a database record containing fields. Searching in individual fields (in-field searching) is one of the techniques that you can use to improve the accuracy of your search. This section describes in more detail how to do this in practice using two commonly used techniques: a command and then a pull down menu.

Commands have to be used where you are only provided with a single box to type into. Usually you type in the keyword you want to find, then the command to look in a specific field, then the field name or label (see Example 4.6).

Example 4.6 In-field searching

Using an example from Silver Platters database software WinSPIRS, the command is IN and the filed label is AU. So:

weinberger IN AU

With this type of search interface you need to know:

* the command that instructs the database software to look in a specific field.
* the fields available for you to search.
* the labels the database uses to identify them.

A look in the online Help should provide you with answers to these questions.

The second approach is to use pull down menus. They offer a choice of all the available fields so there is no need to use commands. Figure 4.5 is taken from ProQuest UMI ABI Inform: keywords are typed in the centre; fields are selected from the pull down menu on the right.

Controlled indexing languages (thesauri)

All records that are entered into a database are first read by a human indexer. He or she assigns subject terms that describe the significant content of each record. These terms are taken from a controlled list to ensure consistency across the database. These controlled lists are called *thesauri*. The terms they contain are controlled language, that is, language that is deliberately chosen to reflect the literature of a subject or the content of the database. There are printed thesauri, such as the

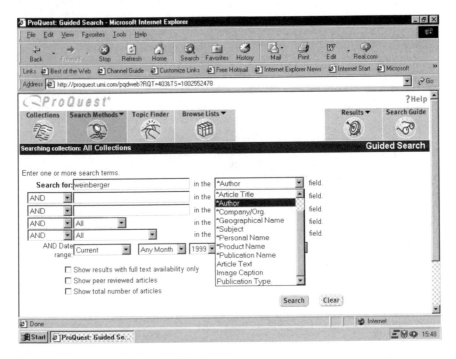

Figure 4.5 An example of a pull down menu.

Source: The screen shot displayed here is published with permission of Bell & Howell Information and Learning Company. Further reproduction is prohibited without permission.

Thesaurus of psychological index terms published by the American Psychological Association (APA) for use with the PsycINFO (Psychological Abstracts), or online thesauri, such as *ABI Inform thesaurus* which is only available online. Smaller databases such as ComAbstracts simply provide a list of keywords.

Thesauri offer other facilities to enable you to select appropriate subject terms. Typically for any given subject term a thesaurus suggests broader terms, narrower terms and synonyms and near terms, also called related terms. To clarify the meaning of a term as it is used in its database a thesaurus might also provide scope notes, that is, a definition of the subject term as it is used in the database (see Example 4.7).

Thesauri can be used to prepare a search by selecting terms from the thesaurus that fit the topic you are researching. Remember that these terms exist in their own field and that field either has to be specified in the command you issue using the database software, or selected from a pull down menu.

An alternative approach is to plan a search and then choose subject terms that occur in the results of your search. If you find a record that typifies those that you would like to find, selecting some of the thesaural terms from within that record enables you to find similar items.

Example 4.7 Sample thesaural entry

This is an example of a thesaural entry. Note that the main heading, *Advertising*, appears at the top followed by a *Scope Note, Broader Terms, Narrower Terms* and *Related Terms* (synonyms or near synonyms). A glance at this gives you an excellent overview of the choice of possible keywords.

Advertising
Scope Note:
   Paid for non-personal presentation and promotion of ideas, goods or services, transmitted through the mass media.

Broader term:
   Marketing

Narrower term:
   Advertisements
   Advertisers
   Advertising campaigns
   Advertising expenditures
   Advertising media
   Advertising rates
   Advertising revenue

Related terms:
   Brochures
   Frequent flier programmes
   Publicity
   Signs

Reviewing your search results

Two outcomes are likely. Either you will get too few records, in which case you need to broaden your search, or you will get too many records, in which case you need to narrow your search. Table 4.1 shows you how to do this.

Citation searching

From your general reading you may already know of a significant article which relates to your topic, or which has provided a foundation for thinking in the area. A search for other articles which have cited this article leads you to articles whose content closely matches the subject you are searching for. This technique can be implemented in the *Arts and Humanities Citation Index, Science Citation Index* and *Social Science Citation Index*. These databases are specifically designed to allow you to search the bibliographies of journal articles to see if your chosen paper has been cited. It takes about three years to write and publish articles for scholarly journals, so the article you use needs to be at least three years old to allow for subsequent authors to include it in their own work (see Example 4.8).

Table 4.1 Broadening or narrowing your search

To broaden your search	To narrow your search
1 Remove a concept. Take the least important concept out of your search.	1 Add in more concepts using AND to further define your research topic.
2 Add in more keywords using OR. This will increase the number of records retrieved for each concept.	2 Eliminate some keywords. Take out keywords which retrieve too many records.
3 Use truncation.	3 Eliminate truncation.
4 Eliminate proximity operators.	4 Use proximity operators.
5 Replace terms from the thesaurus with your own keywords.	5 Use terms from the thesaurus.
6 Search the entire record. Take out instructions to search in only one field.	6 Search in specified fields. Search in the appropriate field such as 'title' or 'abstract'.

Example 4.8 Citation searching

An early article in the *Journal of Advertising Research*:

Madden, T.J. and Weinberger, M.G. (1984). 'Humor in Advertising: A Practitioner View'. *Journal of Advertising Research* 24, 4: 23–30.

This retrieves twenty-one articles on the topic of humour and advertising using the Social Science Citation Index.

Recording essential information

You won't be surprised to learn that the problems of recording, storing and managing references are not new. In fact, there are software packages on the market designed to store and manage references and documents, many of which are in their fifth or sixth version. They are collectively called Personal Bibliographic Software (PBS) (Mulvaney 2000). The three most popular packages are ProCite, Endnote and Reference Manager. Currently all three packages are owned by a single company, ISI ResearchSoft (ISI ResearchSoft 2000). For an extended research project with perhaps many thousands of references you should consider one of these packages.

PBS have many advantages over using either a general-purpose database management package, or not using one at all. They enable you to:

- store and retrieve records using a sophisticated retrieval interface.
- input data manually, directly from the Internet or download from databases.
- work with Microsoft Word to cite references directly from PBS databases into your word documents.

Key point: Personal Bibliographic Software

Personal Bibliographic Software (PBS) are database packages designed to manage bibliographic references to all kinds of information:

- printed sources: books, journal articles, conferences and reports.
- non-print materials: videos, CDs and tapes.
- electronic resources: web pages and emails.

- choose from citation styles used by professional institutions and publishers to produce reference lists and bibliographies.
- seamlessly download into your personal ProCite database from many major bibliographic databases.
- share files of references with colleagues and publish your own databases on the Internet.

For an undergraduate piece of work where you might have perhaps only fifty to 100 references, they are not really necessary; you can get by by using a word processor or database package. Usually the databases you search, such as ABI Inform, will allow you to email references and full text to your email address or download it to your computer. It's easy to transfer this information from your email box into your own recording system.

Most important is to have a system for recording that will deliver your references in the format needed for your final report or thesis. This is likely to take the form of either a number system or the name–date system, as illustrated in Example 4.9. A number system is where each reference in the text is numbered corresponding to references in the bibliography. The name–date system is where each reference in the text includes the name of the author and the date corresponding to a bibliography arranged alphabetically by author. In Chapter 3, we have already mentioned that the Harvard System is a commonly used academic reference system.

The organization or publisher to whom you submit your research will require certain elements of the citation to be present in a given order. There may also be stipulations about style, for example, using italics or underlining for journal titles. Be sure that you know what the requirements are and can store your references using the correct citation style.

A word processor enables you to store your references in a table. Using columns such as Record Number, Reference, Abstract/Notes or Keywords, you can create a usable document for recording your references. You can sort your references alphabetically or numerically depending on which reference system you are using to produce a final bibliography. When you come to produce the final bibliography, make a copy of the document and then remove your own additions, notes, abstract and keywords, leaving just the references. You can either transfer the table into text or simply make the table borders invisible to produce the final version. See Example 4.10.

Example 4.9 Referencing systems

Number system
In the text:
Early research in the use of humour in advertising (1) focused on . . .

In the bibliography:
(1) Madden, T.J. and Weinberger, M.G. (1984) 'Humor in Advertising: A Practitioner View'. *Journal of Advertising Research* 24(4): 23–30.

Name–Date System (such as the Harvard System)
In the text:
Early research in the use of humour in advertising (Madden and Weinberger, 1984) focused . . .

In the bibliography:
Madden, T.J. and Weinberger, M.G. (1984) 'Humor in Advertising: A Practitioner View'. *Journal of Advertising Research* 24(4): 23–30.

Example 4.10 Storing references in a table

Rec. Num.	Reference	Notes	Keyword
1	Alden, D.L. Mukherjee, A. and Hoyer, W.D. (2000). The effects of incongruity, surprise and positive moderators on perceived humor in television advertising. *Journal of Advertising Research* 29, 2: 1–15.	Two studies, using television advertising: 1) schema familiarity moderates the effect of surprise – other aspects of the ad moderate the effect of surprise on humour 2) surprise can have different affective outcomes such as fear and humour. Full text in file adv.doc [Hyperlink]	advertising; humour; surprise

If you feel confident about using your word processor software, you could create hyperlinks from the document that contains your bibliography to the documents that contain the full text articles you have downloaded from databases. Most modern word processors will allow you to do this. At least, record the names of the documents which contain the downloaded full text so you know where they are.

Table 4.2 Bibliographic and full text databases

Style	Subject	Scope
ABI/INFORM [Full Text]	Management and business	Coverage of *c.* 1,000 journals in business and related areas with full text of recent articles.
ASSIA: Applied Social Sciences Citation Index	Social science	English language journals including such topics as social services, politics, employment, race relations and health education.
ComAbstracts	Media and communication	Abstracts *c.* 40 communication journals. Topics covered include communication theory, mass media, and politics and social policy. Abstracts are brief.
ComIndex	Media and communication	Indexes 65 key international journals in communication. Topics covered include mass communication, journalism and broadcasting.
Communication Abstracts	Media and communication	Communication related journals from *c.* 200 journals, books and conferences. Contains full abstracts.
Emerald Fulltext	Management and business	*c.* 110 full text journals published by MCB, a significant number cover PR, marketing and advertising.
Emerald Reviews	Management and business	Coverage of management journals including such areas as organizational behaviour and public relations.
Market Research Abstracts	Marketing	Coverage of scholarly journals in advertising, public relations and marketing. The electronic version of this service is available through WARC.
PsycINFO (Psychological Abstracts)	Psychology	Comprehensive coverage of scholarly journals, books, chapters and dissertations in psychology; including the areas of advertising, business and communications.
Public Relations Review Bibliography	Public relations	Printed index to PR journals, and related journals that cover PR topics.
Social Science Citation Index	Social science	Indexes 350 international English language journals. Topics included are business, politics, psychology and sociology.
Sociological Abstracts	Sociology	Comprehensive coverage of the literature of sociology. Topics of relevance include groups and society, culture, politics, education and the environment.
World Advertising Research Centre [WARC] [Full Text]	Advertising	The site contains case studies, statistics, conference papers and full text of selected journals including the *Journal of Advertising Research* and ADMAP.

Bibliographic and full text databases of relevance to public relations and marketing communications

A significant amount of recent material is available in full text from ABI Inform and Emerald Fulltext (see Table 4.2). The World Advertising Research Centre (WARC) occupies a niche in the area of advertising but provides full text access to a number of journals and an extensive collection of case studies. The full text databases, however, do not represent the totality of literature available and need to be backed up with Indexes and Abstracts and, of course, visits to the library.

Summary

- The process of searching begins before you actually use a database.
- Your search starts when you identify what you want to search for, leading to a written statement of your search question.
- The next step is a search plan that identifies concepts and keywords.
- Your approach needs to be systematic. However, be prepared to revisit your search and revise it in the light of what you find.
- In general, start with a broad search using keywords you have chosen. Then modify your search using one or more of these techniques: Boolean AND, OR and NOT; truncation and wildcards; phrases and proximity; in-field searching.
- Consider using a Citation Search when you come across an article in your reading that might have been cited by other authors writing on your subject.
- Make use of Personal Bibliographic Software (PBS) or a word processor to manage your references.

5   Access and ethical issues

The attainment of high standards of ethics in research is an essential goal of any research project and the subject of this chapter. The chapter encourages you to consider how you might plan and carry out your study with integrity, honesty and a concern for the welfare of participants in your research.

This chapter deals with:

- strategies for gaining access to participants, research settings and resources. It notes the difficulty of recruiting informants and negotiating with gate-keepers.
- basic ethical principles and conventions related to:
  - the right to free and informed choice
  - protection from harm to individuals and equipment
  - privacy: anonymity and confidentiality
  - autonomy: voluntary informed consent
  - honesty: omission, interpretation and plagiarism.

Introduction

When collecting data through human interaction, it is important to pay close attention to ethical issues because there are inherent problems and dilemmas related to the inductive and holistic nature of qualitative research. Because research is initially inductive, it is not always possible for you to fully inform participants in advance about the potential consequences of the research, or even the particular areas you intend to study because changes occur as your research unfolds. The holistic, humanistic nature of qualitative research means that you are involved in a relationship with research participants – in some cases this can become quite close – and it is your personality, experiences and perceptions, together with your interaction with informants, that shapes what data are collected and how you interpret them. Therefore, as you navigate between 'the illusion of objectivity and the borders of subjectivity' (Fine 1998: 141), you will continually face a host of ethical issues.

Among ethical considerations are those concerning the intrusive nature of research and the welfare of participants. Unless you have acted honestly and in a trustworthy manner, your research will be unethical. Furthermore, unless you have addressed ethical issues explicitly in your research report, your project will lack professionalism. Ethical issues must be carefully thought through in detail, in advance of your fieldwork. They should be clearly discussed first in your research proposal and later in the methodology section of your report or dissertation. Even if you have addressed the more obvious questions of anonymity and confidentiality, and ensured that no psychological harm to participants has been intended through your research, it is not advisable to make a start on your fieldwork without first thinking about ethics because, before too long, you will meet an ethical dilemma.

The attainment of high standards of ethics in research should be an essential goal of any research project. This begins with a discussion with your research

---

Example 5.1 Some ethical dilemmas

- You are carrying out a series of interviews with public relations consultants. You were given some information in a previous interview which, if released into the public arena, could seriously damage the reputation of your next interviewee. Should you tell her about it in the course of your interview? Should you include the information in your published research report?
- Your research is in a sensitive area. You are unlikely to get access if you state your real purpose. Do you hide the goals of your research from informants and tell them you are studying something else?
- You are likely to have difficulty gaining access for research if your potential informants realize they will be involved in a student project. Do you send an introductory letter on university letterhead, leaving out some of the details of your project, in the hope that they will think this is a university-funded project?
- You are in the middle of an interview when your interviewee interrupts the conversation to take a telephone call. He presumes you have turned off your tape recorder and goes on to discuss some highly sensitive information which would be useful for your research. Do you use the information?
- You have been granted access to shadow a public affairs director as she carries out her normal work routines. She goes to lunch and you are left alone in the office. There are confidential documents lying on her desk which would usefully inform your research. Should you read them? Should you photocopy them while she is out?
- You are studying young people's attitudes to brands. A tobacco company offers you £30,000 to sponsor your research. Do you take it?

How you answer the last question will depend on your own stance towards smoking and the ethics of tobacco companies. The answer to all the other questions is 'No'. Don't even consider it! The rest of the chapter explains why.

supervisor or research colleagues about the ethical issues that are likely to arise at the initial access stage, during the research process, in the writing up stage and, finally, in publication. It involves keeping detailed records about ethical dilemmas that confront you. It includes making decisions that are ethically sound and which are articulated in your writing. It is important, therefore, that ethical issues are not merely understood and taken into account but also made explicit in the research report, dissertation or thesis.

Example 5.2 Making ethical issues explicit in a proposal

The following is an extract from a student proposal by Belinda J. Tucker for research into the perspectives of adolescents regarding the influence of their teachers:

> Due to the nature of the research questions, the confidentiality pro-vided through carefully maintained participant anonymity, and my status as a graduate student with no connections to the teachers or school administration, there is minimal threat to the well-being of the students in the study as a result of their participation.
>
> My stance of 'empathetic neutrality' should minimize the threat of 'interviewing as exploitation' – a process that turns others into subjects so that their words can be appropriated for the benefit of the researcher (Seidman 1991: 7) that presents ethical problems in some studies.
>
> (Quoted by Locke *et al.* 2000: 261)

Researchers often believe that it is sufficient to deal with ethical considerations only at the planning stage of their work. However, ethical problems occur right through the research process. Unless you have explained the steps you took to deal with these, then your work is inadequate.

In the area of ethics, guidelines and rules exist which should not be trans-gressed. Some of these standards are set by professional bodies such as the Market Research Society, or sociological, psychological or communications associations in various countries. Others are established by universities themselves.

Some ethical principles are simple and clear, for instance, obvious infringe-ments of ethical guidelines such as plagiarism or manufacturing the data. Others, however, are unusual or unique and cannot be solved by reference to established texts or sets of guidelines. In cases such as these, you may be tempted to 'bend the rules' in order to gather valuable evidence. Indeed, some well-known researchers have succumbed to this. This highlights the tension between the obligation to extend knowledge and the need to respect the rights of others. However, it is essential that you maintain this balance with honesty. There is never any excuse for unethical behaviour in research. It is unacceptable and unprofessional.

The neglect of ethical questions could result in:

- harm to participants.
- damage to the reputation of the department, university or organization in which you are registered.
- conflicts with funding agencies and grant-holding bodies.
- denial of access to organizations and participating institutions.
- problems for your supervisor.
- litigation.
- non-completion of the research.

In the following sections, we discuss some of the ethical issues you will encounter in your research.

Access to participants, settings and resources

Recruiting participants

Gaining access to informants, settings and materials for research is one of the first steps in the research process and ethically can be the most problematic in qualitative research. The ethical issue is linked as much to the acceptability of your conduct as to other ethical considerations. People can be vulnerable, they have rights that must be protected, settings may be dangerous or difficult to access and materials may be confidential. In all of these instances, it is crucial that you carry out your research with integrity, honesty and with a concern for the welfare of participants.

When seeking to gain access, you must ensure that:

- participation is voluntary.
- people in the setting (such as a geographical area, an organization or a particular context) are not harmed or inconvenienced.
- resources that you use are freely committed, such as confidential company documents or personal diaries that you read. Be aware that access to certain materials and their use in research may have harmful consequences, such as the release of information that is valuable to competitors, or the public exposure of private issues.

Before starting your research, take the following steps:

1 gain access to the setting.
2 obtain permission from gatekeepers – those who are able to give permission for the research to be carried out (e.g. account directors, marketing or corporate communications directors, leaders of organizations, or human resource directors).
3 ask participants for permission to undertake the research and explain how you will protect them.

4   explain early and clearly the type of project in which they will be involved.

Gaining access means gaining permission to enter the setting, set up and obtain samples, interview or observe participants, and read formal documents relevant to your research. You might ask your supervisor to advise and support you in obtaining access to gatekeepers and participants and to gain permission from ethics and other organizational committees, if this is necessary. Formal permission is important in any research and protects all sides – researcher, participants, supervisors and the university in which you are enrolled or the organization commissioning your research.

Access is sought in various ways. Some researchers pin up a notice on a public board in the organization in which they wish to carry out their research or put an advertisement in the local newspaper asking for volunteers to participate. Where you advertise will depend on your research sample. For example, if you were seeking the views of film-goers about cinema advertising, a good place to advertise would be on a noticeboard in the local cinema or in a newspaper advertisement positioned next to the film guide. It is important to advertise in a public space where the advertisement can be seen easily; it should be readable and interesting with inclusion criteria clearly stated. Remember that you may have to obtain the permission of gatekeepers to advertise (such as the cinema manager). If you are a student, your supervisor's signature on a letter of introduction may help in your application for access.

Example 5.3 Advertisement for research participants

DO YOU GO TO THE CINEMA AT LEAST ONCE A MONTH?
A university research team would like to hear your views on cinema advertising – and pay you for them. We're looking for people who are regular film-goers, and who have an hour to spare next Friday to take part in a group interview held at the University of New South Wales.

For further information, contact the research coordinator, Joe Bloggs, University of New South Wales, on 01202 524 111 before Wednesday 16 December.

Participation in research by individuals or groups should be entirely voluntary; participants must not be pressurized. Talk or write to people, tell them about your project, ask them if they wish to take part. Try someone else if they don't.

Dealing with gatekeepers

Participants often have to be approached through the mediation of 'gatekeepers', that is, people who have the power to grant or withhold access. They control information and grant formal or informal (sometimes verbal) entry to the setting and participants; they may also impose certain conditions for access, such as the requirement to read your report prior to publication. It will be up to you to convince them of the relevance of your research and the benefit of their involvement. Gatekeepers may hold official positions, such as the corporate communications manager of an organization or the partner of an advertising agency, or they may have an unofficial gatekeeping role, such as those persons with the informal power and influence to grant and deny access or information. Secretaries and personal assistants are often powerful, but unrecognized, gatekeepers in organizations.

Gatekeepers may be found in any hierarchical level of an organization. There is no point in seeking access only from management if you are interested in undertaking an ethnographic study which requires you to explore the whole organization. Say you wished to investigate an organization's communication networks and the managing director had guaranteed you access. Without your realizing it, there may be deep rifts in the organization between management and other stakeholders. Your project, therefore, could come to a standstill if the workforce, customers or clients refused to take part. Therefore, it is wise not only to ask the person directly in charge but also others elsewhere in the organization who are likely to hold the power to start or stop your research.

Example 5.4 Seeking access

The study of a new organization was undertaken by one of us, Daymon (2002), who began the research six months before the company officially started operating with a staff of 400. She first approached the executive responsible for education liaison (the company's training officer) with a letter explaining her proposed research. This was followed by a meeting with him where she outlined the research objectives and explained the implications for the company and participants of being involved in the three-year research project. The training officer forwarded her proposals to the director of regional development and to the chief executive who eventually granted her access to the company. No conditions were placed on her research although a request was made by both the chief executive and director of public affairs to view the draft report in order to check for accuracy of facts. Over the course of the next three years, she approached individuals and departmental heads, seeking their participation, outlining details of the project, and guaranteeing the anonymity and protection of informants.

All gatekeepers have power and control of access, but those at the top of the hierarchy are most powerful and usually they should be asked first because they can restrict access even if everybody else agrees. Their decision is likely to be based on whether the benefits of involvement in research will be outweighed by the costs to the organization (such as the time involved in employees being interviewed. For a start, just calculate the hourly rate charged by consultants to their clients and then consider the hidden cost of their interviews with you!). If gatekeepers agree to co-operate in your research, the path of your research is smoothed because their recommendations can encourage others to collaborate. They might, for instance, explain your research at a regular company meeting and ask potential informants to take part. A danger with this strategy, however, is that participants may see the research as originating from management and therefore be reluctant to disclose their thoughts.

Example 5.5 Problems with permission

John Giddens asked permission from the managing editor of a group of radio stations to interview news journalists about their work and social relationships with public relations practitioners. The chief executive granted access and announced John's research in an open meeting. The journalists decided that the research was management-led and infringed their journalistic autonomy. John found it very difficult to persuade them otherwise, as they were concerned about issues of confidentiality.

Negotiating access

Gatekeepers may deny access for a variety of reasons.

- *As a researcher, you are seen as unsuitable by gatekeepers.* Depending on the organization, you may be considered an unsuitable researcher because of your gender, youth, appearance or behaviour. However, just because you don't 'fit in' to the culture of an organization does not mean that you are untrustworthy or unable to cope with the study. Therefore, friends or acquaintances who are already involved in your chosen location may sometimes be able to persuade those in power who doubt your credibility. A letter from your research supervisor also helps.
- *It is feared that your presence might disturb the setting.* In some settings, relationships and dynamics can be subtly altered by the presence of someone new. Imagine a meeting called to resolve a conflict: levels of concentration and trust would be threatened by an 'outside' researcher sitting in with a notebook or a tape recorder.
- *There is suspicion and fear of potential criticism.* Research findings may not be favourable to an organization and could damage its public image. In this case, you would need to consider phrasing your critical discussion diplomatically without damaging your own integrity. Remember that even if you do not publish a paper from your research, in general your research report will be publicly accessible.
- *You are investigating sensitive issues.* These may involve commercial confidentiality or might be of a more personal nature where participants, researchers, or even society as a whole could be harmed if results are published (Lee 1993).
- *Potential participants in the research may be embarrassed, fearful or too vulnerable.*

- *Gatekeepers may not know about qualitative research methods and see them as 'unscientific' because surveys and numbers are not involved.* According to the culture of many companies, numbers have high validity and research which does not produce statistics is deemed to have little value.
- *Economic issues – the research may take up too much time for the organization involved.*

For these reasons, access should be negotiated with a great deal of diplomacy, honesty and tact. Ideally, you should expect to articulate the purpose of your research and the methodology in order to explain your project. However, the inductive nature of qualitative research often makes this difficult. Initially, you may have only a general idea of the area of research. Say you are interested in studying how integrated marketing communications are managed in a large multinational organization but you don't yet have a central research question. After several weeks of conducting unstructured interviews at different sites, you discover that there are major tensions caused by differences in cultural expectations. Therefore, you end up focusing your research on how national cultures affect the extent to which marketing communications are integrated. In your early discussions with the organization, it would not have been possible to explain exactly what your eventual focus would be. Therefore, in order to gain access to some contexts, researchers sometimes have to be rather vague or ambiguous about their proposed research, providing only general, not specific, information.

Helpful hint
In some cases, it is not possible to provide full and frank details about the research purpose and direction prior to the commencement of your research. However, you should fully inform participants after the research is completed.

Another reason why full explanation of your purpose is problematic is if participants know exactly what you are seeking to investigate, they may be directed towards certain issues raised by you, rather than allowing their own ideas and perceptions to emerge. They may become unnaturally sensitive or responsive to material that they might otherwise view only casually or indifferently (Deacon *et al.* 1999). In some observation studies, modifications in behaviour may occur if participants are aware of your primary focus. This invalidates the data. A solution offered by the British Psychological Society is to withhold some of the details of your project. Is this deception? Some would argue yes. Others contend that as long as participants are given detailed information *after* completion of the data collection, then such a tactic is ethical. The British Psychological Society suggests that the withholding of some details is ethical as long as there is a distinction between this and 'deliberately falsely informing the participants of the purpose of the research, especially if the information given implie[s] a more benign topic of study than was in fact the case' (BPS 2000: 6). The protection of the dignity of participants is paramount, however, and therefore the BPS go on to state that the withholding of information is inappropriate if it is likely to lead to 'discomfort, anger or objections'.

Key point
Most gatekeepers will only grant access if they are assured that there are no risks to themselves, their organizations, their customers or their clients.

Gatekeepers sometimes give permission for research on the basis that they have the opportunity to view and comment on your draft report. This can put you in a difficult position: do you agree to provide a draft and risk the organization denying you the right to publish, or do you look elsewhere for another research setting where the gatekeepers are more relaxed about your findings? Bryman (1989) writes that sometimes it is better to offer a draft and face the risk of eventual restrictions rather than not secure entry to an organization. We have followed his advice when carrying out our own investigations and have gone on to use gatekeepers' comments on our drafts as further primary evidence which we have then analysed and incorporated into our reports.

Sometimes you may be asked to give details about how your research will be disseminated. To some extent, future problems can be avoided if you are able to negotiate this before research starts. However, if you intend to publish articles where the company and informants cannot be identified (because you have changed some details and used pseudonyms), you can feel confident about progressing in this direction without informing the research organization.

If you are carrying out sponsored research where you have financial and social support from the organization where your research takes place, there is a danger that gatekeepers and other participants will have their own agenda and may attempt to manipulate the research – intentionally or unintentionally. For example, institutional objectives may take precedence over individual research interests because of the prioritizing of resources, such as the costs of staff time. If you are influenced by these expectations, your direction and interpretation of the data will be affected. Resistance can be difficult because of the powerful position that gatekeepers hold to facilitate or prevent the progress of your investigation. Unfortunately, there is no ideal solution to this problem.

In attempting to gain access to organizations, groups or other contexts, a variety of ethical issues are likely to arise. To whom do you turn if you discover anything unusual or dramatic in your research that requires an ethical decision to be made? Your supervisor or research colleagues should be your first port of call, but don't forget to refer to professional codes of ethical practice. The research discussions and writings of other researchers working in similar fields will also provide useful insights.

Ethical principles and conventions

A number of basic ethical principles provide benchmarks against which to judge your study as you move through the stages of planning, implementation and outcome. These concern the right of free and informed choice, protection from harm to individuals and equipment, and principles of privacy, autonomy and honesty. If you choose not to follow these ethical guidelines, or adopt inappropriate procedures, you are likely to affect your future or ongoing employment in a negative way.

The right of free and informed choice

People whom you ask to participate in a study have the right to give or withhold their co-operation. They can do this at any time, either at the outset or during the course of research. In online research, participants may not offer a reason for withdrawing; they may simply disappear, leaving you wondering if the reason was due to unclear communication or faulty technology. An ethical dilemma then is whether or not to try to find the participant when this might be construed by them as an unwelcome intrusion. In accepting the principle of free and informed choice, you recognize that your need to collect data is always subordinate to a person's right to decide whether to provide it or not.

Protection from harm

No emotional or physical harm should come to the people you study, either in the course of conducting your research, or in its outcome. For instance, in certain circumstances, in-depth interviews may carry emotional risks for participants because they can be problematic, stressful and taxing. The onus is on you to be aware of this, to ensure that your research procedures are just and fair to the individuals who take part, and that you care for their well-being. This extends to the way in which you treat people involved in your study. It is tempting to slip into a mode of seeing informants as sources of data, or research chattels (Locke *et al.* 2000) rather than as interesting human beings. Violating their person through disrespect in this way may scar them for a long time, and cause them to see future research in a cynical or negative light.

In some instances, you may be collecting data from people who cannot take complete responsibility for their own decisions, such as children or consumers with learning difficulties. They need special protection.

For your own protection, make sure that you are aware of health and safety issues. You are responsible for protecting not only informants (and your own health) but also any equipment which you use or come into contact with.

One of the risks involved in Internet research relates to its public–private

---

Example 5.6 Undertaking sensitive research

In an investigation into teenage lifestyles and responses to public relations messages about contraception and AIDS, Greg Parker conducted interviews with forty people between the ages of 15 and 20. He ensured that he had the consent of the individuals as well as their parents. Where possible, he held the interviews in schools, in rooms where the doors were left open or in open plan areas. This helped his participants to feel more comfortable and secure.

---

nature. Online research carries the potential for public exposure of participants, especially when personal or sensitive information is involved or when reports or messages are distributed that are commercially confidential. Researchers do not have the same extent of control or intervention as they do in face-to-face group discussions and therefore potentially harmful contributions to online focus groups may be read and sent elsewhere before you even get to read them. In the same way, if participants' email addresses become known to one another they could be used for purposes unconnected with the study without the consent of participants. Your ethical role is to emphasize the dangers inherent in online research before participants give their consent to take part (Mann and Stewart 2000).

Whether your research is online or face-to-face, it is worth remembering that eventually your study will end up in the public domain, and others who evaluate or review such research studies will assume its integrity. As long as you are careful not to expose informants to unnecessary risks, to respect the privacy of participants' thoughts and actions, and value the co-operation that has been extended to you, then you will have demonstrated your concern for the protection of the people involved in your study.

Privacy: anonymity and confidentiality

Privacy and protection from harm are closely related ethical principles because, if you betray participants' rights of privacy, then you are failing to protect them from harm. Rights of privacy are neglected if you publish research findings which present confidential information, or if you expose confidences which can be traced back to participants. However, even if you have published with integrity and sensitivity, two questions remain: how is it possible to guarantee that your findings will not be misused by outsiders, and can you guarantee that your conclusions will not be harmful if read by people with different sets of cultural values (Cieurzo and Keitel 1999)? Your responsibility then is to ensure anonymity and confidentiality for organizations and individuals. This applies to all participants whether they are consumers, clients, managers, academics or your peers.

Maintaining *anonymity* means that you do not divulge the identity of research participants to others. It includes not identifying the institution or location in which the research takes place when you are writing up the research report or dissertation. If you are using email or online conferencing for research, it may mean not identifying real names, user names, domain names, signatures and even ISPs. If, on the other hand, you wish to identify individuals or organizations, it is necessary to first obtain permission. This is sometimes granted to you prior to the data collection. It is good practice, however, to reconfirm this if you are writing for publication.

Anonymity is maintained through:

- the use of pseudonyms.
- a change of the names of location and organization.
- a change of minor detail in the description of participants, if necessary.
- a change of demographic factors that are unimportant to the study (this should only be done if demographic factors are not important to the focus of the study).
- the protection of data by applying labels with letters or numbers, not names.
- secure storage of tapes, lists, scripts, transcripts, etc.

To guarantee anonymity, give participants and settings (including Internet lists, etc.) pseudonyms, and only you or the members of your research team should be able to match these with the real names. Provide labels for tapes, notes, transcripts or participant lists and store these securely. For example, you might label interviews according to the order in which they were conducted, matching tapes and transcripts with the same label. When writing up your findings, identify any quotations according to the interview code and refrain from disclosing too many details about informants so that they cannot be identified.

Confidentiality is different from anonymity. It means that you do not disclose issues or ideas that participants wish to keep confidential. As Sieber states: 'Confidentiality refers to agreements with persons about what may be done with their data' (1992: 52). This refers not only to how you eventually use the data, such as in the writing of your research report, but also to how you conduct yourself in interviews. Many informants share confidential information that could jeopardize their careers or even the future of their organization. It is vital that you honour their trust in you and do not release this information to other members of the organization. It is sometimes tempting when interviewing to let something slip especially if you are keen to gain the confidences of subsequent interviewees.

On similar lines, on one occasion we were on the receiving end of an attempt by a senior manager to coerce us into revealing what we had learnt about the personal motivations and relationships of his staff. We had spent a day at a major record company interviewing the managing director, the general manager and a record promoter. We returned home to receive two telephone calls from the managing director demanding that we tell him what his staff had said in interview about his style of leadership and how they perceived their relationship

---

Example 5.7 Anonymizing informants and their responses

The following are examples of two different ways of anonymizing informants. The first provides a letter and numbers instead of a name, the second a pseudonym.

- A former factory worker explained that no official statement had been made about the company's closure: 'The first we heard was when the local radio announced that 5,000 jobs were to go. We received no communication from management' (A1.3).

Label: interview A, page 1, line 3.

- A former factory worker explained that no official statement had been made about the company's closure: 'The first we heard was when the local radio announced that 5,000 jobs were to go. We received no communication from management' (Joe, assembly line operator, Luton site).

Pseudonym and changed details: pseudonym, only general role provided but no specific details given of job title or department.

---

with him. This was despite our insistence in verbal and written communication at the outset that all interviews were strictly confidential. Needless to say, we told him nothing further, and used the telephone calls as further data for our research project!

The issue of confidentiality also becomes important with respect to data from confidential documents such as work records, client contracts, letters of complaint or statements made about powerful people in organizations. In the latter case, remember to keep the identities of people strictly confidential. There must be no chance that they can be recognized.

Computer-mediated communication poses a threat to confidentiality because, when electronic messages are in transit, they can be accessed and used by unscrupulous others (Mann and Stewart 2000). Messages can also be copied and distributed to unintended recipients without the knowledge of either the sender or even, in some cases, the researcher. Therefore, if research in public relations and marketing communications is commercially sensitive, investigations carried out over the Internet may not be appropriate. In any case, take care with the assurances of confidentiality that you give to participants.

Be aware that ethical principles and rules are implicit in the research itself, for instance, carrying out the research or presenting participants' viewpoints without fraud or distortion. The research should be used only for the purpose which you have presented to participants, and you should only disclose that which participating individuals permit you to share publicly.

Autonomy: informed consent

One of the most important issues related to the principle of autonomy is that of voluntary informed consent. This is an explicit agreement between the researcher and research participants whereby participants agree to take part in the research project and allow data to be collected for use by the researcher. Their permission is based on an understanding of what the research is about and the potential risks or benefits to them.

Traditionally, informed consent has meant a one-off event prior to the start of research (when information is given by the researcher and consent received from participants). However, more recently, researchers have begun to view informed consent as a process whereby participants are offered multiple opportunities to evaluate their involvement and the direction of the research (Cieurzo and Keitel 1999). This relates first to the longitudinal nature of much qualitative research where you may interview participants more than once, or observe them over a period of time. In this case, it may be appropriate to seek renewed consent from informants if the settings or focus of the research change, or if the relationship between you and participants changes. Second, it relates to the difficulty of establishing a clear direction at the start of much qualitative research because, as we have discussed earlier, your research develops from the interpretations of participants and therefore often you cannot describe the path of research in detail before it commences. In this case, you seek to gain consent at the beginning of

---

Key point

The basic components of informed consent are:

- name, credentials and contact address.
- identity of your sponsor or funding agency, if there is one.
- research strategies and aims.
- expected duration of the individual's participation and/or the researcher's presence in the setting.
- potential risks and benefits to the organization or individuals.
- promise of anonymity and confidentiality. Steps through which these will be ensured.
- assurance that participation is voluntary and that participants can withdraw at any time from the research process.
- promise to answer any questions that participants have about the research.
- reassurance that the research will not adversely affect the people involved or the organization where they work.
- details of how the data will be disposed of at the end of the study.
- description of how the findings will be disseminated at the end of the study.

---

research (based on a general aim) and then also at the end when you are able to provide full details about the aims and direction of the research.

When gaining initial consent from potential participants, it is best to have a written consent form. The following list offers some basic components of informed consent.

It is usual to give your name, credentials and university or funding body so that participants know that they are dealing with a bona fide researcher. The reason for providing an address is so that participants can contact you if they experience difficulties during the research or want to withdraw. Most individuals will want to know why they specifically have been selected and will expect an honest answer. By setting out the research strategies, aims, potential risks and benefits, you go some way to answering this. It is usual to promise anonymity to participants in your research unless, of course, they wish to be identified. For example, we are currently carrying out a longitudinal study of issues of organizational growth in a London public relations consultancy, Abel Hadden & Company. When we were seeking consent for the study to take place, the partners of the company readily agreed to their identity being divulged in all future publications, in the expectation that this would generate some additional awareness of their corporate brand.

Participants confirm their agreement to participate through a signed information and consent form or by oral consent. It is more desirable to obtain signed consent rather than oral agreement although sometimes it is not always convenient to do this. However, a simple tear-off statement and space for a signature helps. If sending by email, you have two options. Participants can be sent a form for printing off, signing and posting back to you. Or your consent form can be downloaded and then emailed to you with a typed 'Yes' or 'No' response. Remember to express the consent form in ordinary language without jargon (this applies especially to the presentation of your aims and research procedures).

With regard to obtaining consent for participation in real-time online focus groups, participants need time to read and digest your consent form before returning it to you. Asking them to do this while the chat session or focus group takes place is not practical as it disrupts the flow of discussion. Therefore, Mann and Stewart (2000) suggest either setting up an asynchronous conference area where your form can be read and agreed ahead of time, or sending participants the form by email or traditional post. The same methods can also be used for online research using conferencing although here there is another method open to you which is to email the consent form to the conference website.

Autonomy: debriefing

Over the course of carrying out your investigation, you will become aware that research relationships do not end on completion of the study. Debriefing gives participants a chance to interact further with you, to ask questions and to hear your explanations. This relates to the principle of autonomy. Debriefing gives you the opportunity to discuss more fully the potential use of the study and share

---

Example 5.8 Providing a debriefing on research findings

In Norway, Kristin Goa (1999) conducted a case study investigation of information sharing in a technology company. Following the completion of her report, she made several presentations to senior managers and to the corporate communications department. She spoke about ways in which their tactics for implementing computer-mediated communications had had diverse consequences. She then facilitated a discussion on the implications for future corporate communications planning and suggested possible practical applications. In providing feedback and a debriefing, Kristin was able to offer a useful contribution to the company which had allowed her open access for her participant observation study.

---

the knowledge that you have gained from your research. If you have been conducting research in an organization, it may be appropriate to offer a workshop or presentation to interested members about the outcomes and implications of your findings.

For reasons of time, money and sometimes confidentiality, it is not always advisable to promise all participants a copy of your completed report. However, many participants welcome receipt of a copy of the transcript of their interview, especially if they are taking part in a longitudinal study where the transcript serves as a tangible reminder of changing circumstances. In addition, a short summary, a copy of the report's abstract or a brief discussion in a letter of thanks is appreciated by those who have given their time to reveal details about themselves and their experiences.

Honesty: omission, interpretation, plagiarism

We have already touched on the need for honesty together with a willingness not to mislead. We have noted how, in some cases, it is problematic if you divulge full information about the research purpose and procedures. Therefore there are grounds occasionally for withholding some information as long as you reveal it at a later time, perhaps in a debriefing session. However, the omission of information should not be done lightly and you need to consider carefully if this ploy is necessary and ethical. There is never any justification for deception and the giving out of false information about the nature of the study or the risks of participation is not an option open to you.

Honesty in research extends to how you collect and interpret the data. It would be easy to manufacture a quote that supports your working hypothesis, or ignore data which are disconfirmatory. Similarly, it would not be difficult to fabricate observations that didn't take place or take a quote out of its context and use it inappropriately. But these would be lies! It may be tempting to do this if deadlines are tight and financial resources make it difficult to travel to meet participants. Nevertheless, it is not worth it in the long run as deception can rebound on both the researcher and also the academic institution or the organization which sponsors your research. Resist the temptation, therefore, allow yourself to live with a clear conscience, and be congratulated on joining the ranks of ethical scholars.

In online research, there is some debate regarding whether or not the principle of honesty is infringed if you choose to assume a false identity in order to gain more 'useful' data, particularly if the area is sensitive. However, if your intention is to mislead others in order to manipulate the content of discussion, then the practice is unethical. If informants find out, it is unlikely that they will consider this acceptable behaviour; indeed many would denounce it as a violation of their personal worlds.

Key point
If you use the words, ideas, phrases or ways of thinking of others and do not credit them, you are acting dishonestly, or *plagiarizing*.

Plagiarism guarantees that any academic work will fail when it is assessed; it may even result in dismissal. Plagiarism, according to Locke *et al.*, includes

> failure to use quotation marks where they belong, omitting citations that credit material found in someone else's work, shoddy carelessness in preparing the list of references, and failure to obtain permission for the use of figures, tables, or even illustrations from another document – whether published or not.
>
> (2000: 34)

Consider your own work and how you would feel if you read about your words and ideas in the text of another researcher without seeing any reference to yourself. Use that as a motivation to cite others in your own work.

However, the issue of plagiarism is complicated where the Internet is involved. No formal procedures have yet been established for crediting the source of information gleaned from computer-mediated communications. Mann and Stewart (2000) set out various views as they exist to date, explaining that some researchers hold that all computer-mediated communication is published written material and therefore sources should be cited. Others, however, see a distinction between email or 'closed' chat rooms (private or semi-private sources) and open access fora such as newsgroups and bulletin boards. They argue that citations should be provided for the former as long as consent for use has been obtained, otherwise pseudonyms are acceptable. For material in open access fora, some form of authorship needs to be cited such as name, note or number, although, because these data are in the public domain, it is not necessary to seek permission for their use.

Honesty: covert research

An area of controversy about honesty and deception concerns covert and overt research methods. Some argue that the use of deception in covert participant observation studies is justified because it allows researchers to acquire knowledge about people, events and places that would not otherwise be accessible or obtainable. We believe that covert research should not be attempted by undergraduates or MPhil and PhD students but only by very experienced researchers.

Example 5.9 An unethical, covert research project

One of the most famous participant observation studies is that of 'The Tearoom Trade' which took place in 1970. Laud Humphreys, a PhD candidate in sociology, examined sexual interactions between men in public lavatories, acting as a look-out to warn of approaching outsiders. He noted down informants' car numbers and approached them in disguise at a later stage to discuss other issues, in particular their sexual behaviour.

The method taken by Humphreys to obtain his results aroused strong criticism on a number of counts, including his failure to disclose his real identity, his neglect of his informants' right to privacy and his use of questionable strategies for obtaining information. Although Humphreys did receive his PhD, there was a later, unsuccessful attempt to have it rescinded.

Covert research of this nature is highly problematic and unethical.

Electronic communication makes it easy to conduct covert research because it is possible to subscribe to and lurk on a mailing list while concealing your identity. It is also possible to participate in online discussions under a pseudonym and with a completely different identity. However, there is a fine line between the benefits of knowledge acquired through covert means, and potential harm, and therefore you need to evaluate the consequences for participants, your profession, and yourself if you are intending to undertake research of this nature (Cieurzo and Keitel 1999).

Honesty: ownership of research and public access

If your research is sponsored by an agency, you should be aware of the potential conflicts that may arise concerning ownership of data. Most universities insist that ownership of data is in their hands although there are some prior negotiated exceptions. Generally, universities retain the right to economically exploit the work of student researchers unless a specific contract has been negotiated with a commercial firm. Funding agencies often impose conditions about the economic exploitation of the research. To prevent conflict, it is wise to negotiate questions of ownership before the start of your research.

Once your research is finished, it is usual to share your ideas and findings with others through published articles, industry reports, or working reports and papers held in university libraries. Although your findings are in the public domain, your raw data remain protected from disclosure, unless, of course, your participants and their organizations have given permission for identification. Protection means ensuring that tapes, notes and transcripts are stored securely, names are not disclosed and participants' identities are disguised. Take care that unauthorized access to sensitive electronic data does not occur. Use a sound password and also keep a backup of your data in a secure place. When data are shared with others, whether funding agencies or gatekeepers, take care to delete all identifiers. It is up to you to decide what information to make public. If there is any doubt or ambiguity, your decision will rest upon participants' wishes, as expressed when giving their written or oral consent.

Summary

- Ethical problems and dilemmas are inherent in any qualitative research that you undertake.
- They should be articulated and addressed in the planning, process and outcome stages of research.
- In the initial stages of research, ethical problems and dilemmas relate to how you recruit participants, deal with gatekeepers and negotiate access.
- The basic principles which provide guidelines for conducting research ethically include:
  - the right of free and informed choice
  - protection from harm to individuals and equipment
  - privacy, involving guarantees of anonymity and confidentiality
  - autonomy, involving informed consent and debriefing opportunities
  - honesty, concerning issues of omission, interpretation, and plagiarism, as well as problems in covert research and issues of ownership and public access.

6   The quality of research
Reliability and validity

Right from the early stage of writing up your proposal, you need to consider the quality of your work because this is the basis on which your research will be judged. Quality is assessed according to a number of criteria which are outlined in this chapter. This chapter focuses on:

- reliability and validity.
- an alternative set of criteria related to authenticity and trustworthiness.
- how to ensure that your research meets these criteria.

Introduction

Conventionally, researchers have referred to notions of reliability and validity to demonstrate the goodness or quality of their studies. However, reliability and validity are complex terms, derived from quantitative research (and a 'realist' or positivist paradigm), and not everyone agrees on their value for qualitative methodologies.

We use the terms reliability and validity in this book because of their common usage in public relations and marketing communications research. However, we also present an alternative stance which relies on the overarching concepts of trustworthiness and authenticity. You will come across both positions during your reading so it is helpful to know something about each, regardless of the terms you opt to use yourself.

Key point

Your research should show that it has been designed and conducted with an awareness of and care for the methodological implications of your research choices. Whatever labels you give to the criteria for quality, be consistent in your use of the terms, and systematic in the way you demonstrate how the appropriate criteria have been applied to your research.

Reliability and validity

Maxwell (1996), Kvale (1996), Hammersley (1998) and Silverman (2001) are among those who promote the value of applying reliability and validity benchmarks to qualitative research. They argue that these offer the most effective means of evaluating the quality of research. This is despite the fact that reliability and validity are measurements of objectivity, which is a central research issue in *quantitative* research. In qualitative research, however, subjectivity is the more salient research issue. On the whole, qualitative researchers appreciate that:

> Research is not a wholly objective activity carried out by detached scientists. It is . . . a social activity powerfully affected by the researcher's own motivations and values. It also takes place within a broader social context, within which politics and power relations influence what research is undertaken, how it is carried out, and whether and how it is reported and acted upon.
>
> (Blaxter *et al.* 1996: 15)

Objectivity and neutrality, then, are impossible to achieve. Indeed, qualitative researchers openly acknowledge their own subjectivity, often writing about their values and research orientations. Rather than concealing subjectivity, they examine it and note its place within research. For this reason, if you choose to apply the criteria of reliability and validity to qualitative research, you need to do so carefully and thoughtfully, recognizing that the distinctive character of qualitative research forces you to redefine some of the features of reliability and validity.

Example 6.1 The subjective nature of research

If you were interested in studying whether a 'glass ceiling' existed for women in advertising, consider how your results and conclusions might be affected if you approached interviewees in a company through the male managing director, the personnel manager, the equal opportunities committee, the Institute of Practitioners in Advertising or a professional women's association. A variety of politics and values are involved depending on the route you choose. Your initial contacts would affect your access to the participants in your research, they may influence what you can write up or publish, and indeed, your participants may themselves be influenced by their perception of you as a researcher because of the person through whom you gained access.

Reliability in qualitative research

Reliability in quantitative research is the extent to which a research instrument such as a questionnaire, when used more than once, will re-produce the same results or answer. However, in qualitative inquiry, you yourself are the main research instrument, and therefore your research can never be wholly consistent and replicable. Although your study could be repeated by other researchers, they would be unlikely to achieve the same results, even in similar circumstances and conditions. This is because your own characteristics and background influence what you see and how you arrive at your conclusions. Other researchers have different emphases and foci even if they adopt the same methods and select a similar sample and topic area.

Therefore, one way to achieve some measure of reliability in qualitative research is to set up an audit trail or a 'decision trail'. This is when you record the data, methods and decisions that you have made during your project.

Key point

An audit trail documents the decisions and steps you have taken during your project. It:

- allows other researchers to follow the same process as you have done.
- helps readers to understand the decisions you have made.
- provides a way of establishing and indicating the quality of the study.
- presents a means of evaluating the entire study.

Validity in qualitative research

Validity in quantitative research has to do with whether the methods, approaches and techniques actually relate to, or measure, the issues you wish to explore. In qualitative research, the concept of validity is more salient than that of reliability. Maxwell (1996: 87) maintains that it is 'the credibility of description, conclusion, explanation, interpretation, or other sort of account'. We deal with three aspects of validity in this section: internal validity, generalizability and relevance.

Internal validity is the extent to which the findings of a study are 'true', and whether they accurately reflect the aim of the research and the social reality of those participating in it. To an extent, you can establish this by showing your findings to participants and asking for their comments (see the section on 'member checks', page 95). This enables you to compare your interpretation with the perceptions of the people involved and note whether or not they are compatible.

Generalizability or external validity is the most contentious concept linked to validity. For some authors, such as Wolcott (1994) and Stake (1995), generalizability is not an issue. For others, it is problematic. However, most funding agencies and research committees demand that the research you propose to do should be generalizable.

Generalizability is usually considered to exist when the findings and conclusions of a research study can be applied to other, similar settings and populations. The term has its origin in quantitative research with its random statistical sampling procedures. Random sampling ensures that the results of the research are representative of the group from which the sample was drawn. However, this type of generalizability is difficult to achieve in qualitative research because the notion stems from a 'realist' worldview, which informs most quantitative research where the discovery of law-like generalities is important.

On the other hand, the interpretive worldview, which informs most qualitative research, prefers to focus on specific instances or cases that are not necessarily representative of other cases or populations. Sampling is purposeful or theoretical rather than being based on a statistically representative sample. Indeed, case(s) may even be atypical. The concept of generalizability, therefore, is likely to be irrelevant if only a single case or a unique phenomenon is examined. Yet the study may still be successful if it highlights specific, non-typical features that can be related and compared to those of other, more typical cases.

Example 6.2 Demonstrating generalizability

In a study of how creativity is managed in public relations consultancies, one of us developed concepts about creativity and the influences that determine how it is managed and organized. Christine Daymon (2000) sought to generalize her findings by relating them to the literature on creativity and by suggesting that the ideas could be verified in other research settings.

Her study found that creativity is characterized by:

- unconventionality.
- autonomy.
- risk.

She indicated that the manner in which public relations consultancies respond to the above determines the extent to which creativity is stimulated or stifled. She also discovered that the styles of management and the forms of organization which accommodate creativity are primarily influenced by:

- the size of the organization.
- client expectations.
- the nature of public relations practitioners.

She concluded the article by suggesting that future research is needed in order to apply the findings more widely to other sectors within the creative industries.

Despite the problems with generalizability in qualitative research, many researchers do attempt to achieve some measure of it because they recognize the desirability of being able to apply their theoretical ideas to a wider context. Morse (1994), for example, claims that theory is able to contribute to the 'greater body of knowledge' when it is 'recontextualized' into a variety of settings. This type of generalization, called 'theory-based generalization', involves being able to transfer theoretical concepts found in one situation to other settings and conditions. If the theory developed from the original data analysis can be verified in other sites and situations, the theoretical ideas are generalizable.

In order for your own work to have external validity through 'theory-based generalization', ensure that you have related the findings of your study to the literature in order to arrive at your own theoretical propositions or concepts. This enables the readers of your study to make connections to their own settings when they read your findings. It also allows you or other researchers to verify your theoretical ideas in other sites and situations, using either qualitative or quantitative research.

Validity: relevance

According to Hammersley (1998), a further aspect of validity is relevance. This means that any research study must be meaningful and useful for those who undertake it and who read it. This criterion has salience for evaluating qualitative research in public relations and marketing communications because it suggests that any study you undertake should provide some sort of solution to problems faced by practitioners in the field. However, not all researchers would agree that investigations should be done to help sort out industry issues. Sometimes, there is merit in undertaking research just to find out how something works or because you want to solve a mystery rather than a problem (Chapter 2 offers some reasons for carrying out research).

Although you can never be fully certain that you have eliminated all threats to validity, having an awareness of them helps you to produce a valid piece of research. On page 95 we offer some strategies for you to follow in order to ensure that your research is reliable and valid.

An alternative perspective: authenticity and trustworthiness

We mentioned earlier in the chapter that there are two different positions related to the assessment of the quality of qualitative research. Reliability and validity are the concern of the conventional position. However, there is some disquiet about their adequacy to encapsulate the range of issues raised by a concern for quality (Seale 1999). Therefore, we now outline the second and perhaps more fashionable position. Guided by an interpretive paradigm, it relies on the work of Lincoln and Guba (1985) and Guba and Lincoln (1989, 1998), and is promoted by Erlandson *et al.* (1993) among others.

According to this stance, the goodness of research is characterized by trust-worthiness and authenticity which are central to the whole research process. Trustworthiness and authenticity are shown by researchers' careful documentation of the process of research and the decisions made along the way.

Authenticity

A study is authentic when the strategies you have used are appropriate for the 'true' reporting of participants' ideas, when the study is fair, and when it helps participants and similar groups to understand their world and improve it.

Trustworthiness

The criteria for evaluating trustworthiness are credibility, transferability, dependability and confirmability.

Credibility

Lincoln and Guba (1985) suggest that you should aim for 'credibility', rather than internal validity. Your study is credible if the people in it recognize the truth of the findings in their own social context. At the proposal stage, you can indicate in two ways how you will endeavour to make your study credible. First, set out the various research methods you intend to use and how each method will complement the others. Second, indicate how you will undertake a 'member check' (on pages 95 and 98, we set out details on triangulation and member checks).

Transferability

Transferability replaces the notion of external validity, and is close to the idea of theory-based generalizability. Many qualitative studies involve very small samples or single case studies and it is your role to help the reader transfer the specific knowledge gained from the research findings of one study to other settings, as indicated in Example 6.2.

For instance, if you intend to explore techniques of integrated marketing communications carried out by a multinational organization, your findings would be specific to that particular setting (i.e. the organization only). You would need to

Helpful hint
Ensure at the proposal stage that you have chosen a topic that can be related to a wider context and to the academic literature. This provides a basis for the transferability of your findings.

consider how any principles or models which might emerge from your study could be applied to similar settings elsewhere (such as the integrated marketing communications practices of other multinational organizations). The beginning of this process of transferability is at the proposal stage where you outline the characteristics of your focal setting, or company, and indicate how you will select your sample (we discuss sampling in depth in Chapter 11).

When you are able to discuss how your investigation is positioned within the realm of pertinent industry or scholarly issues or concerns, the salience of your work is demonstrated. This helps you, later, to show how your findings relate – or are transferable – to other settings in the same industry. For instance, you may be broadly interested in integrated marketing communications. This has been studied before by other researchers. What do you think is missing from existing studies? Is there a particular aspect of the practice that has been insufficiently studied (for example, how does integrating all types of communications affect the role and responsibilities of the marketing communications manager?). Findings from your narrower study of one aspect of the practice should be related to other studies which articulate ideas about the overall functioning of integrated marketing communications.

Dependability

Credibility and dependability are closely linked, the latter replacing the notion of reliability. If the findings of your study are to be dependable, they must be consistent and accurate. This means that readers will be able to evaluate the adequacy of the analysis through following your decision-making processes. The context of your research must also be described in detail. One of the ways of achieving dependability is by demonstrating an audit trail, a technique which we describe later in the chapter.

Confirmability

Confirmability is more suited to qualitative research than the conventional criteria of neutrality or objectivity. Your research is judged by the way in which the findings and conclusions achieve the aim of the study and are not the result of your prior assumptions and preconceptions. Therefore, for your study to be confirmable, you need to be able to show how the data are linked to their sources so that a reader can establish that the conclusions and interpretations arise directly from them. Again, auditing or a 'decision trail' are pertinent because they require you to be reflective and to provide a self-critical account of how the research was done. To indicate at the proposal stage how confirmability will be demonstrated in your research, it is sufficient to outline the early intentions of your study, that is, your proposed research, your expectations, and a recognition of the need to be reflexive throughout.

Strategies for ensuring the quality of your research

There are a number of ways in which you can check and demonstrate the quality of your research. Whether you choose to apply the criteria that are clustered within the reliability and validity position, or the trustworthiness and authenticity position, the following strategies will be helpful. We should point out that not all of these are accepted by all qualitative researchers. Once again, it depends on your own preference, research orientation and research aims as to which of these you apply.

- Longitudinal research design.
- Member checking.
- Peer debriefing.
- Demonstration of an audit trail.
- Thick description.
- Searching for negative cases and alternative explanations.
- Triangulation.

Longitudinal research design

Your study will be more likely to be valid or trustworthy if you have been involved in the setting for a lengthy period of time. This may be the result of choosing an ethnography research design (see Chapter 9) or because you wish to trace a social process over the course of its development (such as the way in which an advertising campaign is created and executed).

Some of the benefits related to validity and validity of longitudinal research are:

- you gain a good understanding of the context and will be more likely to present a convincing account of participants' perspectives.
- participants learn to trust you and are more likely to tell the truth.
- over a prolonged period, you are more likely to examine and reflect on your own assumptions.

Longitudinal research with its extended periods of engagement in the field, therefore, goes some way to eliminating bias in research.

Member checking

A member check (Lincoln and Guba 1985) or member validation is when you check your understanding of the data with the people you study, by summarizing, repeating or paraphrasing their words and asking about their veracity and interpretation. It provides feedback to participants, enables you to check their reaction to the data and findings, and helps you to gauge their response to your interpretation of the data.

Example 6.3 An extended period of engagement in the research setting

The British National Health Service has undergone considerable change. Wendy Button and Graham Roberts spent five months in a hospital, exploring how managers, doctors and nurses perceived the change processes and how changed management practices affected internal communication.

They carried out semi-structured interviews and observations of meetings, writing that:

> Through the use of multiple data-collection methods, it was felt that we would get a better composite picture of the organization than we would obtain using quantitative methodology. Analysis of multiple data would allow a clearer insight into the underlying structures and interactions occurring within the organization, transcending what would otherwise be a rather notional view.

(1997: 150)

They concluded that there were a number of tensions within the organization that related to organizational change and communication. However, the managers of the NHS were aware of these and were implementing new strategies to improve communication.

The specific purposes of member checking are:

- to find out whether you are presenting the reality of the participants in a way that is credible to them.
- to provide opportunities for them to correct errors which they might have made in their discussions with you.
- to assess your understanding and interpretation of the data.
- to challenge your ideas.
- to gather further data through participants' responses to your interpretations.

Feedback from others ensures the validity and credibility of your research, helping you avoid misinterpreting or misunderstanding the words or actions of participants. By carrying out a member check, it is more likely that you will present their point of view. To an extent, this acts to empower your participants because you are giving them a form of control of their words, and thus some control in the study itself.

In Table 6.1, we set out the different ways of carrying out member checks with their associated difficulties. With each technique outlined, you request participants in your study to comment back to you.

Alvesson (1994) used the second technique identified in Table 6.1 when he studied a Swedish advertising agency. He wrote: 'Towards the end of the empirical research process, we confronted respondents with observations and statements from previous interviews and asked them for comments.' Under-graduate and

Table 6.1 Techniques for carrying out a member check

Technique	Problems	Comments
1 Present participants with transcript of their interview or fieldnotes on your observations.	– Time consuming. – Participants do not see your interpretation of the data.	– The procedure is an acceptable one but too time consuming for undergraduates.
2 Present participants with a summary of their interview and your observations, plus your interpretation of their words and actions.	– Time consuming. – Requires you to write summaries and accounts specifically for the purpose of member checking.	– Useful for confirming ideas and meaning of your account. – Participants can suggest adaptation to your interpretation. – Their comments can clarify, trigger or extend your ideas which can be fed back into your final report.
3 Present copy of final report or substantial sections of it to participants.	– Lengthy process. – Demands time commitment from participants. – Value of feedback on academic reports depends on participants' familiarity with this style of presentation.	– Has potential to be very valuable as it allows participants to read the study in its entirety and comment. – A risk that some organizations may withdraw funding or support if they consider your conclusions to be unfavourable.

masters students may also find the second technique most appropriate because of the time-consuming nature of the process. If, however, you follow the third strategy and provide your informants with rough drafts of your writing to examine, don't be too disappointed if you don't receive much feedback. Sometimes participants are either satisfied that your interpretation adequately conveys their experiences, and therefore they don't bother to comment further. Or they may be unfamiliar or uncomfortable with an academic style of writing.

Searching for negative cases and alternative explanations

The validity and credibility of your study is enhanced when you identify and analyse any discrepant data or 'negative cases'. We deal with this further in Chapter 16. Briefly, however, when you find data which are inconsistent with what you have already discovered or which are contrary to your own view of reality, don't ignore them. Instead, allow them to challenge your ideas and to offer an alternative explanation for the evidence you have collected. In some cases, 'negative cases' or disconfirmatory examples will cause you to revise your working propositions and reconsider your theoretical framework. By indicating in your final report that you have considered dissenting voices, your study will be seen to be more plausible.

Searching for negative cases and alternative explanations always presents challenges. It is not easy to become aware of discrepant data and negative or alternative cases. On the other hand, at some stage you will have exhausted the alternative possibilities, and that's when your search should come to a halt.

Peer debriefing

Sometimes it may be useful to employ the strategy of 'peer debriefing'. This involves colleagues re-analysing your raw data and discussing any concerns you might have about their interpretation. You might also give your peers a draft copy of your report to read at the end of your research. Make sure, though, that you select colleagues who have a good understanding of qualitative research. The benefits of peer debriefing are:

- peers may detect bias or inappropriate subjectivity.
- peers might provide alternative explanations to your own.
- peers may warn against inappropriate attempts to produce interpretations that are not substantiated by the data.

Triangulation

A combination of more than one perspective is often used to corroborate the data because, traditionally, it is claimed that this strategy provides a more 'complete' picture. Denzin (1989) claims that triangulation comes in different forms which he defines as:

Example 6.4 Peer debriefing

Advertising associated with cause-related marketing was the topic of Minette Drumwright's research in which she interviewed sixty-three people from advertising agencies and client companies. She also undertook document analysis. After analysing the data, she asked two expert colleagues to review a sample of the materials and code the data for the dimensions she identified. In the methodology section of her report, she wrote:

> The coding agreement was 98.4%. The auditors then were asked to read this manuscript and note disagreements or questions concerning any conclusions I drew or any quotations that did not fairly represent attitudes of other informants. In the few instances that this occurred, the statement or quotation was removed from the manuscript. (1996: 74)

- *data triangulation*, where you use multiple data sources, such as collecting data from different groups, settings or at different times. The study in Example 6.3 collected data over a long period; the researchers entered the research organizations on many different occasions. In Example 9.2, the researchers carried out a case study of one Swedish advertising agency but endeavoured to relate their findings to the wider setting of the Swedish advertising sector by testing out emerging ideas in interviews with senior executives from other agencies.
- *investigator triangulation*, when you are involved with more than one expert researcher in the same study. This is illustrated in Example 16.3.
- *theoretical triangulation*, when you employ several possible theoretical interpretations of the study, developing and testing competing propositions against each other. One of our own studies follows this strategy because three competing perspectives were used to analyse the same phenomena (Daymon 2002).
- *methodological triangulation*, when you use two or more methods in the same study, such as observations, interviews, documents and questionnaires. See Examples 6.3 and 8.2.

The latter strategy is most often used in a small-scale dissertation. If your findings are based on one method, you might consider confirming them by using another method. It is not usually necessary – though occasionally desirable – to use quantitative methods to confirm qualitative findings, that is, 'between-method' triangulation. Instead it is more common to stay within the same methodology; this is called 'within-method' triangulation.

For example, in ethnographic research, triangulation is often used by researchers to check their observations against answers to interview questions. This helps them to ascertain that they are clear about what they have seen. In documentary research, everything needs to be checked from more than one angle, which includes using an array of texts collected at a variety of times, in different locations, and from different authors or participants. This is important because nothing can be taken for granted. A document may not be what it appears to be, an archive may have been collected for motives that you do not understand, and a context may be crucial in determining the nature of a document or the way in which people express themselves (Macdonald and Tipton 1993).

Be aware that merely mixing methods is insufficient for triangulation and does not automatically demonstrate validity. Triangulation only takes place when the same phenomenon has been examined in different ways or from different perspectives. In some research approaches, such as discourse analysis, it is inappropriate to employ triangulation because what you are concerned about is not an 'accurate' or comprehensive account, but the various culturally defined stories and narratives that individuals use to describe, for instance, their work or consumer experiences.

The audit trail

All research should have an audit trail by which others are able, to some extent at least, to judge the validity of the research. The audit trail is the detailed record of the decisions made before and during the research and a description of the research process.

It is worth reminding yourself, even at the earliest stages of designing your research, that it is a good idea to compile a running record of all your activities. The audit trail begins at the proposal stage of your research where you highlight any explicit decisions you have already taken about the theoretical, methodological and analytical choices of your study. As you begin to collect data, make a note of extended transcripts, extensive fieldnotes (including how and in what context these were recorded), notes of reflexive and analytical thoughts, as well as a research database. These all contribute towards the dependability of your research.

Thick description

When you provide a 'thick description', this helps to establish the quality of your research and is linked to the audit trail. A term coined originally by Geertz (1973), it means a detailed description of the process, context and people in the research, inclusive of the meaning and intentions of the participants. The reader of your study should be able to feel, hear and see exactly what it is like to be in the setting you are describing.

Reflexivity

The process of critically reflecting on your own role and preconceptions is one that is ongoing through all the stages of data collection, analysis, interpretation and writing up your research report. Because you yourself are the main tool of qualitative research, you are part of the phenomenon to be studied, and therefore need to reflect on your actions, feelings and conflicts that you experience during the research. Reflexivity also requires you to take stock of your relationships with participants and examine your own reactions to their accounts and actions. If you adopt a self-critical stance to (i) your research, (ii) your research relationships, (iii) your personal assumptions and preconceptions, and (iv) your own role in research, the study will become more reliable and valid, in other words, more trustworthy and authentic.

Summary

- The benchmarks against which the quality of your research is judged relate to either reliability and validity, or authenticity and trustworthiness.
- Each is measured according to different criteria. Choose one set and follow it in your own research.

1. Reliability and validity	*2. Authenticity and trustworthiness*
Based on a realist or positivist paradigm. Criteria include reliability, internal validity, generalizability, relevance, objectivity.	Based on an interpretive paradigm. Criteria include authenticity, credibility, transferability, dependability, confirmability.

- Strategies which enable you to ensure that your research is reliable and valid – or authentic and trustworthy – include a longitudinal research design, member checking, peer debriefing, demonstrating an audit trail, providing 'thick' description, seeking out negative cases and alternative explanations, and triangulating the data.

Part II

Selecting the research approach

7   Case studies

Case study inquiry is usually associated with an intensive investigation of a location, an organization or a campaign. Different theoretical frameworks and methodological approaches are often incorporated within the design. This chapter outlines:

- key characteristics of case study inquiry.
- types of case studies.
- how to make sampling choices based on the setting and the research focus.
- the contentious topic of generalizing from case studies.
- criteria for interpreting and evaluating case studies.

Introduction

With the exception of some investigations across many sites, much qualitative inquiry is considered to be a form of case study research. Indeed the meaning of the term has overlapped substantially with that of others, notably with ethnography. However, we argue that case studies differ from other qualitative approaches because of their specific, in-depth focus on the case as an object of interest in its own right.

Key point
A case study is an intensive examination, using multiple sources of evidence (which may be qualitative, quantitative or both), of a single entity which is bounded by time and place. Usually it is associated with a location. The 'case' may be an organization, a set of people such as a social or work group, a community, an event, a process, an issue or a campaign.

The purpose of case study research is to increase knowledge about real, contemporary communication events in their context. Questions about how and why things occur in a particular situation, or 'what is going on here?' are your primary concern when you opt for this research approach. In effect, you are aiming to bring to life the nuances of managed communication by describing a chunk of 'reality'. You do this by:

- undertaking a detailed analysis of a particular case and its setting.
- trying to understand it from the point of view of the people working there.
- noting the many different influences on and aspects of communication relationships and experiences.
- drawing attention to how those factors relate to each other.

Case study inquiry enables you to collect 'rich', detailed information across a wide range of dimensions about one particular case or a small number of cases. A good case study, therefore, highlights the numerous factors governing managed communication in a particular setting, portraying something of its uniqueness while also – but not always – attempting to offer insights that have wider relevance.

In sociology, anthropology and increasingly in organization studies, case studies are often accorded a central role in research with the case being allowed to stand on its own in order to generate theory, test theory (is theory applicable to all contexts, for instance?), enable findings from other studies to be confirmed or achieve insights into territory that is previously uncharted or not well documented. For example, Crane (1998) whose research is outlined in Example 7.1, justified his application of a single case study approach on the grounds of its complexity and its exploratory nature.

Despite Crane's interesting study, and some others like it, public relations and marketing communications research, on the whole, has been less keen to offer a primary or central role to case studies. Traditionally, these disciplines have relied on 'case studies' to illustrate or provide an example of something else, or to provide a pilot study for a wider, quantitative research project.

To some extent, this is explained by the preference of many public relations and marketing communications researchers for quantitative survey research. It also comes down to the fact that the term 'case study' is not used consistently, nor is it restricted to the research context. In public relations consultancies and advertising agencies, for examples, 'case studies' are compiled of good practice or award-winning campaigns and used for promotional purposes or to generate new business. In education, 'case studies' act as a teaching tool to stimulate discussion and debate. Used in this way, they are examples of professional practices within industry contexts. Finally, we note that we ourselves, like other researchers, are inconsistent in our utilization of the term, applying it not only to a research approach but also to examples of discrepant data, e.g. 'negative cases' (see Chapter 6).

When the term is applied to a research approach it describes the following distinguishing characteristics:

- deep, narrow exploration.
- focus on real events in their real-life context.

Example 7.1 A single case study

An interest in ethical marketing led Andrew Crane (1998) to carry out an investigation of a green alliance to find out if relationships of this nature can help to solve marketing problems associated with environmental issues.

Aims of the study
To define the concept of a green alliance and to place this within the context of green marketing; to provide a theoretical basis for studying green marketing alliances; and to develop insight into the management processes associated with their practical application.

Research design
A single case study approach using grounded theory (see Chapter 8) with the focus on WWF 1995 Plus Group, a UK green alliance between seventy-five companies and the World Wide Fund for Nature.

   Case study sampling: based on a 'test-site for theory' (see sampling section on page 109).

   Methods: seventeen semi-structured interviews, informal discussions, company documents, marketing artefacts and archival materials (see Chapters 12 and 15).

   Time: 1996.

   Analysis: from inductive to deductive (see Chapter 16)

Findings
Cultural factors led to differences and similarities in how members perceived the environment, their relationships with each other and their roles. Not all of the members involved in the alliance were primarily motivated by social responsibility. Some had economic goals; others wanted to avoid potentially bad publicity. There were difficulties in supply chain relationships and competitor relationships. Therefore concepts which aid analysis of a green alliance are stakeholder relations, competitor relations, motivations and objectives, and culture.

- bounded in place and time.
- either a snapshot, or a longitudinal study of events with a past and a present.
- multiple sources of information and multiple viewpoints.
- detailed and descriptive.
- holistic view, exploring relationships and connections.
- focus on the taken-for-granted as well as the significant and unusual.
- useful for theory building and theory testing.

Each of these characteristics is discussed as we move through the different headings in the next section.

Designing case study research

A strength of case study research is that it is able to produce multiple sources of evidence. One reason for this is that different theoretical and methodological frameworks can be incorporated into it. For example, Crane in Example 7.1 drew on grounded theory and case study approaches to examine relationships and practices in a green marketing alliance. Hackley in Example 10.1 applied discourse analysis and a case study approach to study the language and communication interactions of a top London advertising agency. Ritson and Elliott in Example 9.1 combined ethnography with a case study to investigate advertising-related behaviours and social exchanges in a school. Depending on the circumstances and needs of the research topic and the particular situation, you might apply both quantitative and qualitative methods. However, if you opt to concentrate on a qualitative approach only, you still need to draw on multiple sources of information such as observation, interviews, documents and audio-visual materials. This evidence should reflect your intimate knowledge of the case, allowing you to build multiple viewpoints and perspectives into the case.

The design of your study, then, involves making decisions about your overall research approach – whether or not to incorporate another research orientation and which methods to use – as well as whether to select a single or a multiple case study methodology.

The single case study

A single case study design offers you the opportunity to undertake a deep (but narrow) exploration of one particular instance (or a few instances) of a particular phenomenon. Your interest, therefore, is on small numbers which are investigated in depth at a single point in time or over a longer period. For example, if your research focus called for a study of communications within a single organization, you might analyse all internal and external communications in all departments on all sites over the course of a year (this would be a *holistic analysis* of the entire case). On the other hand, you might concentrate instead on a single aspect of the case, such as communication in one department only, and then compare your findings with those for the organization as a whole. This would be an *embedded analysis* (Yin 1994).

The collective or multiple case study

The use of two or more case studies enables some measure of generalization to a wider universe. It also allows you to identify distinctive features by exploring similarities and contrasts between cases. It is not usual to choose more than four cases because the larger the number, the more the benefits of the case study approach will be diminished. When researching multiple cases, typically you would give a detailed description of each case, identify themes within the case, followed by a thematic analysis across the cases. You would then provide an interpretation together with 'the lessons learned' from the cases. However, the more cases studied, the greater the lack of depth in any single case, and the more the overall analysis will be diluted (Creswell 1998).

Sampling

The process of sampling for case study research occurs on two levels: the case itself and the informants or participants. We consider sampling in Chapter 11 but in this section we discuss specifically how to make choices concerning the case itself.

Key point
Sampling for case studies is purposeful. You should always provide a rationale for your sampling strategy.

It is not uncommon to select a case for primarily practical reasons. If you are confident about what you wish to study, you might select a case because it is the most convenient or accessible setting for exploring your research topic. The fact that a case has intrinsic value – it is interesting in itself – is also a logic for selection (Stake 1995). This is a useful rationale if you want to build theory, particularly if you have chosen a grounded theory methodology.

On the other hand, the setting itself may be of less interest than the focus of your research. Your search for an appropriate case may be driven less by the accessibility or interest of the setting than by your determination to find a context which illustrates some feature or process in which you are interested.

Therefore, your final selection – which must be justified – will probably be based on a large number of possibilities which Silverman (2000) suggests might relate to:

* the particular setting to be studied.
* the elements or processes on which you want to focus.
* how the study might generalize further (this will not be applicable in all studies, as we explain in Chapter 6 and later in this chapter).

Settings

That a particular context is *convenient* or *accessible* can make it an attractive setting to study. Convenience is likely to be a crucial factor if you are a student because, faced with alternatives which are equally suitable, it is not unreasonable for you to select the one that requires the least travel, the least expense and which has the easiest access. However, don't use these criteria on their own to justify your selection; they should be subordinate to the other criteria as outlined in the previous paragraph.

Another basis for selection might be because the setting is *intrinsically inter-esting*. Although Stake (1995) argues that it is sufficient to study a case 'in its own right', his stance ignores the debate about theoretical generalization. There-fore, it is perhaps wiser to use this as a criterion for selection only if you are deciding between instances that in all other respects are equally suitable.

The logic for selection of a *revelatory* case (Yin 1994) is because the research focus within the case is unique, or because this is the first time that a case of this nature has been studied. A potential problem, however, is that, over time, the case may not turn out as you thought at the outset of your research.

The research focus

When you make a theoretically guided choice to study particular individuals, events, processes or campaigns within a particular theoretical framework, you are following a process of purposeful sampling. The logic for selection may rest on one or more of the following factors: problematic situations, significant or unusual events, everyday goings-on and a test site for theory.

You might select a case because it allows you to focus on *problematic situations*. Your aim would be to identify factors that cause problems in managed communication in order to offer practical solutions. However, while there is merit in learning about the difficulties involved in managing communication strategies and activities, you risk seeing only half the picture if you fail to attend to situations where communication has been organized effectively and managed successfully.

The focus of some case studies is on *significant or unusual events* which chal-lenge or support current thinking about managed communication. *An extreme case* is one that is in contrast to the norm. For example, working within an integ-rated marketing communications conceptual framework, you might choose to study a communications campaign that has an exceptionally large budget (which encourages the extensive use of all communications methods). Your choice would be justified on the basis that the case enables you to uncover how the dif-ferent communications tools complement each other.

Arguably, however, case studies should also focus on the routine, the taken for granted, the *everyday goings on* of those involved in sending and receiving managed communication. Analysing how and what things become ordinary or generally acceptable can make a significant contribution, for example, to your understanding of why consumers in a particular region stay loyal to a specific brand, or why email is used extensively in one consultancy and not accepted in another.

If your focus is on building theory, then you would look for a case that is able to act as a *test-site for theory*. For example, when reading for her masters degree, Katrine Jaklin discovered that concepts about identity management were derived from research in the private sector only. Therefore, for her dissertation, she decided to apply identity management models to the study of two British and Norwegian monopoly organizations. She subsequently revised current con-ceptual models about organizational identity and its management. When considering a test-site for theory, don't select a case on the grounds that it is likely to support your argument. Deliberately seeking out a *deviant* case can offer you the opportunity to undertake a crucial test of theory.

A focus on the need to generalize elsewhere is the logic behind the selection of a *typical case*. Because it is similar in key aspects to others that you might choose, its findings can be generalized to others in the same class or universe.

Example 7.2 A single case study

A case study carried out in Malaysia by Maureen Taylor (2000) evolved out of her desire to find out what governments can do to build relationships among people of different ethnic groups in order to stop ethnic violence before it begins.

Aims of the study
To develop theoretical propositions about the role of public relations in helping to build national unity. Taylor suggested that public relations could be useful for building relationships between different ethnic groups and between government and its publics.

Research design
A single case study approach with the focus on a Malaysian government communication campaign that had attempted to build inter-ethnic relationships.

Sampling: based on a 'significant event' and also on a 'test-site for theory'. The Malaysian government consciously uses communication campaigns in order to improve ethnic relations. Their 'Neighbourliness Campaign' was one such campaign.

Methods: analysis of archives and interviews with ten officials involved in the campaign, together with a citizen survey using open- and closed-ended questions to measure the attitudes of Malaysians.

Place: in order to define the boundaries of the case, the author provided a description of the campaign and also of the setting in which it was launched, that is, Malaysia. She outlined the divergent ethnic relations and tensions endemic to Malaysia.

Analysis: from inductive to deductive.

Findings
Taylor's comparison of her findings with similar published studies enabled her to generalize beyond the Malaysian context. She found that, to some extent, campaigns do foster co-operative relationships between different ethnic groups and encourage national unity. However, communication alone is insufficient if it is not operating in a social and political context which supports relationship-building messages. Therefore, she proposed a public relations approach to nation-building which uses communication, not as a channel, but as a means of encouraging people to negotiate their own relationships. Both interpersonal and organization–publics communication then become important.

Noting the boundaries of place and time

Case studies are bounded, or fairly self-contained and, therefore, when you have selected your case or cases, you need to be able to identify, and write about, the relevant boundaries of time and place. Imagine the case as a picnic basket where everything inside the basket is the subject of your investigation, and everything outside is excluded. It is important, therefore, to carefully outline the boundaries of your case (i.e. the shape of the picnic basket) in order to show where your research begins and ends. Boundaries concern both place and time.

Place

If the case is a company, you need to describe the organization. Depending on the focus of your research, you might choose to define its *social boundaries*. This includes staff membership or the organization's formal structure, both of which define the organization as a distinct entity. You might also outline *physical boundaries* such as a specific site or building. This allows you to concentrate your research efforts on the activities, processes and relationships that take place within those physical boundaries. On the other hand, if the case is a specific event such as a major promotional activity along the lines of a sponsored exhibition, you might identify the client and consultancies involved in the event and note its target audiences.

However, while these boundaries are practical, they are also artificial; organizational membership changes, temporary and contract workers are only partially attached to organizations, and many communication activities take place outside your identified social and physical boundaries (a communications campaign might be devised by a freelance publicist at home while sitting in the bath!). There is a danger, then, in treating your case like a sealed unit, impervious to the influence of outside factors. These might include:

- events which happen to participants when they are away from the defined setting.
- outside factors which temporarily intrude on your zone of research (for example, the study of employee attitudes to a company's management communication activities would need you to take into account any repercussions if the company changed its consultancy).

> **Helpful hint**
> Be aware of external factors which might have an impact on your case.

Time

Case studies should have a clear beginning and end. Note the period during which your study takes place. Is your investigation, for instance, a snapshot of an event or an issue at one brief moment in time? Or is it perhaps a longitudinal study of a situation that has developed over time, where you examine the series of occurrences that have led up to and resulted from a specific incident? If the latter, you need to justify why the case started and ended when it did. A longitudinal approach is more common in case study research because the nature of the case study allows you to pay attention to the process by which things come to be as they are rather than on what things are at the present point in time. This focus is one of the greatest advantages of a case study.

Generalization

We covered generalization in Chapter 6 but, because the topic is contentious with regard to case studies, we refer to it again in this context.

Traditionally, social scientists' preoccupation with generalization as an essential aspect of research has led to some criticism of case studies for their limited generalizability. However, endeavouring to transfer ideas into a broader realm is not always the concern of case study researchers. They may be more interested in focusing only on the arena of the case itself in order to provide a 'thick' description of the complex processes and influences within a particular context. The ability to offer a rich portrait in this manner is a major advantage of case study research. Readers of your study should be made to feel as if they have been there with you in your research, seen what you have seen, and concluded what you have concluded (Geertz 1988). However, a danger is that, whilst a case may be interesting in itself, few relevant insights are likely to emerge if the reader is unable to transfer these to another setting. On the whole, then, it is desirable to try to generalize the relevance of case study findings.

Yet the quantitative notion of *generalizing to a universe of similar contexts* (or cases) is inappropriate for qualitative case study research because qualitative case studies are not statistically selected to represent a larger population. For instance, you might choose to study a Formula One sponsorship campaign because it is essentially interesting and enables you to assess how sponsorship models operate in the dynamic context of international motor racing. You would not choose it on the basis that it represents all types of sponsorship campaigns in all sectors. Because public relations and marketing communications processes and relationships are an intrinsic aspect of specific situations, such as the organizations where they occur, treating a case study as a sample of one and then trying to generalize to other situations would tear the case's findings out of the particular real-life context which gives them their meaning. However, if your contextual description is rich (or 'thick') and your analytical language comprehensive enough to enable both you and our readers to understand the various processes and interactions involved in the context of Formula One sponsorship, then it might be possible to

---

Key point
The concern by social scientists with the notion of generalization has implications for case selection. The study of a single case is an appropriate research design if the case draws sufficiently on other similar work which allows connections and contrasts to be made. However, if you wish to generalize further from a single case study, you could choose to:

- extend the research methods used (e.g. conduct a wider survey).
- add a second or more cases to the study.
- conduct a case-within-a-case.

---

generalize to the extent of stating that other Formula One campaigns might 'tend' to operate in similar ways under similar circumstances.

Seale (1999) suggests that qualitative researchers cannot possibly study every context to which readers might wish to generalize results. However, if you are able to provide sufficient 'thick' description when writing up your cases, then readers, like travellers returning home, will use their human judgement to establish whether the conditions they have encountered 'abroad' (i.e. in the case study) have any relevance for their present circumstances. The onus, then, is on the reader rather than on you as a researcher to assess how far the findings might transfer into their own context. Your responsibility is to provide sufficient information to allow the reader to make an informed judgement.

Generalizing to a theory

Theory-based generalization is a more accepted rationale for generalizing from qualitative case studies. We have discussed this in Chapter 6. The idea here is for case studies to be used to uncover patterns and linkages to theory in order to generalize to theoretical propositions or concepts. Theoretical concepts from one setting can then be verified in other sites and situations, using either qualitative or quantitative research. For instance, an investigation of the experiences of marketers in the Formula One case study mentioned earlier, might lead you to conclude that current prescriptive models of sponsorship are inadequate for this type of context. In suggesting a revised model of how sponsorship operates, you might then test this through further research on sponsorship campaigns in other sectors, such as the arts or the media.

Theoretical generalization, however, concerns not only 'generalizing to a theory', but also *generating theory*. When you combine a case study approach with a grounded theory approach, new theoretical concepts and categories are likely to be found. However, you should always consider theories generated from single cases to be fallible propositions that may be modified in the light of further experience (Seale 1999). Therefore, you need to establish the relevance of your newly generated theoretical propositions through subsequent research.

This requires you to include within the text of your case study your recommendations for further research.

Criteria for interpreting and evaluating case studies

In addition to the criteria for judging the quality of research which we discussed in Chapter 6, there are several other considerations which relate to case studies.

Case studies need to offer a comprehensive account. This does not necessarily mean that you have identified all the possible influences and aspects of the case but that you have taken into account the historicity of the case, paid attention to the nuances of the observed phenomenon, and called attention to the different perspectives on your interpretation, such as highlighting 'negative' cases and their alternative explanations, or by allowing hidden 'voices' within a case study to be heard in your report. Furthermore, by employing a strategy of triangulation (see Chapter 6), you can corroborate evidence from different sources in order to shed light on a particular theme or perspective. The triangulation of ideas is useful in helping you achieve a measure of validity, comprehensiveness and also interconnectivity (Chen and Pearce 1995). When the interconnectedness of various aspects and influences in a case study are discerned and articulated, the complex nature of managed communication is illuminated.

The case should aim to provide probable and plausible interpretations within the context of our inquiry. The reader should be able to judge that the interpretation provided is likely and reasonable in both the situation and period in which the study took place.

Because case studies aim to capture something of contemporary events and situations, they can never have the 'final say' on the case under investigation. Your interpretations will only ever be provisional and fairly incomplete, constructed from your own particular stance which takes into account certain things and not others. Your case study, therefore, should highlight its open-endedness in order to generate a forum for further dialogues (Chen and Pearce 1995).

Stake (1995) recommends that you ask the question, 'Is the role and point of view of the researcher nicely apparent?' As in all qualitative research, it is important for the reader to understand your position and any biases or assumptions that may impact on the inquiry. You need, therefore, to comment on relevant past experiences or orientations that are likely to have shaped your interpretation and approach to the study. For instance, a case study focusing on the practice of public relations in a pharmaceutical company is likely to achieve different insights when conducted by a student without work experience, or a researcher with previous managerial experience in the pharmaceutical industry.

Limitations and problems in case study research

In some cases, the boundaries of a case are difficult to define, such as who is an organizational member and who is not, or when a case study begins and ends. This poses difficulties for deciding what aspects and sources of data to include.

Because case studies require you to undertake intensive examination often over a long period, negotiating access to settings may be problematic. Companies are often unwilling to allow researchers entry on the grounds that confidential information may leak into the public arena.

Case studies are sometimes accused of being too descriptive. However, in some instances, description is your intent, say, if you wish to develop understanding of how a theory works in practice in a particular setting, or if you are attempting to illustrate a case that is unique. Nevertheless, be sensitive to accusations of this nature because they relate to the credibility of generalizability, a realm where case studies historically have been criticized. By ensuring that your report is explicit about connections and contrasts to other similar work, you can show how your findings apply beyond the boundaries of your case focus.

Summary

- Case studies are able to incorporate different theoretical and methodological frameworks.
- Case study inquiry facilitates the collection of detailed information across a wide range of dimensions about a single case or a small number of cases.
- Sampling is purposeful, based on the setting or the research focus.
- Case studies are bounded by time and place. These should be made explicit in the case study report.
- The generalizability of case studies is the subject of much debate. Generalizing to a universe is inappropriate for case study research. Generalizing to theoretical concepts or propositions is more acceptable.

8   Grounded theory

As a research approach, grounded theory co-exists with some of the other research orientations outlined in Part II of this book. For example, it may be incorporated within a case study, and it shares some methodological procedures with ethnography, phenomenology and discourse analysis.

This chapter notes that:

- grounded theory is both a set of research procedures and the emergent theory that develops from that research.
- theory is generated from the data rather than from pre-existing theoretical frameworks.
- procedures and specific techniques are carried out in great detail in a step-by-step fashion.
- it is a particularly suitable approach for public relations and marketing communications research because it allows practice-based theories to be built that extend or modify existing theory.

Introduction

Grounded theory is an open, reflexive approach to research where data collection, analysis, the development of theoretical concepts, and the literature review occur in a cyclical process. While these features apply to some of the other qualitative research orientations, there are three aspects of grounded theory which distinguish it from other approaches:

- *researchers follow systematic, analytical procedures in most versions of the approach.* Grounded theory is more structured in its process of data collection and analysis than other forms of qualitative research even though their strategies are similar (such as thematic analysis of interview transcripts, observations and written documents).
- *researchers enter the research process carrying as few assumptions in advance as possible.* This means eschewing pre-existing theories in order to concentrate on discovery and emergent knowledge.
- *researchers do not aim merely to describe but also to conceptualize*; they are keen to generate and develop theory.

Grounded theory studies, therefore, are based on the premise that the strategies and products of research are shaped from the data rather than from any preconceived theoretical frameworks and hypotheses that you might bring to the research. Many studies claim to have followed this approach because they have grounded their theory-building in the data. However, unless they have conformed to the operational practices of grounded theory, their claims are likely to be unfounded.

A grounded theory approach enables you to undertake processual research, that is, research that focuses on 'a sequence of individual and collective events, actions and activities unfolding over time in context' (Pettigrew 1997: 338). For example, grounded theory studies have the potential to offer original insights into how things happen, such as how a particular advertising campaign is created, or how internal change is effectively communicated over time, or how negative Internet communications impact on a company's reputation, and so on. Grounded theory is useful in situations where little is known about a particular topic or phenomenon, or where a new approach is needed in familiar settings. Although it can be applied to any area of study, it is especially suitable when the purpose of research is to discover consumer- or employee-based theories and constructs.

Usually, the aim of grounded theory is to build new theory although it is also used to modify or extend existing theories. For example, you might further develop your own grounded theory, or that of another researcher, by revisiting the same data at a later date with a different set of questions and interpretations.

Typically in a grounded theory approach, you start with an area of interest and go straight into collecting the data. You then analyse and reflect on them, while exploring the literature at the same time. This allows you to make comparisons and contrasts between the concepts emerging from the data, the scholarship and the work of other researchers. As you collect new data and integrate new con-

---

Example 8.1 Building on existing theory

Denise DeLorme and Leonard Reid (1999) engaged in grounded-theory building in their study of brand placement in movies. Their study elaborated upon their earlier analytic framework on how brand props are interpreted within the everyday lived experience of moviegoers (DeLorme, Reid and Zimmer 1994). They argued that most studies of brand placement in movies neglect to explore the meanings that moviegoers give to the brand props they see on screen. To investigate this topic, they used depth interviews and focus groups to gather first-person accounts. They also kept a reflective journal. Data collection, coding and analysis were simultaneous. They continually compared differences and similarities of specific instances in the data, generating concepts, categories, properties and their interrelationships. Their findings on moviegoers' interpretations of brands provided new insights into the role that brand placement can play in building brand image. See also Example 2.2.

cepts, your grounded theory is modified and reformulated. Research of this nature allows you to make shifts of emphasis early in the research process so that the data gathered 'reflects what is actually occurring in the field rather than speculation about what cannot or should have been observed' (Glaser 1978: 38). Later in this chapter we set out the procedures for following this research process.

The background

Grounded theory was initially developed in the 1960s by the sociologists Barney Glaser and Anselm Strauss whose seminal work, *The Discovery of Grounded Theory,* was published in 1967. Later their ideas diverged. Strauss was keen to prescribe procedures for following the approach, while Glaser resisted any modification of the original idea. Two versions of grounded theory have therefore emerged, Glaserian and Straussian. In management and communication-related research, the Straussian approach (Strauss and Corbin 1990, 1998) is more popular, although both forms have continued to evolve over the years as other researchers have worked with the approach.

The disciplinary tradition that informs grounded theory is sociology, particularly the symbolic interactionist school of thought. Symbolic interactionism focuses on interaction between human beings and attempts to understand how individuals interpret each others' behaviour and language, how people give meaning to their own actions and thoughts (by communicating) and reorganize them when interacting and negotiating with others. The theoretical and methodological presuppositions of symbolic interaction about the nature of the world and the way it can be studied are reflected in the research practices of grounded theory and its product (Locke 2001). Researchers try to observe and understand the point of view of participants about themselves and their worlds in order to uncover the dynamic properties of interaction.

The process of developing grounded theory

To apply this approach successfully, Glaser and Strauss (1967) contend that you need to be flexible, approach the study with an open mind and make no assumptions before the research starts. By choosing to follow a grounded theory approach, you opt to operate as an interpreter of the data, not just a reporter or describer of a situation. This means that you continually search for relationships between concepts in order to generate patterns and links from which you go on to develop theories or, at least, theoretical ideas.

Although you start without a hypothesis or theory, your work develops both inductively and deductively (Alvesson and Sköldberg 2000). This is because during the course of analysis, provisional hypotheses – or early hunches – or propositions arise (they are sometimes called 'working hypotheses') which you check out against further incoming data.

During the process of investigation, you develop 'theoretical sensitivity', gaining insight and awareness of relevant and significant ideas while collecting and analysing the data. Your sensitivity is built up over time in two major ways, first, by acquiring more information through reading and, second, by increasing your knowledge through your experiences. The literature linked to your study sensitizes you in the sense that documents, other research studies or autobiographies highlight relevant and significant elements in the data and stimulate your thinking. Your professional and personal experiences also enhance your awareness – although having an open mind in the first place is a major criterion for examining the data. During the course of managing your data, you will find that theoretical sensitivity gradually develops as you think about the emerging ideas and ask further questions. These ideas are provisional until you have examined them many times. They must always be related and linked back to the data. Grounded theory develops through this constant comparison of data and ideas in an orderly and systematic way.

Some distinctive features of grounded theory which we explain more about in the next sections include working hypotheses, theoretical sampling, memoing, theoretical sensitivity and constant comparison.

Data collection

Traditionally, data collection is based on observed events. Therefore, it is usual to collect your data from observations in the field, diaries and other documents such as letters or even newspapers (which you supplement with literature searches). However, in much contemporary research, it is common practice to include interviews, even though these are based on participants' accounts of events rather than your own observations and experiences. Use of the interview method is justified on the basis that grounded theory is concerned to capture tacit knowledge which is gained from the reflexive accounts of relevant interviewees (Partington 2000).

From the moment you commence your research, your data collection and data analysis go hand-in-hand. Analysis starts as soon as you take the first few steps in data collection. As you collect data from your initial interviews or observations, you use cues from the first emerging ideas to develop further interviews and observations. Similarly, the gathering of your data does not finish until the end of the research process because ideas, concepts and new questions continually arise which guide you to new data sources. In this way, the collection of your data becomes more focused and specific as the research process proceeds. Example 8.2 provides a good illustration of this.

Memoing

From the beginning of data collection, throughout the course of your project, you should be writing memos to yourself about your observations and interviews. There will be certain occurrences in the setting, or ideas which you get from speaking to participants, which seem vitally important or highly interesting

---

Example 8.2 The interwoven process of data collection and analysis

Joana Machado (2000) followed a grounded theory style of research in a study of identity and identification in the British Council's worldwide offices. Unusually for a grounded theory approach, she complemented interviews, observations and document analysis with a questionnaire. This methodology provided her with both a wide and deep knowledge of the topic. Her research proceeded as follows:

- she conducted three exploratory, face-to-face interviews.
- transcribed, analysed and read the literature.
- analysed corporate publications.
- developed a more focused interview guide with questions that took account of concepts about identify and identification.
- began to design the questionnaire based on interviews and reading.
- reviewed the literature.
- conducted some informal interviews via email.
- analysed websites.
- conducted face-to-face interviews and carried out analysis, searching for themes.
- continued reviewing the literature and corporate documents.
- discovered themes relating to how nationality, occupation, tenure and type of contract influence informants' understandings about identity.
- refined the interview guide to take account of developing concepts.
- conducted more face-to-face interviews and also some online interviews.
- continued analysis: undertook some recoding and continued to make comparisons across the data sources, themes and concepts.
- refined the questionnaire and piloted it.
- conversed informally by email about questionnaire design and suitable contacts.
- completed the questionnaire, distributed it worldwide.
- developed questions to guide further analysis.
- qualitatively analysed returned questionnaires, built a quantitative database, undertook quantitative analysis.
- reviewed the findings and reviewed the literature.
- integrated all aspects into the report.

---

at the time. Don't lose track of these thoughts – write them down as soon as you can. Later, they will serve as a reminder of events, actions and interactions that trigger your reflective thinking.

It is also useful to write memos that comment on and explain the analytical codes and categories that you derive from analysing the data. These memos help you trace patterns in the data and emerging themes. They make a valuable contribution to your analysis, by forming the basis of your written theory.

Theoretical sampling

In grounded theory, 'theoretical sampling' is used. This type of sampling is guided by ideas which have significance for the emerging theory. One of the main differences between this and other types of sampling is time and continuance. Unlike other types of sampling which are planned beforehand and where a sampling frame exists from the very beginning of a study, theoretical sampling continues throughout the process of the research. (Theoretical sampling, though originating in grounded theory, is also often used in other types of qualitative analysis.)

At the start of the project, you make sampling decisions for the initial stage only. Choose the setting or phenomenon you wish to study, and select particular individuals or groups of people who are able to give you information on the topic under investigation. Once the research has started and you have analysed the initial data, new concepts will arise. These inform your choices about the events and people you next select in order to gain further illumination on the research topic. Then you can set out to sample different situations, settings or individuals and focus on new ideas to extend the emerging theories.

Theoretical sampling continues until the point of saturation, when no new information of relevance to your study is found in the data. Just because a concept is mentioned frequently in interviews or because the same ideas arise repeatedly does not mean that saturation has taken place. It occurs only when you are convinced that your theory is able to fully explain variations in the data. Saturation is achieved at a different stage in each research project and cannot be predicted.

Coding and analysing the data

The process of data analysis goes on throughout the research from the first interview and observation to the last. Analysis initially consists of coding and categorizing, with coding taking place from the commencement of the study. Coding allows you to transform your data and reduce them in order to build categories; as major categories emerge, your theory evolves.

Throughout the study, each section of the data are compared with every other section as you search for similarities, differences and connections. This is called 'constant comparison'. Included in this procedure are the themes and categories identified in the literature. All the data (primary and secondary) are coded and categorized, leading to the formation of major concepts and constructs. Your aim is to search for major themes which link ideas to find a storyline for the study.

Key point

Coding in grounded theory is the process by which concepts or themes are identified and named during the analysis, that is, the data are coded into categories.

There are three steps in the coding process. These concern:

- open coding (fragmenting the data).
- axial coding (putting data back together in new ways).
- selective coding (selecting a core category and relating it to other categories).

Open coding is the process of breaking down and conceptualizing the data. It starts as soon as you receive the data and examine them. Each separate idea in the data is given a label. Similar ideas are named with the same label.

The words and phrases used by participants themselves to describe a phenomenon are called '*in vivo* codes'. These give life and interest to your study and are immediately recognizable to participants as reflecting their reality. An example of an *in vivo* code might be 'starting from scratch' or 'focusing on the customer'. Although *in vivo* codes are used occasionally, most often researchers develop their own codes – always being mindful, of course, that these reflect the experience and perspectives of participants.

Code the data line by line or paragraph by paragraph in interviews and field-notes, basing the codes directly on the data in order to allow them to speak for themselves. This avoids any preconceived ideas entering into your analysis. Your initial codes will probably be provisional because you are likely to modify these over the period of analysis.

At the beginning, there will be many labels. However, after coding the data and pulling the codes together into groups with similar characteristics, you will end up with a set of categories. Although categories tend to be more abstract than initial codes, they still have to reflect social reality so they must be grounded in the data. Keep referring back to the data to check that they are found there. Whenever you identify a category, you also need to be able to articulate its main features or aspects (properties).

At this point, you go on to *axial coding* where you reassemble the data broken down through open coding. By reviewing and re-sorting your common themes, you group categories together in a new form in order to build major categories, which you then label. Occasionally you might use labels that others have already discovered and written about in the literature. Example 8.3 indicates how a major category emerged from a variety of themes found in the data.

Example 8.3 Axial coding

In a study of organizational culture (see also Example 5.4), one of us identified a major category called communication which emerged out of a number of subcategories (external communication, internal communication 'coordination', public relations, press office, relationships, 'the internal brand', systems, uncertainty, understanding of the mission, internal problems). The category also developed from reading the literature related to communication and culture (Daymon 2002).

Although there is no initial hypothesis in grounded theory, during the course of the research you generate working hypotheses or propositions. These are your first hunches about what the data means and need to be checked out throughout the course of the research. Don't overlook deviant or negative cases which do not support a particular proposition (these are explained in Chapter 6). Whenever you find such exceptions, modify the hypothesis or find reasons why it is not applicable in this particular instance.

The process of coding and categorizing only stops when:

- you find nothing new about a category of relevance for the developing theory even though you have attempted to search for new ideas.
- you have described the category with all its properties, variations and processes.
- you have established links or relationships between categories.

The third step to take is *selective coding* which is coding for the main phenomenon, the core category. In grounded theory, the major category links all others and is called the *core category* or *core variable*. Like a thread, the category weaves through the others, integrating them and providing the storyline. This linking of all categories around a core is called selective coding. This means that you uncover the essence of the study and integrate all the elements of the emergent theory. Included in the core category are the ideas that are most significant to participants.

Coding and categorizing involve constant comparison. This enables you to clarify the relationships between the different aspects of the theory. Once you have analysed your initial interviews by developing codes and concepts, you start making comparisons between the concepts and subcategories. You then group them into major categories and label them. As you gather code and categorize new data, you constantly compare the new categories with those you have already established. Thus, incoming data are checked for their 'fit' with existing categories. Each incident of a category is compared with every other incident for similarities and differences. The comparison also involves the literature linked to the study. Constant comparison is useful for finding the properties and dimensions of categories. It assists in looking at concepts critically as each concept is illuminated by the new, incoming data.

A point to note is that not all your categories will be relevant or robust enough to fit into your developing theoretical framework. If your study is highly complex, there may be too many categories to deal with adequately in the final written report. Once you have made a commitment to a particular focus in your study, 'some conceptual categories [will] end up being immaterial to the analytic framework and research story. Consequently, towards the end of analysis, as [you] work to integrate and delimit [your] theory and its constituent categories, [you] will be able to identify those immaterial categories and drop them from the framework' (Locke 2001: 53).

Some researchers prefer to write up coded information onto cards which are

Example 8.4 Developing codes and categories

The behaviours and underlying motivations of Belgian consumers and business people surfing the World Wide Web was the topic of research by Steve Muylle, Rudy Moenaert and Marc Despontin (1999). With little theory and few empirical studies to guide them, they decided to use grounded theory for an exploratory study. They observed and videoed people navigating the web and then retrospectively interviewed them, confronting them with video images of their own navigation behaviours.

The researchers developed their theoretical ideas through a series of three types of memos.

Memo 1: code note

Here they noted their emerging concepts, writing a memo for each one. Each memo contained a reference and date, it identified a particular concept or category, its general properties and its possible dimensions. It also noted the reference number of each interview or observation which the concept related to. For example, one memo identified the concept 'waiting' which had the properties of 'duration' (dimensions: 'short . . . long') and 'degree of continuity' (dimensions: 'continuous . . . intermittent'). The finished research article described this as '[Duration] indicates how much time elapses between a course of action and the information offered, whereas [continuity] describes whether the information is offered in whole (continuous waiting) or in parts (intermittent waiting)' (1999: 149).

Memo 2: theoretical note

This type of memo built on one or more code notes and set out some working hypotheses. For example, two code notes relating to 'waiting' and 'purposiveness of information search' informed the following working hypothesis: If web users have to (a) wait a long time for the information they require to be displayed on the screen and (b) they have low search purposiveness, then they won't wait but will move on to make a new information search.

Memo 3: operational note

This type of memo worked as a reminder for aspects that the researchers needed to look for in further interviews or in analysis of the next round of data. (Based on Muylle 2001 personal correspondence.)

colour coded and then stacked into emerging categories. This allows you to draw comparisons and contrasts by simply looking at the different colours of the cards. At the selective coding stage, coloured cards enable you to study the data on the cards line by line, marking words and phrases that are particularly relevant for strengthening and refining the emerging interpretation. However, other researchers, including ourselves, prefer to carry out coding and categorizing on a computer, creating new files and folders for our categories and sub-categories.

Generating theory

To be credible the theory must have 'explanatory power', with linkages between categories, and specificity. Categories are connected with each other and tightly linked to the data. Researchers do not just describe static situations but take into account processes in the setting under study.

Two types of theory are produced: substantive and formal theory (Glaser and Strauss 1967).

Substantive theory emerges from a study of a concrete social situation such as customer relationship management, professional practice, gender relations, leadership, or Internet communications. It can also emerge from a study of one particular context such as a marketing department or an advertising agency or a retail outlet. Because this type of theory represents a close connection to empirical reality, it is very useful for researchers in the professional or business arena. Substantive theory has specificity: it applies to the setting and situation studied and hence is limited.

Formal theory is developed from substantive theory. It is generated from many different situations and settings, is conceptual and has higher generality. Because it holds true not just for the setting of the specific study but also for other settings and situations, it is said to have general applicability. Examples of formal theories are systems theory, organizational culture theory and network theory.

In a small student project, it would be difficult to produce a formal theory with wide applications. However, substantive theories can also be important and may have some general implications.

Example 8.5 Substantive and formal theory

The idea that there are stages through which public relations executives proceed when they enter a new employing organization and become accustomed to its norms and practices is *substantive theory*. This becomes *formal theory* when it is linked to the existence of a 'status passage' which can be applied to many situations where people pass through stages.

Additional sources of data

Data that are used to generate grounded theory is both primary and secondary. Secondary sources include company and industry documents (to find out more on documents as data sources, see Chapter 15) and the literature. As you discover categories, you should trawl the literature to confirm or refute these. You are seeking to discover what other researchers have found, and whether there are any links to existing theories. Although you may have undertaken an initial literature review to demonstrate that there is a gap in knowledge and therefore a reason to undertake your research, the rest of the literature becomes integrated into the final write up of your study.

On some occasions, researchers draw upon personal or occupational experiences as sources of data. Locke (2001) provides an example of this with regard to research on the topic of new employees and their mentoring experiences. She suggests that researchers could recall 'all their own newcomer experiences in different kinds of organization and use them in a comparative way to think about what their data might mean. Parallel personal experiences, thus, may be a source of theoretical insight' (p. 90).

We have already mentioned analytic memos earlier in the chapter. Because they are the thoughts and ideas that occur to you as you observe and interview participants, they provide a valuable source of data and the theoretical substance for your final, written report.

How do you know when to stop collecting data and finish generating new concepts and categories? When any new data provide no new information, you have reached 'theoretical saturation'. This means that you have arrived at the point where any subsequent data fit into the categories you have already identified. In effect, this occurs when there are no indications of the need for you to provide further categories, or refine those you already have. In this case, you have reached the limits of your data collection and analysis.

Limitations and problems in grounded theory-building

The process of grounded theory-building has been accused of being bewilderingly complex. Many find it difficult to follow in practice except in 'a loose, non-rigid, non-specifiable fashion' (Partington 2000: 95). One problem is linked to theoretical sampling. Often researchers use sampling procedures which they decide on before they start collecting the data, forgetting that 'sampling in grounded theory proceeds on theoretical grounds' (Corbin and Strauss 1990: 8). Theoretical sampling is necessary because of the inductive–deductive nature of the research. This is linked to the emerging theories which you are trying to advance through theoretical sampling.

Many researchers produce good categories and interesting narratives but often neglect underlying social processes, or they fail to develop abstract concepts. The aim of grounded theory is expressly to develop new theory or modify existing theory. This means providing explanation and conceptualization, not mere description. It is not enough to describe the perspectives of the participant to develop a 'grounded' theory. You need to move on to the next stage where you advance concepts.

Locke (2001) draws attention to the inherent tension in grounded theory between the need for you to hold in abeyance your existing theoretical orientations and presuppositions – so they do not influence your interpretation of the data – and the need for you to be theoretically sensitive in order to compose categories and a theoretical scheme. Being sensitive means being theoretically aware. But it is difficult for researchers to acquire this without drawing on the knowledge they already have from their life experiences, their disciplinary training, and their possible commitment to a particular school of thought. These orient you towards particular aspects of your research, such as phenomena that others overlook because their different interests cause them to focus on different features. The need to stimulate insights from contradictory sources – outside as well as inside the field – is one of the greatest difficulties of following a grounded theory approach. It is likely to be only by trial and error that you find a way to deal with this in your own work.

Although the grounded theory approach is particularly appropriate for research in public relations and marketing communications, there are few examples where this methodology has been applied successfully. The difficulty of operationalizing a grounded theory approach leads many researchers to follow a simplified version of its principles and procedures. For instance, the various stages in coding and categorizing may be condensed, or the sample may be selected in advance of data collection, or the development of a conceptual framework may precede data collection. If such research has developed theoretical concepts that are grounded in the data, it can be said to have employed a grounded theory *style* and, despite neglecting a full-blown grounded theory approach, such research may still hold value for public relations and marketing communications knowledge.

Summary

- Grounded theory is an under-utilized but potentially important research approach for public relations and marketing communications. It holds great potential for tracing social processes in their context.
- It begins without hypothesis and allows both the data and theoretical sampling to guide the choice of conceptual framework and the emerging theory.
- Researchers follow a systematic, structured process of data collection and analysis.
- There is a constant comparison of joint data coding and analysis.
- Two types of theory are produced: substantive theory emerges from a study of a particular context; formal theory is more abstract and has higher generality.

9 Ethnography

As a research approach, ethnography may be used on its own or combined with other orientations such as grounded theory or discourse analysis. This chapter highlights that:

- ethnography entails researchers immersing themselves in a group, organization or community for an extended period of fieldwork.
- ethnography refers not only to the process of doing research but also to the written description of that research.
- in public relations and marketing communications, an ethnographic approach to research has the potential to reveal how communication exchanges and interactions are influenced by culture.

This chapter covers:

- the background and nature of ethnography.
- types of ethnography.
- collecting and analysing the data and writing up an ethnographic report.
- conducting online ethnographic research.

Introduction

The word *ethnography*, which is derived from Greek, means a description of a people or, literally, 'the writing of culture' (Atkinson 1992). However, in contemporary research usage, there is a lack of consensus over its definition. To some extent, its meaning overlaps with that of other research approaches (Hammersley 1998), and therefore it is perhaps not surprising that it has become fairly commonplace to use (inappropriately) the term as a generic descriptor for all types of qualitative research.

Ethnography has its roots in anthropology, which means that, as a research discipline, it is based upon culture as an organizing concept, and therefore uses a mix of observational and interviewing tactics as well as document analysis to record the behaviours and communication of people in particular social settings. It is distinguished from other forms of qualitative research by its emphasis on

Key point

Ethnography is both a research methodology and the product of that research, that is, a written description of a culture which is based on the findings of fieldwork. Ethnographic research may be both qualitative and quantitative, but in public relations, marketing communications and other people-focused approaches, it is usually qualitative.

culture and on a people's particularity, that is, what essentially characterizes one group of people and what differentiates them from others. Above all, ethnography relies upon researchers immersing themselves in a group or community for an extended period of fieldwork. They observe and ask questions about the manner in which people interact, collaborate and communicate – including with the researcher – in regular ways. In ethnography, a group (such as an organization, a department, a project or consultancy team, or a social group) is defined as a social aggregation whose members share a co-created social reality and whose actions are coordinated around that reality.

The background

Modern ethnography emerged in the 1920s and 1930s when anthropologists such as Malinowski (1922), Boas (1928) and Mead (1935) – keen to preserve aspects of vanishing, foreign cultures by living with them and writing about them – explored a variety of non-western cultures and the ways of life of the people within them. When cultures became more linked with each other, and Western anthropologists could no longer find homogeneous, isolated cultures abroad, they turned to research their own cultures, acting as 'cultural strangers', that is, trying to see them through the eyes of an outsider in order to bring a new perspective to that which was already familiar. Sociologists, too, adopted ethnographic methods, immersing themselves in the culture or subculture in which they took an interest. The Chicago School of sociology had an influence on later ethnographic methods through its members' studies of marginal cultural and 'socially strange' subcultures such as the slums, ghettos and gangs of the city.

Key point

Culture is the commonly-held tacit knowledge, beliefs, values and shared meanings of a group, organization or community which account for their particular 'way of life'. Culture is expressed in their behaviours, such as their language or jargon, their rules and norms, their rituals, the ways in which they interact communicatively with each other, their expectations concerning relationships, and their use of products and services, for instance.

The nature of ethnography

Ethnographic analysis of communication within organizations attempts to do what few other research agendas do, that is, to uncover the structures of meaning in the setting, synthesize a picture of a group's reality that characterizes them and sets them apart, and make it more widely available for consideration (Whitney 1994). In the field of managed communication, ethnographic studies have explored topics as wide-ranging as public relations in Bangalore, India (Sriramesh 1996), the consumption experiences of an ethnic minority, Pakistani group in England (Jamal and Chapman 2000, see Example 17.6), professional identities in a Swedish advertising agency (Alvesson 1994, see Example 9.2), and the interpretation of advertising by English school pupils (Ritson and Elliott 1999, see Example 9.1).

Other areas that hold great potential for further ethnographic research are brand experiences and loyalty, internal communication, consumer interpretations of marketing communications, and inter-personal and cross-cultural communication. For example, different (sub)cultural groups attach diverse meanings to constructs such as 'decision making', 'leadership', and 'communication'; therefore, a sensitivity to organizational and societal culture is essential for decoding these meanings. A further, developing application of ethnographic research is the study of virtual communities, such as those that emerge via the Internet.

Ethnography is not merely fieldwork, however. It is also a description – a written story or report – about a particular group of people that is the result of

---

Example 9.1 An ethnographic study in a high school

The contribution of advertising to the everyday interactions of high school students in the north of England was the subject of an ethnographic study by Mark Ritson and Richard Elliott (1999). Ritson spent six weeks with sixth formers in their school context, observing a wide range of advertising-related communication and social exchanges amongst the students. He made detailed fieldnotes and also carried out group interviews.

Amongst their findings, Ritson and Elliott noted that students' choice of favourite advertisement took on a great degree of cultural significance. For example, all the sixth formers possessed a continually updated personal portfolio of favourite advertisements that was socially evaluated and endorsed by the wider group. Through their shared knowledge and interpretation of the advertising text, members reinforced their self-image along with their affinity to the social group they interacted with. Ritson and Elliott concluded that different social contexts are just as likely as different media contexts to have an influence on advertising effect. Therefore, they suggested that consumer research should be directed to more 'fully accept and explore the social contexts that contain, constrain, and convey the meanings of the advertising text' (p. 275).

one or more researchers spending an extensive period of research immersed in a group or community context. It aims to render a group's social reality intelligible to readers of the ethnography.

One of the major characteristics of ethnographic reports – which you should strive to achieve from the outset of your study – is 'thick' description (Geertz 1973). As we noted in Chapter 6, 'thick' description goes beyond recording what participants are doing. It is a dense and detailed account of experiences, and the patterns and connections of social relationships that join people together. Geertz states that the aim of 'thick' description is 'to draw large conclusions from small, but very densely textured facts' (p. 28) – yet it goes beyond the merely 'factual', so that it is both analytical and theoretical in its description.

An ethnography is theoretical on two levels (Philipsen 1989):

- it is a theoretical statement about the people studied, a theory about a culture.
- it is designed to become part of a body of comparative knowledge about public relations and marketing communications from which wider generalizations can be made. For example, when you read ethnographic studies about how advertising is accommodated into everyday social practices in Africa, Asia, America and Europe, this knowledge guides the design of your research project in your own country and also the interpretations of your own primary data.

In summary, ethnographies are theoretical, descriptive, comparative and cultural.

Types of ethnography

Sarantakos (1998) and Thomas (1993) suggest that there are two types of ethnography:

- descriptive or conventional ethnography.
- critical ethnography.

Descriptive ethnography is the type outlined in Example 9.1. This focuses on the description of communities or groups and, through analysis, uncovers patterns, typologies and categories. Critical ethnography, on the other hand, involves the study of macro-social factors such as power and examines common sense assumptions and hidden agendas. It is meant to generate change in the setting it investigates by, for example, giving a voice to the disempowered, or to bring about change in the researcher who studies it. It therefore has a political focus. For example, you might describe a problem connected with a group or community, help them clarify their needs and then provide information that will enable them to facilitate change afterwards. Whichever type you choose depends on the phenomenon or the group you wish to study.

Common to most types of ethnography are a number of steps which we have adapted from the work of LeCompte and Schensul (1999a). They are:

- find an adequate and appropriate sample in the group under study.
- define the problem, issue or the phenomenon to be explored.
- examine how individuals interpret the situation and the meaning they give to it.
- describe what people do and how they communicate.
- document the process of ethnography.
- monitor the implementation of the process.
- provide information which helps to explain the outcomes of the research.

We incorporate these stages into our following discussion of data collection, analysis and report writing.

Collecting the data

Ethnographic data collection, called *fieldwork*, takes place mainly through observations and interviews although documents are also used fairly extensively (see Chapters 12, 14 and 15 for more on how to carry out these methods). The first stage in collecting the data is to find an adequate and appropriate sample. Once you have achieved this, you can go on to define your research problem or issue, or identify the phenomenon you wish to explore.

Sampling

As in other types of qualitative research, ethnographers generally use purposeful sampling (see Chapter 11). This means that, according to the purpose of your study, you choose a specific group and setting for research, and then use criteria to select who and what will be studied. The criteria for sampling must be explicit and systematic and will often be based on some perspective that you have gained from spending time with the group. Choose 'key informants' carefully to make sure that they are representative of the group under study, and have been in the group long enough to have expert knowledge about the group's rules, routine and language. Key informants are active collaborators in your research rather than passive 'respondents'. Much of your interaction with them is likely to be informal.

Time and context also need to be considered in relation to sampling. Arrange to observe the group or community at different times of the day and different days of the week, otherwise your findings will not be valid. Imagine, for example, if you observed a public relations consultancy only on Monday mornings between 9 a.m. and 10 a.m. It is probable that you would sit in on their regular weekly planning meeting and discover interesting data about this particular activity. Your findings, however, would only be able to draw inferences about behaviour that was unique to one morning in the overall week.

Sampling also needs to take account of context because people's behaviour is influenced by situational factors. Therefore, make sure you carry out observations in a variety of natural settings. For instance, if you were exploring the culture of people in public relations consultancies, you would probably want to observe client meetings that take place in clients' offices, join informants when they go out to lunch, watch how they interact with journalists at press conferences, as well as observe consultants' activities in their own offices.

Participant observation

Gaining access to settings is often problematic, especially as you expect to spend a lot of time *in situ*. Turn to Chapter 5 for more on this aspect. As in other qualitative approaches, you as the researcher are the major research tool. This is especially apparent in participant observation (the favoured method for collecting data) where, over a prolonged period of time, you endeavour to become part of the culture, taking note of everything you see and hear but also interviewing people in order to grasp their interpretation of the situation. A difficulty at the early stage of research is to learn to 'speak like a native' – or learn the jargon – so that you can fit in. Familiarizing yourself with the socially constructed local world in this way means getting to know it like an insider.

As a participant observer, you are interested in watching participants' actions and the ways in which they interact with each other. Do this by paying attention to special events and crises, the site itself, the use of space and time, and any change that occurs over time. Don't overlook regular, mundane activities; these

---

Example 9.2 An ethnographic study in an advertising agency

Mats Alvesson spent 'a few months' in a small Swedish advertising agency studying how advertising professionals describe themselves, their work and organizations, the advertising profession and their clients. His research process was characterized by:

- planned and spontaneous observations.
- planned interviews and spontaneous conversations.
- document analysis.

As interesting themes emerged from his observations, he asked people to elaborate on these themes in interviews. Towards the end of the fieldwork, he fed back to participants some of the ideas to come out of the interviews, asking people for further comment.

He also carried out formal interviews with senior members of other agencies in order to 'give a wider profile to advertising agencies and to avoid getting caught in the more idiosyncratic pattern of the agency studied' (1994: 540). This enabled him to conclude that the advertising industry in Sweden is relatively homogeneous because most of what he found in one organization was also found in others.

are just as important as the more unusual. For a detailed discussion of the participant observation method, turn to Chapter 14.

As in Example 9.2, observations are the starting point for in-depth interviews. Initially, you may not understand what you see and therefore need to ask members of the group you are investigating to explain it to you. You may want to set up formal interviews, or ask questions on the spur of the moment when talking informally. Ritson and Elliott (1999), whose study is outlined in Example 9.1, describe their experiences of fitting in to the life of college students as follows:

> Within a few days ... [the researcher's] presence was accepted, and relationships with sixth formers began to develop. These relationships generally varied from daily conversations on a first-name basis to occasional group interviews. This research, like any other form of ethnographic study, can not claim that the researcher's presence did not alter the behavior of the informants to some degree. However, within the six-week immersion period the sixth formers' initial sense of unease at the presence of a stranger within the group was replaced with either a general obliviousness to his presence or partial acceptance of him as a surrogate member of the sixth form who was sometimes included in a conversation or debate.
>
> (p. 264)

In essence, your ethnographic study involves a partnership between you and the people you are investigating.

Making fieldnotes

Fieldnotes are 'a form of representation ... a way of reducing just-observed events, persons and places to written accounts' (Emerson, Fretz and Shaw 2001: 353). There are four different types of fieldnotes, according to Spradley (1979) all of which should be written as you go along:

- the condensed account.
- the expanded account.
- the fieldwork journal.
- analysis and interpretation notes.

Condensed accounts are short descriptions which you make in the field during data collection. They are important because they help you to learn about the things that members of the group see as important. Expanded accounts extend your descriptions and fill in the detail. They are crucial if you have been unable to make any recordings during data collection, and should be written as soon as possible after any observation or interview session. The fieldwork journal is the place to note your own biases, reactions and problems during fieldwork. There are also other ways of recording events and behaviours, such as tapes, films or photos, flowcharts and diagrams. Writing is a key activity in all phases of field research.

Collecting data from online groups

A potentially exciting, new area for ethnographic research is the study of 'virtual communities', such as those that congregate via computer-mediated communications. There is some debate about whether such loose networks of people can be referred to as 'groups' for the purpose of ethnographic research because they lack a sense of physical place and communicate only through text-based discussion. However, Ward (1999) argues that communities do not necessarily have to be based on shared territory or geographical location (such as an office or suburb), but can rely instead on a common interest. Indeed, her participant observation of interactions on two women's bulletin boards showed that participants experienced a sense of shared understandings that transferred from the virtual realm to their physical lives. Some of her responses were:

> I find the Cybergrrl [web]site to be a very positive place for women to explore the internet and participate in the creation of a community.

> It's so weird it's like we're all just sitting at our computers and we have created this world. It's almost spiritual.
>
> (Ward 1999: 101)

Ward studied virtual communities using ethnographic methods that she adapted for Internet research. She argued that traditional ethnographic methods were likely to enforce inappropriate, preconceived ideas about group culture onto the investigation of virtual groups. Therefore, rather than study culture and its various expressions, she sought instead to explore the shared meanings that were held by participants on websites. As in regular ethnography, she employed participant observation, conversational interviews and focus groups but noted that the online researcher does not have as much control over the interview process because there is a more equal power distribution. Participants as well as researchers ask questions, and the final interpretation of the data remains open to constant renegotiation by both researcher and researched. For more on online researching, see Chapters 12 and 13.

Analysing the data

As in other qualitative approaches, the processing of your raw data begins when you code them. You then search for patterns, themes and connections between ideas. In this way you begin to develop analytic categories and themes which can be related back to the data to check that there is a good fit. Turn to Chapter 16 to read about how to do this, noting the section on using computer software for analysis.

The stages of describing and analysing are intertwined with that of interpretation which is where you endeavour to gain insight on your data by giving some meaning to them. This involves making inferences and giving an explanation for the communication phenomena you have explored. Interpretation involves theorizing and explaining by linking emerging ideas derived from your analysis to established theories by comparing and contrasting others' work with your own. Eventually your research story is put together through an integration of your descriptions, analyses and interpretations. It should form a coherent storyline.

Key point

Theory emerges from the *reflexive* nature of the ethnographic experience. As a researcher, you are a part of the world that you are studying and you are affected by it. The combination of your 'outsider's' perspective with the 'insider' perspectives of your informants provides deeper insights – and leads to the development of theoretical concepts – than are possible solely from participants or from you alone. See Chapter 6 for more on reflexivity.

The notion that theoretically informed descriptions emerge from a combination of insider/outsider perspectives is at the heart of ethnography and is related to the idea of *etic* and *emic* points of view. The etic perspective, that is, the scientific, conceptual framework that you develop from both your reading and your primary research, acts as a system of categories for your observations. However, the constructs of participants – the emic, or insider view – is also used to support the etic perspective. Insiders' accounts of reality help you to uncover reasons why people act as they do and inform your descriptions and interpretation. By putting insiders' ideas into an etic framework, you are able to interpret them according to your theoretical perspective rather than adopting a simplistic stance in which you merely summarize the words of participants. Fetterman (1998) describes this process of moving back and forth from the world of the participant to scientific reflection as 'iteration'. It is important to appreciate that emic and etic are not necessarily dichotomous but, as Pike (1967) puts it, they often represent the same data from two points of view.

Writing the report

Although ethnographies are written in various styles and formats, if you are an undergraduate student, it is more appropriate to adopt a fairly conventional approach to writing the research report, as outlined in Chapter 17.

We have already referred to the ethnography as a picture or a story of the communicative actions, interactions and events within a cultural group. Van Maanen (1988) refers to it as a 'tale', and differentiates between three main types:

> **Helpful hint**
> Illustrate your narrative with excerpts from your interviews, from naturally occurring conversations that were observed and recorded, and from your fieldnotes. Use these to represent a distillation of your wider empirical base.

- the realist tale.
- the confessional tale.
- the impressionist tale.

Van Maanen's ideas are summarized in Holloway (1997) as follows. Traditionally, *the realist tale* excluded the ethnographer from the text in order to provide a sense of neutrality and objectivity to the story. Therefore, it was written in the third person. It focused on the mundane details of everyday life, the ordinary ways of life and routines of the informants, and generated the 'native's' point of view. It lacked reflexivity (see Chapter 6) and relied upon only the author's interpretation of the phenomena under investigation. However, in recent years, realist tales have become more personalized, and, if you were to write in this style today, you would be expected to be self-reflexive and probably write in the first person using 'I' (Holloway 1997). Sriramesh's (1996) account of ethnographic research in southern Indian organizations is a traditional realist tale because it is written with no acknowledgement of the presence of the researcher and nor is there any attempt at self-reflection. Ritson and Elliott's (1999) account (outlined in Example 9.1) takes a more contemporary approach because the researcher is introduced into the text and there is some reflexivity.

Confessional tales have become more popular over the last two decades. If you were to follow this style, you would use very personal language to describe in detail the techniques and strategies that you carried out in the field. You would articulate what you have done in order to demonstrate the adequacy of your work. You would tell how you gained the knowledge presented in the ethnography, demonstrating the 'respectability' and disciplined nature of your fieldwork. Your confessions would show awareness of your own stance and biases. It is probable that the writing of your tale would have been stimulated by a surprise or shock that you experienced in the fieldwork, or through mistakes you made that caused problematic situations. These you would discuss in detail. Examples of confessional tales are presented in Shaffir and Stebbin (1991). Realist and confessional tales are now often published in parallel or sequentially.

According to Van Maanen, *impressionist tales* are creative, artistic and contextual. Your aim in writing an ethnography of this nature is to present the culture under study in a creative and imaginative way. It is probable that, as the fieldworker and author, you would give yourself a place in this story. You would give names and personalities to the people in your impressionist tale, and describe their actions. You would attempt to draw your readers into the story by developing a storyline which enables them to learn about the culture gradually. Hackley's (2000) ethnographic study of an advertising agency, outlined in Examples 10.1 and 17.1, follows the style of an impressionist tale. Van Maanen claims that some of the best ethnographies are written in this way because they are read like a work of fiction with a strong and lively storyline.

Limitations and problems in ethnographic research

Ethnography is a demanding methodology which requires a commitment of time to participant observation. It can be stressful as, despite your best attempts to immerse yourself into a group, it is possible that you may never completely succeed, and will always be viewed as someone on the margins of the culture. This is likely to be compounded by having to manage the role of researcher while simultaneously attempting to 'fit in'.

A problem exists if you wish to examine your own cultural group because to do this successfully means becoming a 'cultural stranger'. This is difficult as it entails questioning the assumptions of a culture that is already familiar to you, and whose rules and norms you have internalized.

Researchers often make statements, based on fieldwork in one group, that seem to be applicable to a whole range of similar situations. However, an ethnography – like other qualitative research – cannot simply be generalized. Findings from one subculture or one setting are not automatically applicable to other settings (see Chapter 6 for more on generalizability).

Summary

- Ethnographic research is the study of the way of life (the culture) of a group, community or organization. It relies on extended periods of field-work.
- It is both a research methodology (which uses participant observation, interviews and documents), and the product of that research, that is, a written description of a culture.
- One of the major characteristics of ethnography is 'thick' description which is both analytical and theoretical.
- Theory emerges from a combination of emic ('insider') and etic ('outsider') perspectives.

10 Discourse analysis and phenomenology

Discourse analysis and phenomenology are two distinct research approaches. Until recently, they have been applied infrequently to investigations of public relations and marketing communications research. However, each is beginning to make inroads into research in these domains and is likely to become more popular in the near future. For this reason we briefly introduce the two methodologies within the same chapter.

This chapter notes that:

- discourse analysis is concerned with the cultural and political context in which discourse occurs, and the way that language is used and organized in order to construct different versions of events and activities.
- phenomenology is interested in the personal 'life world' of individuals and groups and how that influences their motives, actions and communication.

Within the chapter is a discussion of:

- collecting and analysing data for discourse analysis.
- collecting and analysing data for a phenomenological approach.
- the philosophical roots of phenomenology.

Discourse analysis

Discourse analysis is a set of broad methodological principles which are applied to both naturally occurring and contrived forms of talk and texts. In research, it may be used on its own, or together with other methodological approaches such as ethnography or the case study. Data sources for discourse analysis include

---

Key point

Discourse analysis appreciates that language, or discourse, is not simply a device for producing and transmitting meaning. It is a strategy which people use purposefully to try to create a particular effect.

interviews, conversations, newspaper articles, media releases, television news broadcasts, company policy documents, letters, reports and even fairly informal chat, such as that involving DJs on the radio.

In general, researchers following this approach appreciate that

> social texts [that is, discourse] do not merely *reflect* or mirror objects, events and categories pre-existing in the social and natural world. Rather, they actively *construct* a version of those things. They do not just describe things; they *do* things. And being active, they have social and political implications.
>
> (Potter and Wetherell 1987: 6)

If you were to use discourse analysis in public relations research, you might study, for example, the rhetoric of a government, such as the way in which it has sought to gain support for cuts in social services by addressing its citizens in their role as tax payers rather than as consumers of those social services (Motion and Leitch 1996). In this case, you would be interested in bringing out the implied meanings and tacit codings in the government's language use in all its various forms of communication.

For research in marketing communications, you might conduct a study that focuses on investigating the stories that companies employ to justify their ethical (or unethical) behaviours towards consumers. In research of this nature, you would note that companies' perspectives shape not only the words they use and the subsequent actions they take, but also the narratives they employ to persuade others of their point of view or the way they see the world.

A preoccupation of discourse analysis research is the cultural and political context in which discourse occurs and the way that language is used and organized in order to construct different versions of events and activities.

As a field of study, discourse analysis comprises diverse perspectives and approaches, some of which are influenced by the work of French philosopher Michel Foucault (1926–84). The version which we discuss here is associated with Fairclough (1995), Potter and Wetherell (1987) and van Dijk (1997). It draws on conversation analysis but is more flexible because there is less of an emphasis on naturally occurring talk than in conversation analysis. The latter approach is rarely used in public relations and marketing communications research. However, discourse analysis is beginning to make its mark in the literature, notably in the work of Motion and Leitch (1996) in public relations and Hackley (2000) in marketing communications.

Researchers who follow this approach recognize that discourse occurs within a social context, and therefore endeavour to examine three aspects in their research. These are:

- the form and content of the language in use.
- the ways in which people use language in order to communicate ideas and beliefs.

• institutional and organizational factors surrounding the discourse under investigation and how they might shape the discourse.

Discourse analysis, therefore, moves beyond textual examination to explore '*who* uses language, *how, why* and *when*' (van Dijk 1997: 2).

Collecting the data

As a discourse analyst, what interests you most is language use rather than the people who generate the various forms of communication. Therefore, the success of your study is not dependent on sample size. Even a few documents or transcripts are likely to reveal a large number of linguistic patterns. Indeed, some classic studies have concentrated on a *single* text, but this is rare. When making decisions about your sample size, be guided by your research question and also by the data that are accessible. In some cases, it may not be possible to get hold of certain material because it no longer exists or because it is confidential. For more on the data collection techniques of interviewing and using documents, see Chapters 12 and 15.

Key point
The goal of interviewing for discourse analysis differs from that for other methodological approaches because you are seeking to find out how communication is constructed and what it achieves rather than aiming to understand what people believe or what they really are.

In discourse analysis, you approach interviews as 'conversational encounters' (Potter and Wetherell 1987) where you encourage participants to talk in the natural, everyday language that they would use outside the interview situation. This means taking an active and interventionist role as an interviewer, rather than being passive and neutral. Potter and Wetherell suggest that one way to do this is to encourage participants to discuss issues from a number of different angles.

For example, if an issue you wanted to consider was equal opportunities in the advertising industry, you might raise this in relation to: the depiction of women in television advertising, graduate recruitment, promotion within agencies. By looking at the same issue in a variety of contexts, participants are more likely to involve themselves in the conversation and put forward less contrived responses. A further strategy is to pose follow-up questions to participants' responses which require them to consider alternative or problematic views or facts. Techniques such as these result in more informal conversational exchanges which are better able to reveal the way language is structured and constructed.

However, the ability to successfully conduct interviews of this type is a skill that takes time to develop. This is because there are two competing aspects involved in interviewing for discourse analysis. On the one hand, you need to systematically cover the same range of topics with all participants and, on the other hand, you need to allow your interviews to remain open-ended enough to engage people fully and naturally in conversation. The first is achievable if you use a detailed interview guide with the same questions, probes and follow-up questions to all participants. The second will occur only if you have excellent interpersonal communication skills.

Analysing the data

Although there are no set procedures for conducting discourse analysis, there are some common techniques. These include focusing on whole segments of language, identifying 'interpretative repertoires', being sensitive to the way arguments are constructed, and paying attention to the context.

Focusing on extended segments of language

Usually when you are undertaking qualitative data analysis, you are concerned to find key words, themes, issues and patterns in your data-texts. In discourse analysis, however, you are less interested in individual words and phrases than in whole chunks of text because you want to explore accounts and language structures.

Identifying 'interpretative repertoires'

Interpretative repertoires (Potter and Wetherell 1987) are the frameworks of beliefs that guide and influence the writers or speakers. To identify interpretative repertoires in communication, look for regularities and variabilities in the language used. Having found them, select a label for them, as appropriate. For example, Billig (1992) researched the ways in which people talk about the royal family. He found regularities in the discourses that people adopted concerning newspapers' role as providers of information about the royal family. On different occasions, his respondents used 'sources of lies' repertoires or 'sources of knowledge' repertoires.

Remember that you are not trying to discover the accuracy of a speaker's or writer's description or whether he or she is distorting 'what really happened'. What you are concerned with is to understand how your respondents use discourse as a device to construct their version of the world, an event, an organization, or a circumstance.

Being sensitive to the ways in which arguments are constructed

When you pay attention to rhetorical detail, you identify descriptive sequences and the ways in which they have been assembled. This indicates the thinking

---

Example 10.1 Analysing discourse in a London advertising agency

Chris Hackley's investigation of a London advertising agency revealed eight mutually-dependent interpretative repertoires which he called: 'corporate way', 'strategic imperative', 'managerial imperative', 'intellectual contingency', 'power of rationality', 'knowledge of the client', 'knowledge of the consumer' and a 'power of creativity' repertoire which was present by its absence, silenced by the others.

He found both regularities and variability in the company's 'corporate way' repertoire. This described and legitimated 'the way we do things round here'. For example, interviewees told him that:

- [the agency] doesn't approve of that system.
- I think [the agency] possibly more than other agencies has an anti-selling ethos.
- I think account managers at [the agency] contribute quite a lot to the planning process.
- [this agency] approach is very thinking and analytical.

Hackley writes that the 'corporate way' repertoire was drawn on by staff in agency discourse in a number of ways including reinforcing their professional identities and the belief that they worked for a company that had a unique way of doing advertising. However, his recognition of variability in the theme enabled him to identify that the 'corporate way' repertoire was employed in different ways within the company according to the seniority of the staff. For example, junior staff drew on it to help them make sense of events and to position them as good corporate professionals. Senior staff used it in a more subtle way to position themselves as 'individual experts rather than slavish followers of convention' (2000: 241–2).

---

and values behind what people are saying or writing, and highlights how arguments are constructed. For example, an extract from a political speech by Norman Tebbit (Atkinson 1984: 60) illustrates how a descriptive sequence is organized:

> Labour will
> spend and spend   1
> borrow and borrow   2
> and tax and tax   3

As Wooffitt (1993) points out, the speaker is less concerned with the detail of spending, borrowing and taxing than he is with conveying the *general* point that the Labour Party's economic policy is inherently flawed. It is possible, therefore, to get an idea of the general features or direction of the discourse rather than the specifics within the discourse structure by focusing on how a sequence of language has been assembled and for what purpose.

Paying attention to context

For example, you might concentrate on power relations between speakers, according to expertise, seniority or gender, or the type of occasion where the language is used, such as a client meeting, political rally or an interview.

For detailed illustrations of how data are analysed using discourse analysis, see Gilbert and Mulkay (1984) and Potter and Wetherell (1987, 1994).

Limitations and problems in discourse analysis

Although a strength of discourse analysis is its tight, micro focus on what is being studied, a tendency in some studies is to consider that the chosen sample of discourse is sufficient unto itself. This fails to take account of the wider social, cultural and historical context in which the sample is situated. To overcome this problem, it is sometimes useful to complement discourse analysis with a complementary methodological approach in order to gain an alternative perspective on the same topic. In a discourse analysis study of the construction of masculinity, for example, Edley and Wetherell (1997) undertook periods of ethnographic observation which sensitized them to subtleties that would not have been immediately obvious in an analysis of language only. This understanding informed their interpretation of the discourse.

Most discourse analysis studies are based on a social constructionist premise which assumes that communication creates reality, that is, we literally manufacture our reality into existence through discourse. However, Reed (1998) is among those who criticize such a view, claiming that this 'non-realist' stance overlooks pre-existing material and social objects or mechanisms which exist and act independently of language. These influence when and how discourse occurs and should not be ignored in research, he writes. While not all researchers go along with his thinking, his comments do draw attention to the different theoretical positions that are held within the same methodological approach.

Discourse analysis is an often difficult and time-consuming method of analysis because you need to engage in a critical reading of texts. This means that you should take sufficient time out to stand back from the text and question the assumptions that you are making.

Considerable expertise is needed for conducting interviews for discourse analysis research because it is necessary to adhere to a detailed interview guide while simultaneously being actively involved in a 'natural' conversation.

Summary of discourse analysis

* Discourse analysis entails the study of the form and content of language, the ways it is used to construct and communicate ideas and beliefs, and the political and cultural context surrounding the discourse.
* Sample size is usually small.

- The research focus is on whole chunks of text, in order to identify 'interpretative repertoires' which are the frameworks of beliefs that guide speakers and writers.

Phenomenology

Phenomenology is both a philosophy and a methodological approach that encompasses a variety of methods. As a philosophy, it is one of the primary intellectual traditions which have influenced qualitative research. As a methodological approach, it has been embraced by researchers from many social science areas, notably psychology and sociology, who draw on one of its many philosophical strands. It is a difficult and complex way of carrying out research, and we would not recommend it to novice researchers.

Key point
A strength of phenomenology lies in its ability to aid researchers to enter into the field of perception of other people in order to see life as those individuals do.

Phenomenology helps you get into the shoes of other people and understand why they experience life as they do. It does more than enable you to see from the perspective of participants; it offers a way of understanding the sense-making framework that each individual has developed over time, which shapes their responses to events and experiences. Whereas other qualitative research approaches also attempt to see things through the eyes of the people they study, phenomenology goes further because it provides a means for you to set aside your own preconceived ideas about an event or an experience in order to understand it from the world in which research participants exist.

Although phenomenology has been popular for a number of decades in health care and educational inquiry it is applied less frequently to research in marketing communications and, unfortunately, almost never in public relations research. Studies utilizing this approach have been mainly limited to investigations of consumers and how their life experiences have influenced their understandings and experiences of brands and advertisements. Yet phenomenology has the potential to be a valuable research tool for investigating a wide range of topics such as how different stakeholders perceive the communication activities of organizations, how the cultural expectations of individuals shape the images they hold of companies, how clients understand and experience the consultancy–client relationship, how male executives respond to female leaders, how employees experience particular episodes of internal communication activity, and so on.

Below we offer a brief overview of some of phenomenology's philosophical roots together with an outline of the process of analysis which differs slightly from other forms of qualitative analysis. If you are interested in following this approach, you need a solid grounding in the philosophical foundations of phenomenology, and therefore we suggest that you read more extensively, starting with texts such as Becker (1992) and Creswell (1998).

The philosophy

Phenomenology has its roots in the European philosophy of Husserl (1859–1938) and in its application by Alfred Schutz (1899–1959). Husserl posited that each of us, as individuals, exists in a unique life world, or *Lebenswelt*, that is made up of objects, people, actions and institutions. This life world is each person's subjective experience of their everyday life, that is, it is their social reality, and this determines the meanings they attribute to their actions and the actions of others. Husserl was interested in how our life worlds get to be the way they are, in other words, how they become natural and taken for granted. In order to find out the essence of things – or the fundamental principles of sensemaking in everyday life – he argued that researchers, or phenomenologists, should attempt to understand phenomena, such as experiences or events, in ways that differ from the usual. This strategy means making strange something that seems normal and natural so that its essential features can be characterized. Husserl suggested this could be done by viewing a phenomenon from an angle that is unusual or outside the norm, as we explain in the next section.

One problem that Husserl never solved was how a human being learns to construct a life world that can be shared with other human beings. If that life world is particular to individuals, how can people share meaning? How can there be so much continuity of meaning in people's actions? Schutz attempted to address these questions through the notion of intersubjectivity. Each person is a unique human being with a specific history who, nevertheless, shares this humanity with others and therefore is linked to the world. Schutz claimed that individuals unquestioningly accept that others share the same perspectives about the essential features of our everyday world. Therefore, in communicating with others, we operate on the notion that 'if you were to trade places with me, you would see situations in the same way as I do, and vice versa' (Lindlof 1995: 33).

Schutz argued that in every situation, we apply a 'stock of knowledge' that helps us make sense of the phenomena we encounter. This knowledge consists of the facts, beliefs, biases, desires and rules we have learned from personal experience as well as from the more general knowledge available to us in the world in which we exist. The first kind of knowledge is personal and unique to us through the encounters we have with others. The second kind is more widely available to all members of a culture, such as knowledge that is transmitted through cultural norms, myths and stories, and common sense. Schutz noted that we organize our 'worlds' by using this knowledge to classify others and events according to what we perceive to be their typical traits. This notion of 'typification' can be seen in the way in which publicists might classify the practices of others within the same industry as professional or non-professional. Social interaction proceeds on the basis of typifications such as this. Intersubjectivity, therefore, is enacted in the kinds of relationships we enter into with others. Each of us defines ourselves through our negotiated relationships and we actively construct numerous life worlds that overlap one another.

Doing phenomenological research

At the core of phenomenological study, then, is the notion of life world, the recognition that the reality of each individual is different and individual actions can only be understood through understanding the life world of individuals and also their shared perspectives. Therefore, it is your task as a researcher to access people's 'common sense thinking' in order to interpret their motives, actions and their social world from their point of view.

Although phenomenology employs no one particular method, there are a number of features that are common to phenomenological studies. These include articulating the underlying philosophical basis, bracketing assumptions, focusing on a main phenomenon, working with small samples, and applying thematic phenomenological data analysis. We discuss these in turn.

Articulating the philosophical basis of the study

Phenomenological studies begin with a discussion of the philosophy underpinning the research. This is important because of the variety of philosophical strands of phenomenology, which include social phenomenology (which focuses on social acts and group experiences), transcendental phenomenology (which emphasizes individual experiences), and hermeneutic phenomenology, where you interpret texts according to the cultural, situational and historical context in which phenomena occur.

Bracketing assumptions

Because you are aiming to look at phenomena in a fresh way, it is essential to state your own assumptions regarding the phenomena you are investigating and then 'bracket' them – or put them aside – so that any preconceptions you may hold do not get in the way of your understanding of the experiences of your participants. For example, if you were exploring the structure of the successful consultant–client relationship from the point of view of clients, you would need to surface your own ideas, prejudices and prior conceptions about the topic, based perhaps on previous reading or experiences. Once you have reflected on this, you should suspend your assumptions so that you can confront the topic on its own terms, that is by seeing it through the eyes of client participants in your study.

Focusing on a main phenomenon

Phenomenological research is concerned with the experiences of people concerning a particular phenomenon. Once you have identified a phenomenon that you wish to investigate, you develop research questions which explore its meaning for your participants. The main phenomenon in the previous paragraph is the successful consultant–client relationship.

Example 10.2 Studying the phenomenon of North American students' experiences of alcohol advertising

The main phenomenon in a study by Betty Parker (1998) was alcohol advertising with regard to North American students' experiences. In interviews with nine college students, she explored their backgrounds, personal history, interests and drinking behaviour. She also showed them alcohol advertisements, asking them to describe their opinions and feelings. Her research found that students' life worlds comprised notions about how they viewed themselves as individuals, their stance on advertising generally, and what they thought about alcohol. Views on alcohol were that it was a 'problem solver', 'party' and 'comfort'. These views influenced how the students interpreted alcohol advertisements.

Parker's findings suggest that the advertising experience is highly personal because it is coloured by people's own life worlds. This points to linkages between advertising, consumption and identity, with subsequent implications for advertisers, not least with regard to social responsibility.

Working with small samples

Although written accounts of participants' experiences are used as data sources, typically data are derived from long interviews with individuals who have experience and in-depth knowledge of the phenomenon under study. For example, in the study outlined in Example 10.2, it would not have been appropriate for the researcher to have interviewed students who did not drink alcohol. Sampling is similar in phenomenology to sampling in other approaches to qualitative research (see Chapter 11). However, because of the depth of research interviews and the extensive analytical process that is required, the sample is generally very small, often no more than ten (Creswell 1998).

Note that when conducting interviews, you are trying to go beyond superficial appearances. Therefore, you should closely observe the language, facial expressions and gestures of participants so that you can better understand their accounts when you come to analyse them.

Applying thematic data analysis

The eventual goal of phenomenological data analysis is to present an exhaustive, analytic description of the phenomenon under study; it should reflect the rich, 'lived' experience of the participants. The description may be in the form of an extended paragraph which indicates the meanings of the phenomenological experience (such as how clients interpret their interactions with consultants) and reveals the essence of the phenomenon (such as the nature of the successful consultant–client relationship). In order to arrive at such a description, there are various practical strategies which you might choose to follow, one of which is detailed below. However, remember that the phenomenological approach to research is flexible and not prescriptive.

A popular and clear procedure for thematic analysis is that offered by Colaizzi (1978) who recommends that you follow seven stages. In common with the phenomenological tradition generally, his procedure is distinguished from other forms of qualitative analysis in that analysis does not interact with data collection. Each interview or written text is analysed separately, although the purpose at the end is to have a sense of the whole, the essence of the phenomenon. Colaizzi's suggested stages are:

1   When you have interviewed participants, listened to their narratives (in transcripts and/or written accounts) and familiarized yourself with their words, try to become aware of the feelings and the meanings inherent in the narratives in order to obtain a 'sense of the whole'.

2   Now return to each of your participants' narratives and focus only on the phrases and sentences that directly pertain to the phenomenon under study. Scrutinize every piece of the data for statements that you consider are significant to the phenomenon, isolate these 'significant statements' from the rest, and list them all.

   For example, significant statements that might emerge from a study about the successful consultant–client relationship from the perspective of clients might include the following:
   a   'They listen to our point of view.'
   b   'They understand our business goals.'
   c   'They give us feedback all the time.'
   d   'They produce campaigns that work', and so on.

3   The next stage is called 'formulating meanings'. Here you take each significant statement, try to uncover its meaning and make sense of it in the participants' own terms. What you are trying to do is to spell out the meaning of each significant statement according to its original context. This helps to bring out meanings that initially may be hidden. For example, following the previous list of statements, the attached meanings might be:
   a   The consultant really tries to listen to what the client has to say, and values his or her opinion.
   b   The consultant does not just pay lip service to the client, but is knowledgeable about the business, its direction, focus and markets.
   c   Once the consultant has been briefed, he or she doesn't ignore the client but constantly keeps him or her in touch with progress.
   d   The consultant delivers campaigns that produce the desired results.

4 Repeat this process for each interview or written account and then organize all the different meanings into clusters of themes. Themes related to the above might be: Consultant Empathy (comprises meanings a and b in the previous section), Constant Communication (comprises meanings a and c in the previous section), and so on.

5 Then provide a detailed analytic description of participants' feelings and perspectives contained in the themes. Colaizzi calls this step 'exhaustive description'. This is where you integrate all the clusters of themes into one account that articulates participants' views of the phenomenon.

6 At this point, you attempt to formulate an exhaustive description of the whole phenomenon under investigation and identify its fundamental structure, or essence, that is, the nature of the successful consultant–client relationship.

7 The last step is the 'member check' (see also Chapter 6) in which you take your findings back to participants, asking them if your description validates their original experiences. Hycner (1985) advises you to do more than this. He suggests that you show participants a summary of each interview with the themes highlighted that you have found. This enables you to modify your ideas or add new ones.

At this point, we briefly draw your attention to the strand of phenomenology called hermeneutics which has its basis in the ideas of Heidegger (1889–1976) and is concerned with the interpretation of texts. Analysis proceeds in a different way from that outlined earlier. Here you are involved in an iterative approach to data analysis, moving back and forth between parts of the text and the whole. By following this approach, you aim to interpret the underlying sense of behaviour, the language of participants and the context in which they occur. The method is culturally and historically informed which means that you need to take account of the cultural, situational and historical location in which the phenomenon under investigation is positioned.

In summary, if you wish to carry out phenomenological research, you need to go beyond the surface to see the essential nature of things. Take nothing at face value but look at everything from the perspectives of other people. This means developing empathy by immersing yourself in the situation in the same way as participants themselves. Focus in on those essential features of the phenomenon that remain constant, reducing it to its 'essence' by getting rid of non-essential elements that are dependent on environment or circumstance. By stripping away the everyday, and going to the very foundations of things, you arrive at a recognition of the essence, or the 'real', 'intended' meaning, of the phenomenon under investigation.

In your subsequent research report, you should provide 'an accurate, clear, and articulate description of an experience. The reader of the report should come away with the feeling that "I understand better what it is like for someone to experience that" ' (Polkinghorne 1989, cited in Creswell 1998: 177).

Example 10.3 Discovering the life worlds of students

Betty Parker's (1998) research which is outlined in Example 10.2 showed how students use advertising to transfer meanings back to themselves. The meanings then become intertwined with pre-existing self-concepts to create advertising experiences that are as individual as the students themselves. She categorized participants' life worlds according to issues that feature prominently in their lives and showed how those issues, or 'life themes', were woven into their interpretation of alcohol. Three examples from her study are:

Student	Life theme	Explanation	Advertisements
Kim: 20, journalism major, upper middle class.	Having control versus not having control.	Kim stressed the importance of control, planning.	Alcohol means being out of control.
Chas: 21, consumer affairs major, oldest of lower class family.	Feeling comfortable versus not feeling comfortable.	Wants to fit in and feel more comfortable around others.	Says that drinking beer will make you feel better.
Ellen: 20, business major, married to air conditioning repairman.	Achieving versus not achieving.	Unsure of intellectual abilities; craves success and works hard.	[Beer brand] is 'for those who push themselves to succeed'.

This illustration indicates how Parker identified (a) themes which enabled her to describe the life worlds of individuals, (b) what those themes meant in terms of how the participants responded to experiences, (c) how these influenced their interpretations of advertisements and, in turn, how those interpretations were interwoven back into their life worlds. From this analysis, Parker was able to provide a more general description of the nature of student experiences of alcohol advertisements.

Limitations and problems in phenomenological research

Unless you have a sound understanding of the philosophy of phenomenology, you will find it difficult to successfully apply this research approach. Many marketing communications studies carelessly fling the word phenomenology into their methodology discussions without a real awareness of its depth, subtlety or methodological requirements.

Finding people who have experienced the phenomenon you wish to investigate and who are willing to spend time in extended discussions about it may be problematic.

The process of surfacing your preconceptions and then bracketing them may not always be successful. Two questions to ask yourself as you go along are: 'Do my descriptions truly reflect participants' actual experiences?' and 'Have I unconsciously influenced these descriptions by my own ideas, biases and preconceptions?'

Summary of phenomenology

- At the core of phenomenology is the study of people's life worlds, their subjective experience of their personal, everyday lives.
- Researchers consciously suspend, or bracket, their own assumptions so they can see through the eyes of participants.
- Sample sizes are usually small.
- In phenomenological research, you try to make sense of a phenomenon according to participants' own terms, identifying the essence or 'real' meaning of the phenomenon under investigation.

This chapter discussed both phenomenology and discourse analysis. To find the summary for discourse analysis, see pages 145–6.

Part III

Collecting the data

11 Sampling

Qualitative approaches to research demand different sampling techniques from those commonly used in quantitative studies. Rarely are they probabilistic or random. Instead they are purposeful, based on the purpose of the investigation. This chapter discusses the strategies that are appropriate for sampling in qualitative research and includes:

• the main dimensions on which sampling takes place.
• different types of samples and sizes.
• what to call the people in your study.

Introduction

It is unlikely that you will be able to collect data from everyone who is connected with your topic of research; time and other resources will prevent this. Also, unless the research 'population' is very small, say a group of people or a small cluster of advertisements which you intend to study, you won't know enough about its characteristics to be able to say precisely who is included within it. Therefore, you will have to collect evidence from a portion (or a 'sample') of the population in which you are interested. You do this in the expectation that your sample will generate adequate and relevant information, with sufficient quality data to offer new insights on your topic.

Sampling decisions begin during the early stages of research. These depend on the focus and topic of the research but include the setting for your study (where to sample), the time and context for your sample (what to sample) and the group of people from which to take your sample (whom to sample). Don't forget to ensure that the people and places are available and accessible to you. To some extent, computer-mediated communications and telephones help to

---

Key point
The term 'population' refers to a totality of units such as people, organizations, brands or advertisements.

overcome some of the difficulties of sampling across a wide or distant geographical spread because interviews can be conducted online or by phone on a global or regional basis. Similarly, busy people are often willing to be interviewed online but not face-to-face. In this way, the Internet is a useful tool in extending the scope of the sampling unit.

Qualitative approaches demand different sampling techniques from the randomly selected and probabilistic sampling which quantitative researchers generally use. They are less rigid and do not start with the establishment of a strict sampling frame, as in quantitative studies. This is because qualitative sampling develops during the research process as you discover new avenues and clues to follow up.

At the beginning of your study, it is not necessary to specify the exact number of informants in the sample, although you are expected to indicate the numbers involved in your *initial* sample, that is, 'the initial sample will consist of x number of informants'. This sampling strategy differs from quantitative research where you choose all participants before the project begins.

Sampling parameters and dimensions

There are a number of dimensions on which sampling takes place. These include people, setting, events, processes, activities and time (Miles and Huberman 1994, Hammersley and Atkinson 1995), as indicated in Table 11.1. The most important element of the research is people. They are chosen on the basis of experience of the phenomenon under study. The context refers to the conditions and situations in which participants are found. Time refers to stages or sequences, or different rhythms of time, or to specific times of the day or calendar. Whatever the sample, the criteria for selection must be clearly identified.

Table 11.1 Sampling parameters

Sampling parameters	Examples
People	People with certain roles, e.g. clients of advertising agencies. People with experience of media relations. People who have been exposed to Internet advertising.
Setting	A country or region where advertising practices are distinctive. A public relations consultancy with novel practices.
Events and processes	Meetings. Communication interactions between managers and staff. New business pitches.
Activities	Watching television advertisements. Producing publicity campaigns.
Time	Six months before and after the execution of a campaign. Morning and afternoon.

Example 11.1 Applying two sampling dimensions

In Scotland, public relations is a highly competitive, multi-million pound industry with a wide range of consultancies servicing a large number of purchasing organizations. Mark Gabbott and Gillian Hogg (1996) wanted to study how companies in Scotland made decisions about which consultancies to select. They conducted twelve in-depth interviews with senior managers in a variety of companies who used PR services.

(**Setting:** Scotland; **People:** senior managers in companies that used PR consultancies)

Purposeful or purposive sampling

The underlying principle of gaining rich, in-depth information guides the sampling strategies of qualitative researchers. Whom you select for your study, where and when depends on certain criteria which are determined by the purpose of your study. Therefore, the term *purposive* or *purposeful* sampling is applied. For example, the criteria used by Gabbott and Hogg in Example 11.1 were (a) Scotland and (b) senior managers in companies that used public relations consultancies. Note how the aim of Gabbott and Hogg's study informed the criteria for sampling. LeCompte and Preissle (1997) assert that 'criterion-based' sampling is a better term for this type of sampling because most sampling strategies, even random sampling, are highly purposive. However, the term purposeful or purposive is used by most qualitative researchers.

Your two main questions concern what to sample and how to sample. People generally form the main sampling units. Identification of a sample provides inclusion or exclusion criteria for the study, that is, boundaries between those who are included in the study and those who are outside it. The members of the sample generally share certain characteristics and experiences which are important for the development of the study.

Example 11.2 Inclusion criteria in sampling

A sample of eight women who were magazine readers were interviewed by Steven Kates and Glenda Shaw-Garlock (1999) in order to explore how women interpret advertising and negotiate personalized meanings.

Inclusion criteria: (a) women (b) magazine readers.

Participants may be chosen by you or self-selected. Sometimes it is easy to identify individuals or groups with special knowledge of a topic. For example, in Canada, Thwaites, Aguilar-Manjarrez and Kidd investigated current practices in the management of sports sponsorship by interviewing ten 'leading authorities on sponsorship issues' (1998: 37). They included the editor of a sponsorship report, senior sponsorship practitioners, sponsorship consultants and academics in the field.

Self-selection takes place when people respond to your requests or advertisements for informants who have insight into a particular situation or those who have particular expertise. For example, they could be students on work placement, or managers with particular professional knowledge and experience, or consumers who have been dissatisfied with the after-sales service of a particular product. In this case, you choose your sample from among those who have put themselves forward as wanting to take part in your research on the topic. Useful informants could be people who have undergone or are undergoing experiences about which you wish to gain information. For example, Jarratt (1996) was interested in understanding how the experience of shopping locally differed from shopping some distance from the home. Therefore, her sample consisted of men and women at differing stages of the family life cycle who were either 'dedicated' shoppers or 'reluctant' shoppers.

Individuals who are willing to talk about their experiences and perceptions are sometimes those who have an uncommon approach to their work. Some have power or status, others are naïve, hostile or attention seeking. Some have lost power and become frustrated. It is wise to remember that these are not always the best informants because they may have an axe to grind or hold a mainly negative perception of the organization or brand which you want to discuss. On the other hand, qualitative research is concerned with the subjective experiences of informants and it is often by allowing such voices to be heard that qualitative research findings challenge the status quo and critique the assumptions that are commonly held in public relations and marketing communications.

When selecting your sample, ensure that your potential informants are willing to share their experiences with you. Some may be jeopardized by uncovering their own practices and ideologies, or the information may be highly sensitive. There may be a reluctance, therefore, to share thoughts and feelings. Respect this stance and look elsewhere for other informants, remembering to make your selection on the basis of appropriate criteria, not on the basis of personal liking or because they seem more articulate. In online interviewing, it is important to ensure that your potential informants have adequate computer access and skills in self-expression as well as the use of email or real-time chat software. Mann and Stewart (2000) note that a further consideration is the amount of access that your informants have to computers. They may have time restrictions on computer usage, or no access to private venues, both of which limit the extent to which informants can provide rich, insightful data.

Sampling types

There are a number of different types of sample and sampling. An overview of a whole range can be found in Patton (1990), Miles and Huberman (1994) and

Marshall and Rossman (1999). The following are the most important and most often used types of sampling, although many sampling types overlap.

- Homogeneous sample.
- Heterogeneous sample.
- Total population sample.
- Chain referral sample.
- Convenience or opportunistic sample.
- Theoretical sample.

A *homogeneous sample* consists of individuals who belong to the same subculture or group and have similar characteristics. Homogeneous sample units are useful when you wish to observe or interview a particular group, for instance specialists in a field or elite group members. In the preceding cases, a homogeneous group is being studied. The sample may be homogeneous with respect to a certain variable only, for instance, occupation, length of experience, type of experience, age or gender. The important variable could be established before the sampling starts. Example 11.3 provides an illustration of this type of sample.

Example 11.3 A homogeneous sample

Although 58 per cent of public relations practitioners in the USA are women, a neglected area of academic research is female leadership in public relations. Linda Aldoory (1998) is one of the few to have investigated the topic. Her study was based on feminist scholarship in which women are studied on their own and their experiences are not compared with those of men. The homogeneous sample consisted of ten women, five educators and five practitioners in the field.

Criterion for selection: women in public relations.

A *heterogeneous sample* contains individuals or groups of individuals who differ from each other in a major aspect. For instance, you may wish to compare the perceptions about work experiences of career copywriters with freelance copywriters who work just because they have to earn a living. Men and women, too, form a heterogeneous sample when their gender is of importance to the study. Heterogeneous sampling is also called maximum variation sampling (Patton 1990, Kuzel 1999) because it involves a search for variations in settings and for individuals with widely differing experiences of a particular phenomenon, as illustrated in Example 11.4.

A variation of a purposive sample is *snowball* or *chain referral sampling* (Biernacki and Waldorf 1981) where you find one participant through another. For example, you might ask someone you have just interviewed to suggest another person who has knowledge of a particular area or topic and would be willing to take part in your study. In turn, he or she nominates other individuals

Example 11.4 A heterogeneous sample

'How effective is the advertorial as a marketing communications tool?' was the main research question in a study by Neil Goodlad, Douglas Eadie, Heather Kinnin and Martin Raymond (1997). They compared the views of members of the press with the views of members of consultancies and agencies. Their heterogeneous sample consisted of nine interviews with press sales managers and editorial staff, and six interviews with public relations consultants and advertising agency account planners.

Criteria for selection: (a) members of the press involved in accepting advertorial copy; (b) members of public relations consultancies and advertising agencies involved in developing advertorials.

for the research. Researchers use snowball sampling in studies where they cannot identify useful informants, where informants are not easily accessible or where anonymity is desirable, for instance, in studies about sensitive or confidential communication issues.

In a *total population sample* all participants selected come from a particular group. For instance, you might interview everyone from an Afro-Caribbean background, working in the British public relations sector. Because there are few people comprising this specific group, it would be possible for you to interview the total population. This type of sample is often used when researchers wish to interview or observe professionals with a scarce skill or knowledge.

Other methods of purposeful or criterion-based sampling:

* extreme-case or atypical-case selection.
* typical-case selection.
* unique-case selection.

In *extreme-case selection*, certain characteristics of the setting or population are identified. Then extremes of these characteristics are sought and arranged on a continuum. The cases that belong at the two ends of this continuum become the extreme cases. For instance, you may examine a very large or a very small organization, or a very successful campaign together with one that has been ineffective. These cases can then be compared with others which are the norm. *Atypical cases* are unusual, different or 'negative' but they may be of significance for the study because they do not fit into a pattern and therefore may serve to disconfirm your working hypotheses. Chapters 6 and 16 have more to say on this.

In *typical-case selection,* you create a profile of characteristics for an average case and find instances of this. This type of sampling is useful for achieving typicality in a study.

When choosing *unique cases*, your focus is on those people who differ from others by a single characteristic or dimension, such as individuals who share a particular trait or occupation or buying habit but come from a minority community, such as a particular ethnic group.

The term *convenience or opportunistic* sampling is self-explanatory. Here you make the most of opportunities (which sometimes occur unexpectedly) to ask potentially useful informants to take part in your study. This sometimes happens when recruiting people is difficult and only a few informants are available. You might, for instance, meet someone at a party who has previously been inaccessible. Rather than let the opportunity slip by, you ask them there and then if they would allow you to interview them at a later date. Of course, to some extent, much sampling is opportunistic and arranged for the convenience of the researcher.

Glaser and Strauss (1967) advocate *theoretical sampling* as a means of collecting data. Theoretical sampling develops as the study proceeds and cannot be planned beforehand. This is because at the basis of your sample are the concepts and theoretical issues which arise during the course of your research. The theoretical ideas control the collection of data. Therefore, if you are using theoretical sampling, it is important to provide a clear justification for why you have included particular sampling units. At the point of data saturation – when no new ideas arise – sampling stops. To find out more on theoretical sampling, refer to Chapter 8 on grounded theory.

To summarize, sampling in qualitative research is:

- flexible: sampling develops during the study.
- sequential: selection of sampling units is not made before fieldwork begins but develops as discoveries are made.
- guided by theoretical development: it becomes progressively more focused.
- continuous: it carries on through the study until no new relevant data arise.
- involved in a search for negative or deviant cases (Kuzel 1999).

Sample size

The appropriate number of participants chosen for research will depend on the type of research question, the type of qualitative approach used in the study, material and time resources as well as the number of researchers involved in the study.

Although there are no rigid rules or guidelines for sample size, generally qualitative sampling consists of small sampling units studied in depth. Some research texts recommend six to eight data units when the sample consists of a homogeneous group, and twelve to twenty for a heterogeneous sample (Kuzel 1999). Most often, the sample consists of between four and forty informants. Some highly insightful studies have been based on very small samples (especially in phenomenological research) because these have allowed researchers to focus in great depth on a few phenomena, rather than more superficially across a wider range (note the small sample in Example 11.5). Smaller samples are acceptable as long as saturation occurs. This is when no new data emerge that are important for the study of the developing theory. In some cases, this occurs fairly early in the study.

From time to time, certain research projects are carried out with large numbers of participants, interviewed usually by a team of researchers. In Example 11.5 we note a large sample of 100. While some qualitative studies with large sample sizes do exist, they are rare and the sample size does not necessarily determine the quality of the study. Personally, we do not see the justification for a very large sample in qualitative research. Students or experienced researchers often use these to appease funding bodies which are used to large samples, or research committees when they do not know much about qualitative research. Wolcott (1994) asserts that the wish for a large sample size is rooted in quantitative research where there is a need to generalize. He maintains that rather than enhance qualitative research, a large sample may actually harm it as the research is likely to lack the depth and richness of a smaller sample. Small samples allow you to capture participants' specific responses and individual interpretations. This aspect is often lost when large samples are used.

Example 11.5 Different sample sizes

Nicola Wade and Sally McKechnie (1999) investigated the impact of digital television on shopping habits. Their research included 100 interviews conducted in shopping malls with a sample of shoppers aged 18 years or older living in Lancashire who had access to both a working television and connected telephone in their household. These interviews aimed to explore consumer attitudes and behaviour towards shopping from different types of outlets. A further sample of ten adult shoppers was then taken for in-depth interviews where these participants were exposed to an extract of digital television programming. This was followed by a telephone interview with a company director in order to explore strategic issues facing the television home shopping industry.

Relatively little research has explored the dynamics of sponsorship of advocacy messages. Therefore, Eric Haley (1996) decided to explore how consumers make sense of such sponsorship. Three researchers were involved in his study which was based on a sample of seventy-two short interviews and twenty-five long interviews with consumers from a range of age groups and education levels. The aim was to define a 'credible' organization from consumers' points of view, documenting a range of constructions of organizational credibility.

Six interviews were carried out by Robert Underwood and Julie Ozanne (1998) in order to investigate the communicative competence of packaging. The six consumers and the researchers walked through a supermarket, discussing whatever packaging was of interest to the participants. The sample was selected on the basis of age, gender and social class in order to obtain a broad range of responses.

What shall we call the people we sample?

It is difficult for researchers to know what term to use for the people they inter-view and observe, especially as this name makes explicit the stance of the researchers and their relationship to those being studied. Most qualitative researchers favour the terms 'participant' or 'informant'. In surveys – both with structured interviews and written questionnaires – the most frequent term has been 'respondents', and indeed, many qualitative researchers and research texts still use it (for instance, Miles and Huberman 1994), but it appears less frequent now in research texts and reports.

Experimental researchers refer to 'subjects', a word that suggests passivity in the people we study. Seidman (1998) argues that this term distinguishes between people as objects and subjects and can be positive, but it also demonstrates inequality between researcher and researched. We suggest that in quantitative studies, this term could be acceptable, but in research with in-depth interviews, it is inappropriate. Indeed the American Psychological Association, which often establishes research rules, no longer uses the term 'subject'. 'Interviewee' can be used but some consider the term clumsy or boring.

Anthropologists refer to 'informants', those members of a culture or group who voluntarily 'inform' the researcher about their world and play an active part in the research, but the term might be seen to have links to the word 'informant' as used by the police. Most qualitative researchers prefer the term 'participant' which expresses the collaboration between the researcher and the researched and the equality of their relationship. However, this term may be misleading as the researcher, too, is a participant. In the end, you make the decision yourself as to which term suits your research. For our own purposes, we have used several of these terms throughout this text.

Summary

- There are a variety of sampling types, all purposeful; that is they are chosen specifically for the study and are criterion-based.
- The sample of individuals in qualitative research is generally small, although this is not a rule.
- Sample units consist of people, time, settings, events, processes, activities or concepts (the latter is called theoretical sampling).
- Sampling is not wholly determined prior to the study but proceeds throughout.

12 Interviews

This chapter discusses interviews as a method of exploring informant perspectives and perceptions. Qualitative interviewing is different from quantitative interviewing in that it is relatively non-directive. The researcher's agenda and the aim of the research guide the interview process.

This chapter addresses issues concerning both online and traditional interviewing, and covers the following topics:

- the process of interviewing.
- choosing appropriate types of interviews and questions.
- the interviewer–participant relationship, including building trust and the effect of the interviewer on the interview itself.

Introduction

Within qualitative approaches to public relations and marketing communications research, interviews are a useful form of data collection because they allow you to explore the perspectives and perceptions of various stakeholders and publics. Bingham and Moore (1959) use the term 'conversation with a purpose' for the qualitative interview where researcher and informant become 'conversational partners'.

Interviewing is more than just conversation, however. There is always a purpose and usually some form of structure. The purpose and the degree of structure are conceived by one person, the researcher, who organizes the interview talk in such a way as to cover the topics of interest to him or her and who moves the discussion in a desired direction by asking most of the questions (Lindlof 1995). However, to think of interviews merely as 'a pipeline for transmitting knowledge from informant to interviewer' (Holstein and Gubrium 1997: 113) is to limit their potential. At their best, they should be conducted in a collaborative fashion so that interviewees are able to articulate the topics and experiences that are of interest to them. Many novice qualitative researchers assume that qualitative research interviews are easy to carry out, but interviewing is a complex process and not as simple as it seems.

The value of interviews is that they are very flexible because the answers

---

Key point

Key features of interviews are that they are flexible and allow you to understand the perspectives of interviewees.

---

given by interviewees inform the evolving conversation. As a researcher, you have the freedom to prompt for more information if something interesting or novel emerges because you are not restricted to a pre-planned, rigid list of questions, as with the use of the quantitative questionnaire method. Similarly, because the ideas of interviewees have priority, participants are able to explore their own thoughts more deeply or exert more control over the interview if they prefer. This means they may either react spontaneously and honestly to your questions or they may spend time reflecting on their answers, and articulating their ideas slowly. You can then follow up and clarify the meanings of words and phrases immediately, or you can proceed more slowly in order to allow trust to develop.

Another benefit of interviews is that the data you collect are situated within their own social context. That is, the responses you derive from interviews are the subjective views of your interviewees. Your evidence, therefore, is based on participants' interpretations of their experiences and is expressed in their own words, using the jargon and speech styles that are meaningful to them. This contrasts with quantitative surveys where responses are treated as if they are independent of the contexts that produce them.

Example 12.1 The voices of informants

In Indonesia, Amos Thomas (1998) interviewed people working in advertising about some of the issues they have to deal with which are particular to their culture. In the words of informants, important issues were expressed as follows:

> It is not a question of whether the advertising of global products has to be integrated with the local culture of Indonesia, but how it is to be done. Indonesian commercials tend to be more entertainment oriented rather than hard sell, more like those in Japan than the US.

> All advertising expenditure figures are somewhat inaccurate in Indonesia because of the widespread practice of discounting.

> It is believed that StarTV [transnational satellite television] does not actively seek television commercials from Indonesia because that would have meant depriving domestic television of income, thus antagonizing vested political interests.

(Thomas 1998: 232, 233)

Interviews, therefore, are an appropriate method to use when you wish to understand the constructs that interviewees use as a basis for their opinions and beliefs about a particular situation, product or issue. Further reasons for their use are summarized by Easterby-Smith, Thorpe and Lowe (1991: 74):

- when the step-by-step logic of a situation is not clear.
- when the subject matter is highly confidential or commercially sensitive.
- when an interviewee may be reluctant to tell the truth about an issue other than confidentially in a one-to-one situation.
- if an aim of the interview is to develop an understanding of the participant's working 'world' so that you might influence it, as in the case of critical or action research.

Different types of interview exist. The one-to-one interview consisting of questions and answers is the most common form. Focus groups, however, are used widely (we discuss this method in Chapter 13). They are groups of people interviewed by one or more researchers. For instance, you might interview a group of people who have shared the experience of buying a new brand, or who share a professional specialism, such as direct marketers. Less common as an interview method is narrative inquiry where 'long stretches of talk', or participants' narratives, are analysed (Riessman 1993). Few questions are asked in research of this type, because you are keen to encourage participants to talk at length about the story of their situation or experience. An example might be the narrative of how a publicist was involved in raising international awareness of a particular issue and getting it onto the international news agenda. (Note also Chapter 10 which discusses interviews used within a discourse analysis methodology.)

In qualitative student projects, dissertations and theses, the one-to-one interview is prevalent, either in a single encounter or in several meetings with individual participants. This may be conducted face-to-face, by telephone or, more recently, online. Online interviews take place by email or by chatting using real-time software.

Although we focus on one-to-one interviews in this chapter, many of the features of this form are common to other interview types.

The interview process

Interviews may be formal and pre-planned, or informal, such as spontaneous conversations that occur in the corridor or canteen. Primarily, they aim to elicit information by delving into the past and present experiences of participants in order to discover their feelings, perceptions and thoughts. In qualitative data collection, interviewees' responses to your initial questions determine how the interview develops. You follow up their answers with further questions along the same lines or by branching out tangentially. This means that each interview differs from the next in sequence and wording, although distinct patterns are likely to emerge that are common to all interviews in your research project. In most qualitative research approaches, you go on to discover these patterns when you analyse the data.

One interview does not always suffice. In qualitative inquiry it is possible to re-examine the issues in the light of emerging ideas and then to conduct follow-up interviews. Also, because relationships take time to develop, sometimes it is 'better to undertake a series of short interviews from which a useful dialogue flows, rather than to act hastily and alienate the interviewees through lots of pushy questioning' (Easterby-Smith *et al.* 1991: 78). In undergraduate projects, the short time span for research means that three face-to-face interviews with one participant over a period of time is probably the optimum number because of the amount of planning that is involved, and because you may lose the interest of your participants beyond this. Usually novice researchers plan one-off interviews only, although postgraduates often carry out more than one with each participant.

Helpful hint
It is easier to set up a series of online conversations, via the Internet, than it is to arrange the same number of face-to-face meetings.

Pilot studies are not always necessary in qualitative inquiry as the research is developmental, but you could try out your interviewing skills on friends and acquaintances to get used to this type of data collection. A practice run is very useful, particularly if you aim to conduct telephone or online interviews and are unfamiliar with the technology or real-time software. Of course you become more confident as interviews proceed.

Many qualitative research projects start with relatively unstructured interviews in which researchers give minimal guidance to participants. This allows issues particular to the situation to be revealed. You can then incorporate these into your questioning in the next stages of interviewing. As interviews proceed, then, the outcomes guide further interviews, allowing that which is important to participants to emerge throughout the data collection. Although you are aiming to uncover patterns and themes, the unique experience of each individual participant is also important.

Types of interview

An early decision you need to make is how much structure is appropriate for your interviews. A continuum exists of interview types, ranging from the unstructured to the structured interview. Qualitative researchers generally employ the unstructured or semi-structured interview because structured interviews tend to stifle the flexibility that is so valued in qualitative research.

Unstructured, non-standardized interviews

In unstructured interviews, there are no predetermined questions except at the very beginning when you start with a general question in the broad area of study. An aide mémoire, an agenda or a list of topics helps you to keep your focus through the course of the interview.

Example 12.2 An aide mémoire for an interview with an entrepreneur

Initial question: Tell me about your experience of setting up a company that specializes in online PR.

Aide mémoire:
- Putting in place systems and procedures (note internal communication).
- Clients.
- Strategic alliances.
- His own leadership style.
- Financial arrangements.
- Future plans.

Because unstructured interviewing does not follow rigid procedures, interviews of this type are highly flexible, allowing you to follow the interests and thoughts of informants as they relate to their own thought processes. Your questioning follows no order but takes a sequence that depends on the responses to early questions. Even though your overall direction and control of the interview is minimal, you still have your own agenda because of the need to achieve your research aim. Therefore, it is important to keep in mind the particular issues you wish to explore and ensure that you cover these during the course of interviewing. The outcome of unstructured interviews differs for each informant. Informants are free to answer at length, so that great depth and detail can be obtained.

Key point
Unstructured interviews generate the richest data and often uncover surprising evidence, but they also have the highest 'dross rate' (the amount of material that is of no particular use for your study), particularly if you are inexperienced at interviewing.

Because unstructured interviewing requires participants to be highly involved, an issue to consider when you are conducting online interviews is how to motivate participants to engage with the conversation and then to continue. Mann and Stewart (2000) suggest that you need to be very clear about the purpose and procedures of your research, outlining these clearly at the start, and then offering reminders along the way. If participants understand the goals and motives of your research, they are likely to feel more secure about their interactions with you. When trust and rapport have been established, then your study is likely to sustain participants' interest and involvement.

Semi-structured interviews

Semi-structured or focused interviews are often used in qualitative research. The questions are contained in an interview guide (not 'an interview schedule' as in quantitative research!) with a focus on the issues or topic areas to be covered and the lines of inquiry to be followed. The sequencing of questions is not the same for every participant as it depends on the process of each interview and the responses of each individual. The interview guide, however, ensures that you collect similar types of data from all informants. In this way, you save time and the 'dross rate' is lower than for unstructured interviews. The interview guide allows you to develop questions prior to interviewing and then decide for yourself which issues to pursue.

Example 12.3 An interview guide

The following are some questions which aim to find out about the process of setting up a new, public relations consultancy:

- How did you come to start up the online-PR company?
- How did you know how to go about managing a commercial organization?
- How did you feel about taking on all this responsibility at such a young age?
- What happened when you gained your first client?
- How did you know what online methods to employ to promote that client's type of business?

And so on . . .

Although the interview guide may be quite long and detailed, it need not be followed strictly. It should, however, focus on particular aspects of the subject area to be examined, but can be revised after interviewing because of the ideas that arise. Although the aim is to gain the perspectives of informants, you need some control over the interview (which the guide provides) so that the research topic can be explored and the purpose of the study achieved. Ultimately, you must decide what interview techniques or types are best for you, the topic and the interview participants.

Structured or standardized interviews

Standardized interviews resemble written survey questionnaires and are rarely used by qualitative researchers. Questions are pre-planned and asked of every informant in the same order. Therefore, they tend to direct participants' responses, prohibiting you and your interviewee from exploring together the meaning of the object of inquiry. Although some standardized interviews may contain some open questions, even then they cannot be called qualitative.

However, there are two reasons why qualitative researchers might occasionally use standardized interviews to supplement other methods:

- to elicit socio-demographic and biographical data, i.e. about age, number of purchases, number of clients, length of experience, type of occupation, qualifications, etc.
- to conform to the demands of research committees who often ask for a pre-determined interview schedule so that they can find out the exact path of the proposed research.

Online interviewing

When deciding to use computer-mediated communication for research, a key question is whether to conduct synchronous or asynchronous interviews. The decision depends on the purposes of your inquiry. Synchronous interviewing occurs in real-time, and consists of 'chatting' (using computers and networks with software such as IRC – Internet Relay Chat). Usually, but not always, synchronous interviewing is conducted with a number of people at once.

If you are conducting a one-to-one synchronous interview, both you and your interviewee read and write messages at the same time although you are in different places. This means that you can pose a question and the response will be immediate because you have organized your informant to be at his or her computer at the same time. Conversations are spontaneous and often 'dynamic, playful and performative' (Mann and Stewart 2000: 192). This method is especially valuable for accessing people in their own environments, such as at home or at work, especially those for whom use of the computer has become a way of life.

Key point
Online interviews are conducted in real-time (synchronous interviews) or non-real-time (asynchronous interviews).

The main advantage of email is that it enables asynchronous communication to take place, that is, conversations which happen in non-real-time. Messages are written and read at different times which may be minutes, hours or days apart. This allows you and your interviewees to choose the times that best suit you for participating in the study. This is beneficial if you are interviewing across world-wide time-zones.

When email is used for asynchronous interviews, it is less immediate than real-time chat, but has the advantage of allowing participants to be more reflective because they can take time to respond in a more measured way. Mann and Stewart (2000) support the use of email for interviews and draw attention to Picardie's (1998) description of email communications as 'a way of expressing thoughts and feelings more spontaneously than in a letter, yet more reflectively than in a telephone conversation. It [has] a quality of being simultaneously intimate and serious, yet transient and disposable' (p. 192).

> **Helpful hint**
> When planning to conduct your research online, consider the experience of your informants in using the technology and their attitudes towards it. Your research will be constrained by the level of computer skills of participants, yourself included.

If potential participants have limited skills in using computers, if they are likely to feel inhibited about chatting freely online because of their fear of technology or because their writing skills are inadequate, you would be wise to opt for face-to-face or telephone interviews instead.

While email might be appropriate for contacting and screening potential participants, it will only be suitable for interviewing if participants have a good level of skills in electronic discourse. Similarly, your own inexperience in setting up and running interviews online could limit the type of data you acquire.

Types of question

There are a variety of techniques for asking questions and most interviews make use of a wide range. Patton (1990) identifies *experience, feeling* and *knowledge questions*. For example:

- *Experience questions.*
  Could you tell me about your experience of using electronic media to distribute press releases?
- *Feeling questions.*
  How do you feel when you know you are going to be interviewed on television?
  What did you feel when you discovered that you were not appropriately trained in communication issues?
- *Knowledge questions.*
  What services are available for this group of clients?
  How did you cope with this?

Spradley (1979) distinguishes between *grand tour* and *mini-tour* questions. Grand tour questions are broad. They ask a participant to reconstruct a routine, procedure, activity, event or cycle of activity that took place at a particular time in his or her life. The participant is the tour guide, describing the steps taken and the thoughts or feelings associated with each step (Davis 1997). Mini-tour questions are more specific. For example:

- *Grand tour questions.*
  Can you describe a typical day in the press office?
  Could you tell me about the events that led to your winning this client account?
  Can you describe the first time you tried vegetarian pre-cooked meals? Start at the time you decided to purchase this type of meal and continue through to your first tasting.
  How did your first attempt go at promoting this client – from start to finish?
- *Mini-tour questions.*
  Can you describe what happens when you have to get press releases signed off by other members of the organization?
  Can you describe what it is like to use this website?
  What were your expectations in this situation?

Idealization questions, or what Schatzman and Strauss (1973) call 'posing the ideal', are used when you want to ask participants to speculate about an ideal state of affairs or an ideal product. Once you have obtained a response to, say, a question such as 'Could you describe the ideal hospitality event for a high performance car launch?', you would then go on to ask your informant to compare the ideal with a specific event that has already occurred. In this case, the gap between the ideal and the existing event's characteristics provides both an evaluation and a potential direction for the design of future hospitality events.

Contrast questions aim to reveal differences in attitudes and perceptions by comparing one thing with another. You might, for instance, ask consumers 'In what ways do Nike trainers differ from Reebok trainers?'. Or you could ask them to describe the opposites of a product, such as, 'Describe the opposite of Nike', in order to uncover perceptions about the Nike brand.

In *hypothetical-interaction questions* (Spradley 1980), your interviewee has to imagine a situation that is based on actual or plausible relationships and describe how he or she would respond. Davis offers an interesting example of this type of questioning:

> Imagine that the director and creator of Calvin Klein jeans' advertising were sitting across the table from you. Describe how you would feel and what you would be thinking. What types of questions might you ask these people? What would you anticipate their answers to your questions might be?
>
> (1997: 204)

Other types of questions are *direct* and *factual*. These are useful for providing background information or the foundation for more extensive discussion. Examples are:

What are the advertisements that you recall seeing on television this week?
or
What are the most important reasons for you buying this type of product?

Structural questions are similarly straightforward but here you are aiming to understand how people organize their feelings and knowledge within a particular area. For example, 'What are all the different ways that you watch television?' or 'What are all the different ways to describe how you evaluate various brands of beer?' By asking several informants the same question, you begin to build up a picture of certain behaviours and meanings with regard to a particular product or service.

Example 12.4 Asking questions in interviews

What not to do
- No leading questions.
- No ambiguous questions.
- No double questions.
- No jargon or technical terms.

What to do
- Guide responses.
- Phrase questions clearly.
- Ask one question at a time.
- Use participants' language.

Be aware of practical difficulties in the data collection phase. In qualitative studies questions should be as non-directive as possible but still guide responses towards the topics that interest you as a researcher. Phrase questions clearly because ambiguous questions lead to ambiguous answers. Unless you are using hypothetical-interaction questions where you need to set out an elaborate scenario, double questions are best avoided to prevent confusion. For instance, it would be inappropriate to ask a double question such as, 'How many colleagues do you have, and what are their ideas about this?' Just as unsuitable are leading questions, such as those which attempt to impose your view on a situation. For example, 'So tell me about the unethical campaigns that are created in this agency?' could be better phrased as, 'What is the agency's stance towards ethics and advertising?'. Or, you might ask a general question with a supplementary question which seeks specific examples, such as, 'What is your view on ethics and advertising?', followed by, 'Can you give me some examples of this agency's work that supports your view?'.

Questions should be aimed at the participants' level of understanding and be phrased in words that are meaningful to them, that is, avoiding the use of specialist or academic jargon or technical terms. In a marketing communications campaign you create messages that will be understandable to your target markets; also in interviewing, you follow a similar process. By putting yourself in the shoes of your informants, you are better able to develop meaningful questions that will motivate interesting, relevant responses.

Probing, prompting and summarizing

During interviews, prompts or probing questions help to reduce ambiguity both for yourself and your informants. Probes help when you are seeking elaboration, further meaning or reasons. Seidman (1998) prefers the term 'explore' over the word 'probe' because it has fewer connotations of the interviewer in a position of power. He also dislikes the use of the word 'probe' for its association with the rather distasteful surgical instrument used in medical or dental investigations. Exploratory questions (or probes) might be:

- What was that experience like for you?
- How did you feel about that?
- Can you tell me more about that?
- Yes, tell me more.
- I see.
- That's interesting, why did you do that?

Such questions follow up on certain points that participants make or words they use. To encourage more talk on a particular point, it is sometimes useful to summarize the last statements of the participant. An example of a summary statement might be:

> You told me earlier that new technology has really changed how corporate affairs is practised in your company. Could you tell me a bit more about that?

In the above example, participants might be asked to go on to tell a story or describe a critical incident. In this way, they often become fluent talkers, reconstructing their experiences about a day, an event, a campaign, an interaction, a lobbying decision, a feeling, and so on.

Helpful hint
Active listening shows you are paying attention and are interested. It encourages responses from participants.

Non-verbal prompts are also useful in encouraging further responses. Sometimes people are reluctant to make their thoughts public for fear that judgements might be made about them. Therefore, they give monosyllabic answers until they have become used to you and to being interviewed. Active listening, together with a non-judgemental manner, helps to overcome this problem by conveying that you value the information being communicated to you. Your stance, making eye contact, and leaning forward all encourage reflection. In fact, it is important to train and use active listening skills such as these because they are an important component of the interviewer's toolkit. In online interviewing, active listening occurs through words such as: 'Yes, I can go along with that,' or 'Yes, I quite understand – do go on' or 'I see what you mean – so what else?' or 'That's interesting – tell me more.' Non-verbal actions can be described such as 'That's funny – I'm laughing', or -:).

In order to round-off interviews, we find that a useful question to ask is, 'Is there anything else you'd like to tell me?'. This sometimes opens up completely new and exciting avenues because, by this time, interviewees have taken stock of us and assessed whether or not they can trust us. Sometimes our interviews have continued for another half an hour or so after this question as we allow conversations to flow on in a completely unstructured fashion. At other times, interviewees have had nothing else to add and we have reached a natural ending.

Once the tape recorder is turned off, interviewees sometimes like to know more about the project in more detail. This is a relaxed way to end interviews. Don't forget to send a thank you letter a few days later.

Length and timing of interviews

The length of time for an interview depends on the participants and the topic of the interview. Of course, you should suggest an approximate amount of time – perhaps an hour and a half – so that participants can plan their day, but many are willing or wish to go beyond this, some up to three or four hours, although this is very rare because even experienced researchers or willing participants tend to lose concentration after a couple of hours. Other interviews may last only twenty or thirty minutes because of the work pressures of participants. Essentially, you need to use your own judgement about an appropriate length of time to explore your topic, although the wishes of informants will always have priority. Qualitative interviews are always time consuming, however, and, if possible, it is worth allowing plenty of time for interviewing. If it is not possible to accomplish your goals in one interview, you might want to re-interview on one or more further occasions.

A word of warning about scheduling multiple interviews: previously, we made the mistake of conducting too many interviews over the course of a working day (up to six one-hour interviews for each interviewer). Although we covered all the intended topics, we found ourselves rushing between interviewees' offices with little time at the start of each interview to develop rapport. Similarly, we found we had only minutes at the end of each interview for extended formal thanks or for explaining more about our research project, something which informants often ask about after they have taken part. Since then, we ensure that we build in extra time, for the sake of politeness as much as anything else. We remind ourselves that participants are giving up their valuable time to offer us insights which enable our research to move forward; therefore, we need to acknowledge their contribution and treat them with respect.

Recording and transcribing interview data

A number of techniques and practical points must be considered so that the data are recorded and stored appropriately. These include:

- tape-recording the interview.
- transcribing the interview.
- note taking during the interview.
- note taking after the interview.
- online interviews are copied and saved onto a disc.

Tape-recording

Before analysing the data, participants' words must be preserved as accurately as possible. The best form of recording interview data is tape-recording for which you need to ask permission when you set up the interview. This applies to both face-to-face and telephone interviews. Even if consent has been given, it is not uncommon for participants to change their minds at the last minute. In this case, their wishes are paramount.

Key point

The principle of respect for autonomy includes choice and free decision making and therefore must be considered first in terms of consent. This applies not only to the use of tape-recording but, more importantly, gives participants the right to refuse to participate in research or withdraw from it. They can exercise this right at any stage of the research process.

Tape-recording is useful because it enables you to capture the exact words of the interview, inclusive of questions; this means that you don't forget important answers and words afterwards. It also enables you to maintain eye contact and pay attention to what participants say, without having to concentrate on note taking.

Initially informants may be hesitant, although they soon get used to the tape recorder, especially if it is small and unobtrusive. However, if a large recorder is all you have available, it can be placed further away so it is not so visible and disturbing. Some interviewees have soft, quiet voices, particularly if they feel vulnerable. In this case, place the tape recorder near enough, but not so prominently that it intimidates the hesitant person. We like to use a small Sony microphone, about two inches high, which looks like an extended matchstick and is very sensitive. It can sit in the centre of a conference table and pick up talk from several feet away. Lapel microphones are another option and these allow a better quality of sound. Take care about outside noises though. An interview will be wasted if there is a jackhammer in the street outside as the microphone will pick up the sounds of the machine and not your voices. A room away from noise and disturbances, therefore, enhances not only the quality of the tape but also the interview itself as participants feel free to talk without interruption.

We have experienced problems with tape recorders. They sometimes break down, or the batteries run out. Remember to pack extra batteries and tapes. Auto-reverse on tape recorders is useful because standard cassettes do not need to be turned over and thus interrupt the flow of conversation. Also, the quality of non-standard tape – for instance 90 minute tape – is not always very good. It is much better to use tape recorders that have a conference facility because this picks up sound from various directions. We are aware, though, that students often find them too expensive. However, many universities are able to lend good quality tape recorders to students for the duration of the data collection.

Helpful hint
Test your tape recorder before leaving home, at the beginning of the interview and also after it has been recorded. Cast your eye over the machine when you are a few minutes into the interview just to check that the tape is going round and you haven't forgotten to release the pause button (we speak from embarrassing experience!).

When you have finished your interview, label and date the tape. If your material is confidential, only pseudonyms should appear on the tape or its transcription, with real names and their pseudonyms stored in a different place from the tapes.

Transcription of tapes

If you are a novice researcher, we would advise you to transcribe (or have transcribed) the full text of all of your interviews. This is not necessarily essential if you are more experienced. You might opt instead to select portions of interviews for transcription, transcribing only the areas which link to your developing theoretical ideas.

However, the fullest and richest data is gained from transcribing interviews verbatim. We suggest that – if possible – you transcribe your own tapes because this allows you to immerse yourself in the data and become sensitive to the issues of importance. Be warned, however, that transcribing is a frustrating business because it takes so much time. One hour of interviewing takes between five and seven hours to transcribe. Often it takes even longer if you are not used to audio-typing. Therefore, it may be worth paying a typist with a transcribing machine to do it. This, however, is expensive. It also means you are less intimately involved with your data. A further point is that a typist may ignore the 'pregnant pauses' and hesitations which are salient to you but not to someone who wasn't there when the recording was made. On the other hand, having tapes transcribed gives you more time to listen and analyse. The decision about this depends on you. Any outsider who transcribes must, of course, be advised on the confidentiality of the data.

Number the pages of your transcripts, ensure the face sheet contains date, location and time of interview, and identify the code number or letter of the informant. Many researchers number each line of the interview transcript so that they can pinpoint specific data when searching for them. It is useful to have wide margins in order to leave room for analysis or notes and comments. Notes in the margins and also within the text might refer to some of the non-verbal signals indicated by informants at various points in the interview, and your assessment of their meaning in relation to their speech.

A minimum of three copies (usually more) should be made of transcripts, a clean copy without comments locked away in a safe place in case other copies are lost or destroyed. The process of listening to the tapes and reading through your transcripts will make you sensitive to the data. At this time, any theoretical ideas that emerge should be written down in the form of memos and fieldnotes (see Chapter 16).

Taking notes

There is danger that researchers who fail to tape record interviews will overlook significant issues which they would uncover when listening to tapes or considering transcripts. An alternative, if less effective, method of recording data is note taking during or immediately after an interview. Some researchers employ both tape recorder and note taking on the basis that this allows them to register participants' facial expressions and gestures, together with their own reactions and comments, alongside the words that are spoken. Taking notes, however, may disturb participants and certainly prevents you from maintaining eye contact. To overcome this, we suggest taking notes only when taping is not feasible or if interviewees do not wish to be tape recorded. Notes can then be written up immediately after the interview.

If participants deny permission to record, interviewers generally take notes throughout the interview, hoping that these will reflect the participant's words as accurately as possible. However, unless you have excellent shorthand, it is unlikely that you will be able to take down more than a fraction of the sentences. Therefore, select the most important words or phrases and summarize the rest.

An alternative form of recording is to write up your notes after the interview is finished. This should be done soon as possible after the interview in order to capture the essence, behaviour and words of the informants together with your own thoughts. It is worth considering how, in your note taking, you can differentiate between your own thoughts and the words of informants.

Online recording

Arguably, the scripts of your computer-mediated communications represent 'actual' communication (Mann and Stewart 2000) because they include both verbal and 'non-verbal' communication (through the descriptions of emotions and behaviours that informants insert into their written conversations). Whereas the transcripts of interviews include the talk of participants and the notes you make about the movements and non-verbal gestures that accompany their words, online interview scripts are uncontaminated reflections of participants' own verbal and 'non-verbal' expressions and constructions.

Example 12.5 Emoticons

Emotions are expressed through 'emoticons' such as:
: -) happy   : -(sad   : -o surprised

Online jargon includes:

R	Are	C	See	L8	Late
OIC	Oh, I see	SPK	Speak	4	For/Four
T2UL	Talk to you later	L8R	Later	RUOK	Are you OK?
2DAY	Today	XLNT	Excellent	B	Be
B4	Before	GR8	great	BCNU	Be seeing you
2MORO	Tomorrow	U	You	2U	To you
FYI	For your info	WAN2	Want to	THNQ	Thank you

The researcher–participant relationship

In qualitative approaches to interviewing, whether face-to-face or online, there is a great degree of closeness and personal involvement between researcher and participant. This reflects the emphasis placed on the researcher as the human instrument of research. A good interviewer–participant relationship, therefore, is crucial to the success of the research. If you are able to establish rapport from the beginning of the research process, the evidence you collect will be valuable and insightful. Issues to consider in the interviewer–participant relationship concern status, trust and your 'communicative competencies'.

Relative status of interviewer–participant

A fallacy exists that the interviewer and the person interviewed work together in a relationship of complete equality. This is not always possible for reasons which include differences in age, relative knowledge, hierarchical status, and the goals of researcher and participant. Nevertheless, your relationships should be based on mutual respect and a position of equality as fellow human beings. The onus is on you, as a researcher, to respect the way in which participants develop and phrase their answers (Marshall and Rossman 1999) because they are, after all, not passive respondents but active participants in an important social encounter.

Access to persons in a position of power can be difficult, especially if you are an undergraduate student. Individuals in 'elite' positions have an overview of an industry, an organization or culture, or may have access to scarce information, such as consumer patterns and trends. However, usually they have little time to spare for research participation or, when they do agree to take part, they are often only interested in pursuing their own personal agenda in interviews. As a student or subordinate employee conducting research, you need to be patient in order to get access, and then diplomatic in how you phrase your questions when you get there.

It is possible that in online interviewing, status issues may be less pronounced because you are not meeting face-to-face. For example, our own anecdotal evidence suggests that cultural issues of power-distance often come into play in face-to-face encounters between people of different nationalities but these are less extreme in email or telephone interactions. Email, especially, appears to be a non-threatening mode of communication to those whose first language is not English. If your electronic communication is relaxed and friendly, then status differentials will be less salient.

Trust

Trust is built up through your involvement and interest in your participants and because of your communication competencies. Having good interpersonal skills and being adept at social interaction is important. For this reason, if you are shy or do not have well-developed 'communicative competencies' you may wish to adopt a quantitative approach instead because this allows distance between you and your informants.

Relationship building begins at the start of the research process, when you make initial contact. A concise, initial letter or email explaining your research project (in non-academic language) should be sent to potential participants, explaining the purpose and value of your project and the reason for making contact. You may wish to follow this with a telephone call.

Helpful hint
Work on building up trust right from the start of your face-to-face or online interview. Begin by engaging in brief, casual conversation. This helps informants to feel relaxed with you. Perhaps say a little about your project. Ask if they've been interviewed in this way before, or perhaps undertaken their own research project at some stage.

We have already discussed some non-verbal and active listening skills. These are important not only for encouraging responses, but also for helping participants to relate to you as an individual. In addition, you need to ensure that you are confident, non-judgemental and careful in your comments. These skills, together with the way you dress and your general mannerisms, tell participants something about your professionalism as a researcher. They serve to shape participants' judgements about your sincerity, your motivation and whether they will be able to trust you or will be damaged in some way by the material you collect from them (Easterby-Smith *et al.* 1991). Taking care with your appearance, so that you fit in to some extent with your participants is a first step in helping them to relate to you.

It could be argued that the Internet provides insufficient social cues to enable the 'human' element to be conveyed in interviews. However, Mann and Stewart (2000) contend that, on the contrary, meaningful relationships can be developed online. As long as you provide clear explanations about your research and continual reassurance so that participants understand the purpose of the research and the salience of their involvement, then virtual relationships can quickly become personal. Over the course of conversations, you reassure participants that they are communicating in an appropriate way, that their contributions are valued and, although they haven't met you in person, you can be trusted with their thoughts and ideas. If participants have met you beforehand, then the research process is already off to a flying start and you are able to build the relationship further online.

Because the nuances of voice, expression and gesture are not available in online interviewing, words or emoticons are used instead to convince your participants that you are not a 'faceless computer' in receipt of their confidences. Responses such as 'That's funny, you're quite a comedian' indicates that you are amused. 'Great, I appreciate your thoughts' is a quick way of saying more than just thanks.

When conducting cross-cultural research over the Internet, there is an ever greater likelihood of misunderstandings which can undermine relationships. To overcome this, encourage your participants to feel free to ask for clarification, or to negotiate the meanings of your questions. Your questioning might be along the lines of: 'If there is anything I say which you find odd, or if there is a question that makes you feel uncomfortable, please do let me know. That's the only way to help me learn or to prevent me making the same mistake again . . .'. This approach flags up that you are sensitive to informants and are committed to developing the relationship.

Peer interviews

There are advantages and disadvantages to interviewing your peers. Shared language and norms can be advantageous or problematic. Concepts are more easily understood if you are already involved in the culture of participants and there is less room for misinterpretation. However, misunderstandings can still arise because of the values and beliefs that you hold in common. You may, for instance, take things for granted and neglect to question the ideas or constructs which arise from interviews with your colleagues. This can be overcome if you take on the role of a 'cultural stranger', or 'naïve' interviewer, asking participants to articulate their meaning and to clarify their ideas.

In interview situations with peers, it is possible that you and your informants may hold a similar status. Again there are advantages and disadvantages. Already there will be a certain familiarity in the relationship. This is beneficial because, hopefully, participants will 'open up' and trust you. On the other hand, there is the danger of your becoming over-involved and identifying with colleagues. Students sometimes interview friends and acquaintances for pragmatic and opportunistic reasons. Although this is useful for overcoming the hurdles of getting to know informants and forming relationships, selection from this group might create unease or embarrassment if the topic is a sensitive one. Informants and interviewers might hold assumptions about each other which could prejudice the information. Therefore we suggest that you take great care in your choice of informants.

Limitations and problems in interviewing

Problems in interviewing concern a possible gap between what informants say they do and what they actually do, the time consuming nature of interviews, and the interviewer effect.

The increased use of interviewing as a method of data collection in the social sciences draws attention to what Atkinson and Silverman (1997) term 'the rhetoric of interviewing'. This, they argue, relates to the assumption that, through interviewing, researchers gain full access to the inner feelings and thoughts, and thus the private self, of their interviewees. Atkinson and Silverman question the 'overuse' of the interview and claim that it is often seen naïvely or uncritically by researchers who take the words of informants at face value and do not reflect or take an analytical stance. For example, some informants may fabricate or elaborate in order to enhance their self-esteem or cover up discreditable actions, and indeed at times you may discover discrepancies between what participants say and what they actually do.

For this reason, it is beneficial to validate the evidence you have obtained from interviews. This is done by discretely checking statements or issues with others involved in the same situations, by referring to documentary evidence, and also by collecting data about social action and interaction from observation, although the latter is obviously prohibitive online. Observation not only complements interviewing but is also a form of within-method triangulation (see Chapter 6 for more on triangulation and validity). The situation itself, therefore, also becomes a source of data.

Although interviews offer the benefit of being very flexible, they are limited by their time consuming and labour intensive nature. This applies particularly to the data analysis stage. You might be very enthusiastic during the early data gathering process and only realize when you are involved in transcribing and analysing just how much time you need for the work. In Internet interviewing, the time commitment may be more onerous on the part of participants. It is easy to drop out of email conversations or real-time discussion groups if there are time constraints, or if interest or motivation levels ebb. For this reason, some researchers debate the value of online, in-depth interviews.

The effect of the interviewer on the interview itself needs to be acknowledged. Sometimes informants react in particular ways to you as a researcher and modify their answers to please or to appear in a positive light, consciously or unconsciously. For these reasons it is necessary to set up a monitoring process so that you recognize the interviewer effect and minimize it (Hammersley and Atkinson 1995). This means spending time with participants so that trust develops.

As a researcher, you too will react to the words you hear in interview, or read on the computer screen in electronic interviews, and your responses will be different from those of participants. This is because, within the framework of the research, you both have different priorities. This has to be recognized so that the perspectives of researcher and informants can be made explicit in the research report. A further issue is the possibility that you may misinterpret the words of participants. However, if you spend long periods of time interviewing for a research project, it is probable that you will come to a reasonable understanding of the viewpoints of various groups and individuals and therefore will be able to interpret your data sensitively.

Summary

- Qualitative interviews are flexible and enable you to understand the topic from your informants' point of view.
- Qualitative interviews are usually unstructured or semi-structured.
- Questions and issues emerge from the preceding answers, creating an evolving, but focused, conversation that does not conform to a rigid plan.
- There are a variety of types of open-ended questions, depending on your purpose.
- Interviews are recorded by taping and transcribing, or by note taking during or after the interview, or by saving onto disc in the case of computer-mediated communications.
- Building a relationship of trust and rapport with informants is essential for the success of your project.
- A critical, reflective stance should be taken towards evidence obtained from interviews because of issues such as the interviewer effect.

13 Focus groups

Focus groups stand on their own as a research approach, but also may be used in combination with other methods. Because focus groups – both conventional and online – are a form of in-depth interviewing, this chapter should be read alongside the previous one on interviewing. This chapter notes that:

- the purpose of focus groups is never to examine a wide variety of issues in one study but to concentrate on one or two clear issues or objects and discuss them in depth.
- questions, answers and ideas are produced by members of the group themselves, inspired by the dynamic of the group setting.

This chapter covers:

- the nature, origin and purpose of focus groups.
- how to make decisions about the composition and size of the sample.
- tips for conducting focus groups.
- specific issues concerning the facilitation of online groups.
- the role and involvement of the interviewer.

Introduction

Focus group research generally aids public relations and marketing communications researchers to gain substantial insights on a variety of issues and strategies, from the macro (such as the influence of national cultures on strategies or strategic decision making) to the very detailed (such as consumer responses to advertisements). The focus group approach does not rely merely on the ideas of the researcher and a single participant; instead, questions and answers are produced by members of the group themselves.

The key features of focus groups are:

- they provide evidence from many voices on the same topic.
- they are interactive.
- they provide a supportive forum for expressing suppressed views.
- they allow you to collect a large amount of data fairly quickly.

> **Key point**
>
> A focus group involves a *group* of people – often with common experiences or characteristics – who are interviewed by a researcher (who is known as a moderator or facilitator) for the purpose of eliciting ideas, thoughts and perceptions about a specific topic or certain issues linked to an area of interest. The ultimate goal in focus group interviewing is to see the topic (which may concern a service, product or issue) from the participants' point of view.

One reason for choosing to use the focus group method is because it provides you with evidence from a range of different voices on the same subject. Focus groups create settings in which diverse perceptions, judgements and experiences on a particular topic can surface (Lindlof 1995). They allow you to see how people interact when they are considering a topic and how they react when disagreeing with each other. They have a special value if you are interested in assessing how several people work out a common view, or a range of views, about a topic. For example, they have been used to investigate the interactional dynamics of small groups. Similarly, they have aided the exploration of consensus formation with regard to topics such as how media interpretations tend to be collectively constructed (Richardson and Corner 1986). They also help in identifying particular attitudes and behaviours, such as consumer responses to advertisements or brands.

Another benefit of focus groups is their interactive nature. When participants hear about the experiences of other members of the group, they are motivated to expand on and refine their own ideas and perceptions of the topic. Each person's comments, therefore, encourage further responses from other participants. Their comments do the following:

- stimulate thoughts in other respondents.
- cause other respondents to view things differently.
- stimulate greater depth of discussion.
- remind individuals of things they may have forgotten.
- help other participants to better verbalize their thoughts and opinions.

(Davis 1997: 200)

Focus group research is ideal for providing access to participants who are traditionally suspicious of research and for surfacing meanings and emotions that might not be articulated elsewhere. The group setting contributes to the building of trustful relationships between participants and researcher and also provides a supportive forum for the expression of opinions that might not be disclosed even in private. This is particularly notable in research conducted over the Internet, even though this is still relatively novel as a research approach. Computer-mediated communications seem to have the potential to engender a heightened permissive environment because of the greater preparedness of group members to more openly discuss personal views and attitudes (Mann and Stewart 2000). It appears that people like the safety and anonymity that is offered by the computer screen.

Focus group discussions allow you to collect a large amount of data in a relatively short space of time. They are quicker and cheaper to conduct than individual interviews with the same number of participants. By bringing together between six and ten people for a specific period, you benefit from a range of insights which can be transcribed and analysed more quickly than if you were conducting a number of one-to-one interviews. These advantages apply equally to online group research. In addition, they can be put together more quickly and easily than face-to-face focus groups because it is possible to recruit, confirm and conduct within the space of only a few days. They also have the potential for quicker analysis because group discussions can be immediately recorded into a file and printed out, producing an instant transcript, or loaded directly into a content analysis programme (Gaddis 2001).

In many cases, focus groups are used together with quantitative methods. For example, they are capable of generating findings that are then applied to the construction of a questionnaire. They also have the potential to obtain in-depth data at the end of a survey. Whether focus groups are used alone or together with other methods, the evidence gained is normally analysed by qualitative methods.

The origin and purpose of focus groups

In the past, focus group techniques have been used extensively for business and market research, but recently they have become popular in other areas of the social sciences. Focus groups have been employed since the 1920s when marketers realized that listening to and acting on clients' ideas not only helped to improve products but also stimulated sales. Despite this early enthusiasm, the first book on this type of in-depth interviewing did not appear until 1946. This was written by Merton and his colleagues and was based on their investigations into war propaganda effects during and shortly after the Second World War. Today focus group interviews are used widely by researchers working in the area of communications, policy, marketing and advertising.

A range of different applications of the method are discussed on page 189.

Example 13.1 Some applications of the focus group method

- The testing of advertising messages or concepts.
- Understanding behaviour and attitudes.
- Exploring strategic policies and strategies.
- Developing and understanding brands, products and services.
- Investigating organizational and industry issues.

Advertising or concept testing

Peracchio and Luna (1998) used focus groups to gain an understanding of teenagers' attitudes and beliefs towards smoking. Based on their evidence, the American Cancer Society developed an advertising campaign to discourage tobacco use initiation among children and youths. The campaign was then tested in a further round of focus groups.

Understanding behaviours and attitudes

Focus groups are invaluable for providing insights into the perceptions, needs, wants and thinking of significant publics or stakeholders. For example, Gwilliam's (1997) research into the lifestyles of 'baby boomers', an influential consumer group, involved seventy-seven group discussions with people aged between 45 and 55 living in sixteen countries.

Exploring strategic policies and issues

Research of this nature investigates the way that organizations and government work, as well as the impact of policies on social, industry and community areas. Increasingly politicians are using focus groups to shape and test policy, image and campaign strategies. The British prime minister, Tony Blair, used focus groups extensively to test public opinion on a range of issues. An example of academic research in this area is that of Fombrun, Gardberg and Sever (2000) whose investigation of corporate reputation and communication applied the focus group technique in order to find out how people think about companies and the value they place on reputation.

Developing and understanding brands, products and services

In industry, focus groups are used extensively to help marketers test new products and line extensions. Marketing communicators gain an understanding of consumers through focus groups, they find new opportunities for reaching their target audiences, and develop new methods of communicating more effectively with them. An example of academic research in this area is that carried out by Evans, Nairn and Maltby (2000) who explored the different responses of men and women to the linguistic elements of marketing communications. Their evidence enabled them to make recommendations for the content and style of direct mail shots.

Exploring organizational and industry issues

This type of research may relate to the views of members of particular organizations, or to wider organizational and industry issues. An example of research on internal staff issues is the work of Gilly and Wolfinbarger (1998) who conducted group interviews in four organizations in order to investigate employees' responses

to their employers' advertising campaigns. They not only listened to how participants expressed their thoughts but also observed their interactions. An example of
research which considers wider corporate issues is the investigation by Stuart and
Kerr (1999) into the extent to which core corporate identity messages are integrated
into marketing communication campaigns. They carried out four focus groups in
Australia with marketing managers, corporate identity specialists, public relations
consultants and members of advertising and graphic design agencies.

Sample composition and size

There are five stages in focus group research: planning, recruiting, moderating,
analysing and reporting (Morgan 1998). In this section, we deal with recruiting,
and then go on to consider planning and moderating. Analysing qualitative data
and writing the research report are discussed in Chapters 16 and 17.

The type of sampling used for focus groups is purposeful (see Chapter 11).
This means that the choice of participants is based on well-defined criteria which
are determined by the aims of the research.

Composing focus groups

Depending on your aims, your first decision will be to select either preconstituted or researcher-constituted groups.

Key point
Preconstituted focus groups are social or professional groups that already
exist (for example, all individuals working within a project team).
Researcher-constituted groups are those that you create for your own
research purposes.

Preconstituted groups may consist of colleagues who share the same speciality
(such as copywriters in the same advertising agency), or members of a particular
department or project team (such as everyone working on a client team), or they
may be members of the same social club or association (such as women
members of the media-related club, The Groucho Club, in London). The advantage of choosing preconstituted groups is that they are more natural, and therefore participants may be comfortable in each other's company. On the other
hand, a group of immediate colleagues or friends may be hesitant about revealing sensitive ideas or private thoughts in front of others with whom they have a
continuing relationship. Another problem with preconstituted groups is that their
past history may inhibit or bias them in a particular direction.

Researcher-constituted groups allow you greater control over the individual
composition of the sample (Deacon *et al.* 1999: 56), but the members will not
know each other and therefore group interaction may take some time to 'warm

up'. On the other hand, if your focus group interviews are taking place online and you have recruited from a pre-existing chat room, conference group or list-serv (an advanced form of electronic bulletin board), participants may not know each other but will be familiar already with computer-mediated communications and 'virtual' relationships.

Once you have decided whether you are going to select preconstituted or researcher-constituted groups, your next choice is between *homogeneous* or *heterogeneous* groups. The former are the most common and are characterized by people with similar interests or experiences, positions or roles, ages or gender, etc. A problem in sampling for online research is that you can never be sure that your participants are who they say they are. However, if you recruit from a website or listserv that is associated with your research topic, then this may not be a problem as it is probable that your participants will share an interest in and knowledge of the area.

Heterogeneous groups consist of individuals with different social, cultural, political and economic characteristics. In many instances, however, group selection combines both similar and different characteristics.

Example 13.2 Preconstituted, homogeneous groups

Jason Berger and Cornelius Pratt (1998) wanted to explore the usefulness of using two feature films (*Glengarry Glen Ross* and *House of Games)* for teaching ethics in public relations. They showed the films to students and then conducted focus groups, consisting of juniors and seniors studying business communication ethics in public relations in two Midwestern universities.

Gender and age are factors which affect the quality and level of interaction in groups, and through this the data. For instance, research suggests that there is greater diversity of ideas in exclusively male or exclusively female groups than in those of mixed gender (Stewart and Shamdasani 1990). This is because men tend to dominate conversations and have different conceptions of the public–private divide from women (Deacon *et al.* 1999: 56). In addition, both genders have a tendency to 'perform' for each other, and therefore there can

---

Example 13.3 Composing focus groups according to gender

The salience of gender in focus group research is highlighted in a study of the link between gender and job satisfaction in public relations. Shirley Serini, Elizabeth Toth, Donald Wright and Arthur Emig (1998) set up men-only focus groups with male moderators, and women-only focus groups with female moderators.

The creation of distinct male and female discussion groups (together with appropriate moderators) is a useful technique for exploring the effects of gender.

---

sometimes be unhelpful or biasing interplay between the different types of participant (Evans *et al.* 2000). In online research, these issues are less likely to occur and therefore mixing participants in heterogeneous groups is more common than in face-to-face interviewing (Gaddis 2001).

Size

The purpose of focus groups influences not only their composition but also their size. If you have a topic that is controversial or complex, then a small group will enable you to deal more sensitively with it. On the other hand, a less intense topic area can be dealt with more effectively in a larger group where there is a wider range of opinion but lower level of involvement by participants. Between six and ten participants is the norm for traditional focus groups, although sometimes groups may consist of as few as three members.

At the top end of the range, the larger the group the more noisy it becomes, making it difficult to distinguish voices when you come to transcribe the interview. On the other hand, if there are only a few participants, group dynamics do not work as well. In our experience, six members is about right for most research purposes associated with traditional focus groups; it is large enough to provide a variety of perspectives but small enough not to become disorderly or fragmented. However, when you are recruiting people for focus groups, it is worth slightly over-recruiting just in case some don't turn up.

In online group interviews, the size will depend on the time sequence you have chosen. Focus groups conducted in real-time can mirror some of the issues of traditional group interviewing, such as too many participants and some voices will be 'drowned out', that is, some members will be denied the space to respond because others' enthusiasm or fast keyboard skills allow them to get in first and frequently (Mann and Stewart 2000). This makes your moderating role more difficult in terms of how you structure and control the dialogue. In addition, if there are too many members, there will be too many 'threads' or strands of conversation for you to follow and moderate. Therefore, six to eight participants is a reasonable number for focus groups conducted in real-time.

However, size is less important in non-real-time research because participants contribute at times to suit themselves. This means that participant numbers can be large; for example, we have conducted asynchronous group interviews with up to thirty people. The problems, however, are that not all participants feel involved enough to contribute, nor will they be inclined to self-disclosure, and also the discussion can become very disjointed (Mann and Stewart 2000). The ideal number, therefore, will depend on the nature and aims of your research.

Number of groups

The number of focus groups used to collect data for a research project depends on the research aims and the demands of the phenomenon under investigation. For one research project the usual number is about three or four, but the actual number depends on the complexity of the research topic.

Example 13.4 Conducting a series of focus groups internationally

In order to better brand Scotland so that export and visitor markets could be developed, Kate Hamilton (2000) conducted an international study using focus groups to find out what images people held about Scotland and the Scottish people. Eight focus groups consisting of consumers and opinion formers were held in England, France, Germany, Spain, the United States and Japan. Twelve further focus groups were carried out in Scotland itself.

Conducting focus group interviews

Plan your focus group interviews carefully. Start by contacting participants well in advance of the interviews and then follow this up nearer the time with a reminder of the venue and timings.

Helpful hint

Time is an important factor in online focus group research. Interviewing takes place in real-time (synchronous) or non-real-time (asynchronous) or a combination of both. Each type generates different data.

Real-time focus groups require participants to be online at the same time and to make their contributions simultaneously. Individuals post their messages to the group so that everyone sees them on a single screen at the same time. Respondents post their comments back to the group and, once again, everyone reads them on the same screen. Chatting in this way is often very fast-paced with less depth or reflection in the responses than in asynchronous discussions. Also, because you take a highly involved moderating role, the direction of discussion is likely to be more focused. Participants enter the discussion either through a universally accessible website where you have arranged for an open discussion to take place or if you wish to restrict access, via conferencing software such as Firstclass Conferencing. This requires a password to enter which you distribute in advance by email to participants.

Non-real-time focus groups do not require participants to be available at any particular time. Instead, people can enter and leave whenever they wish. This can be done by using email or accessing online bulletin boards and conference sites. Because there is no pressure to respond immediately to questions, asynchronous interviewing is valuable when you are seeking detailed and highly reflective comments (Mann and Stewart 2000). However, a danger is that it is possible for participants to refer questions to friends, or seek information elsewhere, presenting the answers back into the focus group as their own opinion.

Your role as a moderator of an asynchronous group is more passive than in synchronous interviewing although you still need to offer encouraging and motivating comments. You are less interventionist because it is impossible for you to be logged on and available every moment of each day that the research takes place.

The length of sessions varies but is usually about two hours for a traditional focus group. This allows you time for introductions and building rapport before you begin the main questioning. If you decide to offer refreshments, this will extend the session. If you are interviewing online, aim for no longer than ninety minutes. This period ensures that participants do not flag but remain interested enough to provide high quality responses. It also helps you maintain your own concentration; any longer and fatigue can set in because of the high demands placed on the moderating role.

Choosing the right environment

The environment for online and traditional focus groups is important. Lindlof (1995) contends that a neutral site makes the best venue although, obviously, this needs to be comfortable and, if possible, familiar. For example, a hotel conference room might constitute a neutral space but, depending on the topic, it may be seen as too formal and alien for some participants to feel relaxed enough to express their opinions openly. Arguably, the 'site' of online discussion groups is a neutral space because participants are unlikely to be aware of the physical location of other group members. In addition, it is probable that they are seated in front of their work or home computers, in an environment in which they are already accustomed. This neutral space, therefore, helps to minimize feelings of bias or alienation.

In selecting rooms for conducting traditional focus groups, ensure that they are big enough to seat all participants comfortably; a spatial arrangement of a circle or semi-circle is usually the most successful seating arrangement. Place your tape recorder in a position where it will pick up everyone's discussion. For focus group work, it is essential to have a top quality tape recorder which is able to record people sitting at different distances and speaking in different volumes

---

Key point
The stages in a focus group interview include:

1   introductory remarks and ground rules.
2   'warm up' stage.
3   outline of the context for the discussion.
4   main discussion.
    –   general questions
    –   more focused questions.
5   summary.

from a variety of positions in relation to the microphone. Note that as well as recording your interviews, it is also usual to make fieldnotes on anything unusual, interesting or contradictory. This helps to jog your memory when you are listening to the tapes and reading the transcripts. In online research, participants' contributions are automatically recorded *verbatim* and can be printed off as an accurate transcript.

The discussion guide

Focus groups have been described as being more akin to brainstorming than structured group discussions because of their spontaneous, interactive nature. Nevertheless, successful group interviews are not totally spontaneous but work to a clearly identified agenda, or discussion guide. This prevents them from deteriorating into chaotic or ambiguous discussions and helps them run to time. The discussion guide serves as a checklist which makes certain that all salient topics are covered and in the proper sequence.

When conducting online discussion groups, it is usual to give out the discussion guide in the first few minutes of the session because this ensures that the time for synchronous interviewing is used well. Of course, you need to make it clear that participants are at liberty to contribute their own topics and questions as well (Mann and Stewart 2000).

The procedure

From the beginning, it is important to establish the ground rules so that all group members know how to proceed. This begins at recruitment and continues into the interview itself. Commence the discussion session (whether it is face-to-face or online) by introducing the topic, outlining the objectives of the session, and pointing out what is expected of participants. This can be done in online interviewing by posting an initial welcome message on the conference site. Included in the online message should be something about yourself if participants have not met you; remember that at this stage they may not even know if you are male or female.

It is helpful to clarify to everyone that there are no correct answers; what individual participants think and feel is what you are interested in finding out about. This signals that you are keen to establish a non-judgemental environment where self-disclosure and uninhibited discussion are permitted.

Rapport

Putting the group at ease right from the start is an important skill, especially if none of them have met before. However, if the group is already established, participants will be familiar with each other and the 'warm-up' time will be shorter. This allows you to focus more quickly on the main topic. On the other hand, if participants are meeting for the first time in the interview session or at the online conference site, you will need to spend some time establishing rapport within the group in order that interaction will be facilitated. This can be done initially by inviting everyone to introduce themselves.

Stimulus material

Strategies such as showing an advertisement or telling a story related to the topic help to stimulate interaction. The introduction of other stimulus material such as vignettes, photographs, mock-up publications, advertisement executions on boards or actual products is also useful (note the section on Projective Techniques in Chapter 15). Many of the same stimuli can be used for online discussions as well as face-to-face interviews. In online researching, participants can be directed to websites in order to view graphics, images or background information. However, a problem with online stimulus is that often the full impact may be lost because of the two-dimensional environment of the computer (Greenbaum 2000). One way around this is to mail samples or tangible items to participants for discussion online at a later date (Gaddis 2001).

Questioning

When asking questions in traditional focus groups, researchers generally proceed from the more general to the specific, just as in other qualitative interviews. For example, you might begin by eliciting general knowledge about a specific product in order to put members at ease, and then go on to a deeper discussion of group members' thoughts or feelings about the product.

Example 13.5 Asking questions in focus groups

An investigation into corporate reputation and communications was made by Charles Fombrun, Naomi Gardberg and Joy Sever (2000). Their questions focused on:

- people's thoughts about companies.
- the extent to which reputation matters.
- the language used to address issues of reputation.
- the wording that target audiences use to discuss corporate reputations.

Online questioning, however, differs in that questions are usually predetermined and follow a set sequence. The reason for this is that 'the high interactivity of real-time focus groups introduces the risk that the data will be superficial' (Mann and Stewart 2000: 122). Chatting online encourages brief, non-reflective responses which may take the discussion along a different route to that which you had intended. Therefore it is worth preparing specific questions in advance in order to ensure that you gain data that are sufficiently rich and focused.

Involving all participants, rather than letting a few individuals dominate the situation, demands that you draw on all your skills in diplomacy. This is easier if you are working with a smaller group. A good moderator will not be abrupt with dominant individuals or this will send the wrong message to other group members, such as 'You'd better be cautious or I will do the same thing to you' (McDaniel and Gates 1995). Instead, when you are in the moderating role, you might encourage others to speak (or write online) by saying, 'Let's hear from someone else now' or 'It would be interesting to know if anyone has other views on this.' In face-to-face encounters, you might also avoid making eye contact with dominant individuals, looking instead at others whom you wish to hear from. Another way around this if you are researching online synchronously, is to send a private message to a particular group member, asking them to 'speak up' or present their opinion. This conversation is read only by the recipient, not by other members of the group.

If you encounter extreme views within a group, these are usually balanced out eventually by the reactions of the majority, although problems can occur if a dominant individual hijacks the discussion and leads the group off in another direction. There is a very real danger of this occurring in asynchronous online research because, by the time you enter the discussion, the topic may have moved on into areas which are tangential to your research. International particip- ants, for instance, may have been contributing for up to twelve hours while you were sleeping and unable to moderate the conversations. This highlights the need for you to regularly monitor the group discussions.

Conflicts within groups can sometimes be illuminating because they highlight contrasting stances towards a topic. However, although effective moderators explore conflict by trying to discover the reasons why participants hold dissent- ing views, you also need to ensure that any personal hostility between members is diffused. To find out more about interviewing techniques both online and face-to-face, turn back to Chapter 12. Note especially the sections on question- ing and probing.

Ethical issues

In focus groups as in all other research, ethical issues such as confidentiality, anonymity and impartiality must be considered (see Chapter 5). Confidentiality can be problematic in group interviews if members of the group discuss the find- ings in other settings and situations. Remind participants to keep their group dis- cussions confidential. Anonymity cannot be guaranteed in traditional focus group research as members of the group may be able to identify other particip- ants even if you only use first names in your written report. A further issue con- cerns the need for you to be impartial and fair in your moderation of group discussions. If some participants make remarks that are hurtful to others, or show prejudice, you have to find ways to deal with this.

Interviewer involvement

As a researcher, you are the facilitator or moderator in group interviews. Generally a single researcher facilitates groups, but two moderators are advantageous if group discussions are very fast-paced or complex. Sometimes moderators split the roles so that one person maintains the discussion while the other thinks ahead to new topics, introducing them at an appropriate moment. On the other hand, each moderator may take the lead for different topics although, when two moderators work together, it is essential that each is familiar with the other's interviewing style.

The qualities of an effective moderator are the same as those of an in-depth interviewer: flexibility, open-mindedness, skills in eliciting information, and the ability to both listen and interpret. In addition, because you take on a leadership role when moderating, you must have excellent social and refereeing skills. These allow you, first, to guide participants towards effective interaction. Then they enable you to focus and control the discussion without coercing participants or directing the debate in any way.

The creation of an open and non-threatening group climate is one of your most important initial tasks whether you are moderating traditional or online groups. You must be able to stimulate discussion and have insight and interest in the ideas of participants. If the group feels at ease with you, the interaction will be open and productive, and participants will be comfortable about disclosing their perceptions and feelings about the research topic.

Morgan (1997) advises interviewers to hold back on questioning if they want to examine the real feelings of participants because, ideally, much of the discussion will evolve spontaneously from the dynamics of group interaction. Participants build on each other's comments and, through the group interaction, remember forgotten feelings and thoughts. In this way new ideas evolve which you may not have thought about before. Even vulnerable informants can be supported by the voices of others.

However, because high involvement from the interviewer leads more quickly to the core of the topic, it may be necessary for you to use this tactic if the discussion is wandering or if time is limited. Also, because of the fast-paced interactivity that occurs in many real-time online discussions, it is probable that you will be highly involved and highly directive if you are facilitating this form of focus group. Non-real-time focus groups, on the other hand, have less moderator involvement because participants enter the discussion at times to suit themselves (which may be according to different work rhythms or international time zones). Therefore, unless you are able to function twenty-four hours a day, you will have to take a more passive role as a facilitator.

Limitations and problems in focus group research

Although there are clear benefits to undertaking focus group research, there are also limitations and some problems. These mostly stem from the effects of group interaction. Indeed, it is probable that you will have greater difficulty managing the group debate and less control over the outcome than if you were conducting one-to-one interviews.

First, one or two individuals within a group may dominate the discussion, introducing bias or influencing the direction if other members are compliant. There are people who know it all, or think they do, speaking up first and not allowing others to give an opinion. Davis (1997) provides an example when he suggests that it would be difficult for participants to admit serving their children sugared cereal if one member of the group began the discussion by saying: 'Only mothers who don't care about their children's health serve their children cereal loaded with sugar' (p. 200).

In a similar way, group pressures can distort the expression of individual opinions. Some participants may be reluctant to express extreme opinions if they feel this will deviate from group expectations, or if they are afraid that they will be ostracized by the group. The result is that participants relinquish their critical stance towards the views of other members and the result is conformity in thinking or convergent answers (Carey and Smith 1994). In group interviewing, therefore, participants affect each other, while in individual interviews the 'real' feelings of the individual informant may be more readily revealed.

The whole atmosphere of face-to-face group discussions may seem very contrived to some participants. The impersonal climate of some settings makes natural, honest conversation unlikely in some cases. For this reason, it is important to ensure that you have selected a suitable room and layout for your interview sessions where participants will feel comfortable.

The moderator's style may contribute to bias. Although researchers endeavour not to express their biases in focus group research, sometimes it is difficult to avoid this. A special relationship with a specific individual, an affirmative nod at something of which you approve, or a lack of encouragement for unexpected or unwelcome answers may bias the interviews. In addition, an aggressive, confronting style may lead participants to say whatever they think you want to hear in order to avoid attack. Or, if you take the style of 'playing dumb', participants may withdraw because they think you are insincere or a fake (McDaniel and Gates 1995). Therefore, your style, gestures and facial expressions have to be controlled in order to show members of the group that you are non-judgemental and that you value the views of all participants.

If the group consists of members who are unable to verbalize their feelings and thoughts, you will have difficulty encouraging group interaction and also generating good data. One of the reasons for certain individuals feeling inhibited about making contributions to group discussions is because members have disparate educational backgrounds. Merton and King (1990) stress the importance of the educational homogeneity of groups because, when educational status differs considerably, then some members are afraid to speak out and may even be silenced. Similar educational backgrounds (and sometimes social backgrounds also) is a factor that needs to be taken account of when determining the composition of groups. To some extent, this is overcome in online researching because, as long as participants are able to express themselves via the keyboard, then status differentials may not be recognized.

It is not uncommon for confrontation and conflict to occur in group interviews. While confrontation can lead to stimulating and lively debates, and conflict can provide rich data, they may also be destructive. In Internet interviews, conflict may be expressed through 'flaming', which includes personal abuse, hectoring or bad language. Not only does this affect rapport within the whole group, but some participants may subsequently absent themselves from the online discussions. Unless you are experienced as a moderator, with a sensitivity to group feelings, it is unlikely that you will be able to diffuse the tension constructively, whether you are facilitating face-to-face or online.

Although it is fairly easy to set up appointments for individual interviews if you are conducting one-to-one interviews, coordinating individuals for group interviews is more difficult. Not everyone who has been invited will attend but you will still have to go ahead with your discussion, even if only a few have turned up.

Transcription can be much more difficult in traditional group interviewing because people's voices vary, and the distance they sit from the microphone influences the clarity of their contributions. For this reason, it is a good idea to take fieldnotes either during or immediately after each session.

The data obtained from focus group discussions represent group, not individual, insights (Carey and Smith 1994, Davis 1997) which have been shared and negotiated within the context of the group. Therefore, focus groups do not provide the deep and detailed data that are more commonly obtained from one-to-one interviews.

There are four further problems which relate specifically to online focus group research. First is the difficulty of knowing if participants are who they say they are. It is not really possible to establish who is behind the computer screen and whether or not someone else has been substituted for them.

In some cases, it is difficult to create group dynamics via computer-mediated communications because participants are reading from computer screens rather than interacting verbally and non-verbally. Online focus groups lack the in-depth emotional information obtained from body language or tone of voice (Heckman 2000) although the use of emoticons goes some way to overcoming the problem (such as the 'happy face': -) or the use of capital letters to indicate frustration or shouting). These, however, must be artificially introduced by participants rather than surfacing naturally in conversation.

The involvement of multiple participants in online focus groups can lead to discussions which are disparate in their focus; sometimes many conversational threads make it difficult for participants to follow. Subsequently discussions can be superficial in their content, as trains of thought are lost, or key input is overlooked because participants are focusing on keying in their own comments, or because the conversation is moving too quickly (Mann and Stewart 2000, Gaddis 2001).

Finally, in traditional focus groups, participants are unable to do anything that will detract them from the proceedings because they are closeted in the interview room for the duration of the session. In a real-time, online environment, however, you are never able to know if participants are engaged in other activities which may affect their concentration, such as watching television, reading a book, or eating dinner while the session is happening (Greenbaum 2000). This may or may not be problematic, depending on the aims of your research.

Summary

- In focus group research, several small groups of people are interviewed by one or two moderators in order to explore participants' points of view, thoughts and feelings towards a certain topic or issue.
- The role of the facilitator is to encourage interaction between group members and ensure the discussion stays focused.
- Stimulus materials or projective techniques are commonly introduced to encourage debate.
- Different types of group include: preconstituted or researcher-constituted, heterogeneous or homogeneous, and online groups in real-time or non-real-time. Different issues confront each type of group.
- The strengths of focus groups also contribute to their limitations especially in relation to their interactive nature, the multiple voices involved and the subsequent group effects.

14 Observation

Arguably, observation is the fundamental base of all research methods. No matter which method you use, in any situation you will always be looking about you in order to gather more evidence to help you understand the research context. Yet, observation as a qualitative method is more than this. Conducted online or conventionally, it involves the systematic and ethical recording of what you see 'in the field'. This chapter discusses the following:

- the nature of observation in qualitative research.
- the central role of participation in the research process, with implications for close or more distant observer involvement.
- the different dimensions of the setting which help to focus the research.
- how to collect the data and raise appropriate questions about what you are seeing.
- the importance of keeping fieldnotes and a field diary.

Introduction

As a method for conducting research in public relations and marketing communications, observation is infrequently acknowledged. Yet the technique of observing pervades most everyday activities and is an intrinsic part of other methods of research. Whether you are conducting interviews or running focus groups, you unconsciously take note of your research surroundings and the way people behave within them, using this knowledge to help you make sense of the data you collect.

Consider, for instance, your arrival at the reception desk of a Sydney advertising agency where you have come to conduct a series of interviews about creativity. As you look around the reception area, you take note of the decor, the colours and style of furnishing, and the posters, campaign photographs and creative awards hanging on the walls. You would be naïve to think that the design of the reception area has happened by chance. Agencies use this space to signal something about themselves, inviting visitors to perceive them in a particular way. The manner in which the receptionist greets you and handles your enquiry is likely to make some form of impression on you too. Even before you get to the office of your first interviewee, you are likely to have begun to get some idea about the implicit statements that the agency is making about its corporate identity.

Observation, therefore, is a familiar process to most of us and, as Adler and Adler (1994) suggest, it is the fundamental base of all research methods. Used systematically to supplement other research methods, or as the primary research technique in a study (such as in ethnography), it provides an important means of accessing and understanding the ways in which people act and communicatively interact.

Key point

Observation entails the systematic noting and recording of events, artifacts and behaviours of informants as they occur in specific situations rather than as they are later remembered, recounted and generalized by participants themselves. Observation methods are rarely used on their own but are often linked to interviewing.

Observation of human action provides researchers with data about consumer behaviours and social processes as they are enacted within the realms of the social reality of participants. Observation enables you to identify the conscious as well as the taken-for-granted actions that informants rarely articulate despite participating in them. For example, imagine questioning informants about their family's evening meal. Probably they would tell you about the food they ate and who was at the table. If you were to sit in on the meal, however, you would be likely to observe the way they discussed the menu, displayed branded products (some of them in their original packaging), partially watched television programmes and commercials that were playing in the background, and talked with each other about mundane and topical issues (Arnould 1998). Observation used in this way provides a technique for distinguishing between what people say they do and what they actually do, and investigating any contradictions between the two.

Observational studies offer a holistic perspective and graphic description of social life. When you actively participate in a setting – such as when you work in an organization for some time and are no longer considered to be a 'spectator' – you are able to record events and activities from the perspective of 'insiders'. By closely engaging with the setting, you find that people become used to you and continue to go about their business in their accustomed ways. This enables you to note their unexpressed intentions and expectations, the significance of events affecting social relations, and the multiplicity of participants' experiences. Critical incidents, dramatic events and language use, such as the choice of words, can be investigated, along with the exits and entrances of members of the group you are studying, their body language, facial expressions and communicative interactions. As a research method, observation has great potential in longitudinal studies such as those which examine social processes and change. A study of changing attitudes and communication practices brought on by the introduction of new technology, or changing media-use contexts, are examples of the type of studies which would benefit from observational methods.

A strength of observation is that it can be less disruptive and more unobtrusive than other methods. Therefore you are less likely to influence the data you are collecting. However, it is rare for a study to be conducted by observation methods alone. Usually researchers observe the situation and listen to what participants have to say by asking questions, as illustrated in Example 14.1. In online research, observation and participation go hand-in-hand because researchers frequently play an active part in online discussions in chat rooms, unless, of course, they are undertaking covert observation.

Example 14.1 A cross-cultural study using observation and interviews

Katsutoshi Fushimi, a judo expert, studied the subculture of judo and the consumer behaviour implications of its extension from Japan to America. While interviewing informants at practice sessions in ten American judo clubs and ten Japanese clubs, he engaged in participant observation. In addition, he visited four judo tournaments. The observations helped him to identify customs common to the local judo clubs and the local judo subculture. One custom involved the bowing ceremony which reflected the strict hierarchies of judo society in both countries. About this he wrote:

> In the United States when the students line up, they are separated into two groups, depending upon whether they are children (usually under 13 years of age) or adults. The position of a participant within a group is determined by the color of the individual belt rankings. Age and gender are given no consideration. On the other hand, in Japan, age and gender determines one's position in the line, reflecting the social hierarchical tradition of Japanese culture (DeVos 1985; Nakane 1972). Although the colored belts represent the length of judo experience and the level of skill, they are of less importance ... students line up in the order of their age. Among the black-belt holders, the older judoists sit at higher positions no matter their degree of black belt ... Females are more likely to be in lower positions within the same age group. The conspicuous segregation of female players was observed in several dojos.
>
> (McAlexander, Fushimi and Schouten 2000: 59–60)

To some extent, the characteristics of observational research differ when it is carried out via computer-mediated communication. This is because '[online] there are no data relating to person or place outside that detectable in the digitally generated script' (Mann and Stewart 2000: 197). The text on the screen, therefore, is the research setting where all the interactions and relationships occur. This makes your observations 'culturally neutral' because you are not able to see the worlds in which participants live or work. In addition, all your data comes from the perspectives of participants, rather than your own direct perceptions. Not only do you need, therefore, to be highly sensitive to the norms of online communication in order to understand the online world, but you also need to be skilled in 'reading' the nuances of written language. In online observation, there are no surrounding cultural signals to give you clues about the phenomena you are watching.

The centrality of participation in observation processes

The issue of participation has been the subject of much discussion by qualitative researchers who have arrived at a variety of stances with regard to the degree to which a researcher participates, or engages, with the setting. This is particularly pertinent to online research where the presence and identity of the researcher may be concealed. Deacon *et al.* (1999) identified *simple observation* as the most detached form of the technique. This, they suggest, is akin to being a 'fly on the wall', that is, having no relationship with the processes or people being observed, who remain unaware of your activities.

While observation of this nature reveals patterns of activity which tell you much about the everyday encounters of people with each other, with brand usage or with cultural institutions, the technique owes much to principles that are fundamental to quantitative research. These concern the need for observers to be detached from settings in order to maintain objective. However, as we have discussed elsewhere, qualitative researchers generally object to the idea of playing the role of an outsider looking in. Instead they seek to be an insider taking part and immersing themselves in the world of participants. This role allows them to lessen the status and activity differences between themselves and the people at the research scene, enabling them to achieve a greater understanding. Observers in qualitative research, therefore, endeavour to participate actively in the settings they study.

For this reason, in qualitative research observation is often referred to as 'participant observation'. This means that you are taking part to some extent in the activities of the people you are observing. At one end of the scale is observation used within an ethnographic approach (see Chapter 9) which requires long-term involvement, sometimes over years, in a setting. Here the aim is to take an unstructured approach to your research, not limiting your observations to particular processes or people, but allowing your research focus to crystallize as the research proceeds. At the other end of the scale are briefer, occasional encounters with a setting where observation may be somewhat more structured because it plays a supplementary role to other methods.

Seale suggests that the most appropriate role for researchers is that of a 'marginal native' (1998: 226) where you are positioned between a strangeness which avoids over-rapport and a familiarity which grasps the perspectives of people in the situation.

The typology of Gold (1958) has been influential in enabling researchers to articulate the distinction between the extent of participation and observation. While it is not without its critics, its use lies in its ability to identify the various strengths and weaknesses of the different forms of participant observation. Gold proposed four 'master roles' for the researcher:

- complete participant.
- participant as observer.
- observer as participant.
- complete observer.

The complete participant

The complete participant is part of the setting and takes an insider role that involves covert observation. At this point, we would stress that this is not a suitable role for novice researchers because it is problematic on a number of fronts. If you are an experienced researcher and choose to employ this method of observation, you become a fully functioning member of the setting, say, an organization or a consumer lobby group, and are not known by others as a researcher. Therefore, they respond to you as a colleague rather than a researcher. Lindlof (1995) promotes the effectiveness of this role by contending that there is 'no better path to knowing the feelings, predicaments, and contradictions of "the other" than to be with the other in an authentic relationship' (p.142).

Research of this nature is valuable if the settings you enter are characterized by beliefs and norms that do not admit criticism, or when the situation is very sensitive, or where there is guarded access. However, there are a number of problems associated with this type of research. First, the scope of your movements as a researcher is limited to what you can experience in your member role, which probably spans only part of the total activity of the group or organization (Lindlof 1995). Second, the use of interviewing techniques is ruled out unless, of course, you wish to 'blow' your cover. Third, because you are actively involved with people at the scene, it is possible that you may 'go native' and lose the ability to critically assess the situation in which you are immersed.

Finally, we would question seriously whether covert observation in any private or closed setting, without the knowledge or permission of the people observed, is ethical. After all, with the exception of easy-to-access online discussion groups, most of the places that researchers enter to study issues in public relations and marketing communications are not public, open situations such as a street corner, concert or exhibition, where nobody can be identified. (In the latter situation, observation through 'unobtrusive measures' is permissible and may produce valuable data.) Instead, they involve individuals where trust, friendships and client confidentialities are likely to be exploited. To find out more about ethical issues in research, turn back to Chapter 6.

Helpful hint
Check your motives before undertaking *complete participant observation*. Is it ethical to conceal your research aims and role?

The participant as observer

You have negotiated your way into the setting by openly acknowledging your exploratory purpose to gatekeepers and asking their permission for you to undertake participant observation. Now you are taking part in the work or consumer group under study, undertaking duties and responsibilities but, to some extent, also holding a special status. This is because, although you are not fully integrated into the routines and subjective realities of the group, you are still allowed to take part. Research of this nature allows you to move around in the location as you wish, observing in detail and depth. If you employ this method for online research, you are considered to be a member of a discussion group but your participation is minimized. Example 14.2 provides an illustration of the method.

Lindlof (1995) notes that a greater degree of reciprocity distinguishes this role from that of the complete participant. You may have to continually adjust the terms of your participation as members find out about, and seek reassurance of, your role and the evidence you are gaining. For new researchers, this type of observation is more difficult than interviewing, and potentially more stressful, because of the ethical issues involved. It is up to you to ensure that you respect participants' right to privacy, including taking measures to ensure people are not disturbed while they are working. Obviously this doesn't apply to online observation. In some cases too, you may have to make it quite clear that you are not a 'spy' for management.

Example 14.2 Observing the social exchanges of students

Mark Ritson and Richard Elliott's study of the contribution of advertising to the everyday interactions of students is outlined in Example 9.1 and an extract about Ritson's experiences of 'fitting in' is provided on page 135. The following quotation from Ritson's fieldnotes indicates his acceptance by students as both a researcher and a participant in their social world.

> Darren showed me how he and his 'mate' Paul had said goodbye the previous evening after rugby practice. Smiling throughout he had recalled, 'So I said to Paul, "Here's what I'm gonna get now," and I did the Chicken Tonight thing ... you know!' Then he tucked his hands under his armpits and ducked out his head a few times, imitating the actors from the *Chicken Tonight* ad for me. The sight was funny and I had begun to laugh. With growing hilarity Darren had then recalled that Paul had mirrored his actions and said, 'Aye, me too'. They had both left the field laughing. (researcher note, January 27, 1995).
>
> (1999: 268)

The observer as participant

As an observer who participates only by being there, you are marginally involved in the situation (see Example 14.3). Your main agenda is to observe rather than to take part, unlike in the previous role. For instance, you might observe a press conference but not be involved in it in a journalistic or public relations capacity. In online research, you would be observing without being a member of the discussion group. Nevertheless, you should still negotiate with gatekeepers or online participants to allow you access and ask permission of all participants to be observed.

Before you enter the setting, you are likely to know the kind of information you need and the amount of time required to collect it. Therefore, participant observation of this nature is often more acceptable to informants because there is less uncertainty over the data that you will gain and less disruption to them. An advantage of this type of observation is the possibility to ask questions, to be accepted as a researcher but not called upon to play a role as a member of the workforce or social group. On the other hand, you are prevented from playing a 'real' role in the setting, a restraint on involvement that is sometimes difficult if it is a particularly busy work situation.

Example 14.3 Observing meetings but not taking part

- A hospital trust was the setting for a study by Wendy Button and Graham Roberts (1997) into communication and change. Their primary method of research was interviews. However, their observation of meetings enabled them to view participants behaving naturally in their accustomed setting. Evidence from observations added contextual information to the data on individual perspectives that they gained from interviews.

- Two social movement organizations were investigated by Kimberley Elsbach and Robert Sutton with a view to understanding impression management tactics. Their methodology consisted of interviews, document analysis and observation of meetings. One author attended three meetings which were open to the public. These provided more detailed information about the structure of one of the organizations and the promotional events that they were involved in.

In the above cases, the researchers took on the role of *observers as participants*.

The complete observer

This role relates to that which we identified earlier in the chapter as 'simple observation'. Here you take no part in the setting but employ a hidden approach, creating no impact on the situation at all. This mainly occurs when you employ a one-way mirror to observe focus groups, make use of static video cameras to observe various activities, as indicated in Example 14.4, or observe online discussion groups without taking part.

For this method of research, some argue that ethically it is essential to gain consent from everyone involved in the setting. This includes seeking permission from those who have power to withhold or grant access, such as managers. This poses problems for online researchers, however, especially as one of the reasons for conducting covert research online is to observe natural behaviours without distorting them through the acknowledged presence of the researcher. Based on your own moral stance, you will have to decide on the best course of action. If you do seek permission, do this by posting a message of your intentions onto the appropriate website. On the other hand, if you decide that this is an inappropriate course of action, you would be wise later on to obtain permission from individuals whose comments you intend to reproduce in your written report. In this way you show concern for the rights of privacy of participants. Yet even this strategy is not without its critics who argue that if messages are posted up in the public domain and can be freely accessed, then there is no need to seek consent to quote them.

On the whole, the issues of access as a *complete observer* are more problematic and complex than for other forms of data collection because of the potential that the method holds to do harm to the interests of participants. Unlike in the complete participant role where you act in ways that conform to the norms and moral order of the group, in the complete observer role you have no meaningful contact with informants. Therefore, they have no opportunity to give you feedback or to have an influence on your interpretation of their actions and experiences. With this method, there is a danger of 'going ethnocentric' or having little conscience about how you interpret the actions of the people you are investigating (Lindlof 1995). For this reason, it is worth designing your research so that

---

Example 14.4 Observing without being seen

An investigation of World Wide Web search behaviour was carried out in Belgium by Steve Muylle, Rudy Moenaert and Marc Despontin (1999). More on this is found in Example 8.4. Their research design involved observations and interviews. The exploratory nature of the study called for unstructured observation but, because of the difficulties of analysing user system behaviour in real time, they employed 'unobtrusive, hidden, mechanical observation' of informant-WWW interactions. This enabled them to record the navigational behaviour of participants on the websites they visited.

The role of *complete observers* taken by Muylle and his colleagues applied to only one stage of their overall project. After videotaping computer usage, they then became more involved with participants in the second stage. Here they replayed the videos back to them, confronting them with their navigational behaviour and asking them to discuss their motivations (1999: 145–6). As in many such studies, observational techniques were employed within a multi-method research design.

the complete observer role is applied alongside other methods, such as interviews. The establishment of rapport with informants before your research begins is also a good way to overcome the problem of ethnocentricity.

While Gold's typology of 'master roles' is helpful in identifying the different involvements of researchers, the framework tends to limit the observer to one role or another. In reality, situations change, roles shift and indeed at times researchers seem to carry out multiple roles. For example, although you may be acknowledged as a researcher in the group you are studying, there may be some aspects of your research that you are carrying out in a covert fashion. In another example, you might begin an online study in the complete observer role in order to gain an understanding of the culture of a virtual community. Once you are familiar with the language, online norms and some of the issues, you may decide to take a more participatory role by engaging in the online discussions. The degree of overlap between the roles depends not only on the stage you have reached in your research, but on the position and role of the people being observed, on your own interest about what you are watching, on the overall research design and incorporation of other methods, and even at times on your own ability to remember the role that you have pre-selected!

The process of observing

Beginning observation means coming to an understanding of 'the field' or the setting. This is best thought of as 'the physical settings and social activity arenas of the research problem' (Lindlof 1995: 155). Table 14.1 identifies some of the

Table 14.1 Dimensions of 'the field'

Dimension	Explanation	Example
Space	the location	a PR consultancy.
Actor	members or participants in the setting	consultants and clients.
Activity	behaviour and actions of people	implementing a crisis campaign.
Objects	the things located in the setting	architecture, decor, documents.
Act	single actions of people	ringing a journalist.
Events	what is happening	a press conference.
Time	time frame and sequencing of activities	beginning and end of the campaign.
Goal	what people are aiming to do	objectives of the campaign.
Feelings	the emotions that people have	attitudes towards journalists.

Adapted from Spradley (1980: 78).

dimensions that make up the field. It is worth taking note of these as they will help to focus your observations.

The main research question, problem or puzzle that you decide to address is very much shaped by the nature of the setting you have chosen to study. In some instances, it may be appropriate to pay more attention to some dimensions than others; this will depend on your area of interest and what is going on in the setting itself. However, it is important to pay attention to some degree to all dimensions as this enables you to provide a holistic description of what is going on.

Participant observation varies on a continuum from open to closed settings. Open settings are public and highly visible such as street scenes, restaurants, corridors, reception areas and many types of online bulletin boards. Closed settings are less accessible and include personal offices, meetings, presentations, private online chat rooms and places where small groups go about their everyday routines.

When you first enter the field, it will seem confusing and you may experience difficulty in relating much of what you are seeing to your research topic. However, be patient and non-judgemental. Don't try to fit your initial observations into a theory about how or why something happens. This is particularly important in cross-cultural research where the activities of participants may carry quite different meanings to those of your own culture. It may take a long time before you are able to reach an informed understanding of the gestures and behaviours of people from different national cultures.

Therefore, spend time getting to know the people in the setting, familiarize yourself with what is occurring, and begin to adopt the perspectives of the participants in your study. Learn to see things as they do. Remember to respect the norms and regulations of the setting in order not to intrude on its routines. This means taking care about where you stand, when you speak, and how you address people. As time goes by, your ideas will start to crystallize, enabling you to develop a descriptive narrative of the events and actions taking place before your eyes.

Key point

Doing participant observation is like working in a funnel structure. Start with a wide view and a broad research question. As you get to know the people and surroundings, your ideas and research questions will develop more focus.

Spradley (1980) claims that observers progress in three steps, using descriptive, focused and, finally, selective observation. Descriptive observation proceeds on the basis of general questions that you have in mind. Everything that goes on in the situation is data and is recorded, including colours, sounds and appearances of people in the setting. As time goes by, certain important areas or aspects of the setting become more obvious; focus on these because they contribute to the achievement of the aim of your research project. Your investigation, therefore, moves from broad to narrow observation as you concentrate on smaller units, such as the similarities and differences in brand purchasing behaviour among groups and individuals. Eventually the observation becomes highly selective as you concentrate just on the key issues which relate to your topic.

In some cases, researchers enter settings with a specific, narrow focus in mind. This may be the result of undertaking secondary analysis and interviews first. Observations are then focused from the outset because researchers already have a good idea of what they are looking for.

Asking yourself questions

Key questions to ask yourself as you observe are listed below.

'Who' questions

Who and how many people are present in the setting or take part in the activities? What are their characteristics and roles?

'What' questions

What is happening in the setting, what are the actions and rules of behaviour? What are the variations in the behaviour you observe? What are the physical surroundings like?

'Where' questions

Where do interactions take place? Where are people located in the physical space?

'When' questions

When do conversations and interactions take place? What is the timing of activities?

'Why' questions

Why do people in the setting act the way they do? Why are there variations in behaviour? (LeCompte and Preissle 1997)

Mini-tour observation leads to detailed descriptions of smaller settings, while grand-tour observations are more appropriate for larger settings.

In some cases, researchers make use of cameras and video equipment to catch movements and expressions of participants more accurately (as in Example

14.4). Bear in mind, however, that video cameras may be intimidating or disturbing to participants, causing them to change their behaviour. A benefit to you as a researcher, however, is that you can re-run a video as many times as you like afterwards, capturing and recapturing important moments. Of course, video tapes must be kept secure and confidential, and cannot be shown to colleagues or friends, only to your supervisor with the permission of participants. Although some researchers like to use still photographs, these are only useful if you wish to freeze a situation in time in order to, say, recall physical surroundings or note spatial relationships among participants or between participants and products. When participants guide researchers' photographic choices or take pictures themselves, this provides you with clues as to the unarticulated significance of events or people. However, photographs are not able to demonstrate the processual character of the situations you are studying in the same way that a video recording can.

Writing fieldnotes and keeping a field diary

In Chapter 9 we noted the importance of making meticulous fieldnotes during and after your periods of observation. These are detailed descriptions of the setting and the behaviour of participants, translating observation into a written record. They should be written as soon as possible after you have observed events to overcome the problem of memory recall. Your own reflections on the situation and your feelings about it are also recorded in fieldnotes. At the beginning, you will probably write down most of what you observe but your fieldnotes will become progressively more relevant to emerging concerns. The extract in Example 14.2 is taken from the researchers' fieldnotes and used as evidence in their published article.

While fieldnotes are as important in online research as in face-to-face studies, the nature of them is likely to differ. First, when you are observing online, there is no need for you to record the salient moment-by-moment occurrences. This is because conducting observation through computer-mediated communications results in an automatic written record of each exchange amongst participants. In addition, there is no need for you to write about contextual influences on behaviours and implicit assumptions, because you cannot observe the setting in which participants live and work. This means that there is no non-written information (such as artifacts and non-verbal behaviour – although emoticons give an indication) to provide you with clues about communicative interactions. Fieldnotes in online research, therefore, are used to help develop your ability to get 'a feel' for what is going on, to practise your intuition about the mood or intentions of participants and to make note of your impressions regarding emerging themes.

A field diary allows you to record your growing recognition of emerging themes, changes in those themes and other comments about how you saw and interpreted the data. The journal is critical in tracing your own growth in the process of data collection and in evaluating the implications of your own background and theoretical orientation to how you relate to the people and contexts you study.

Analysis

Analysing observations follows a similar process to that of interviews. Turn to Chapter 16 for more on this. Observational data are the events and actions which you have seen, heard and recorded in the setting, and which you have recorded in your field diary. Further data are the explanations and comments you have recorded in your fieldnotes and analytic memos. Recall that, as in all qualitative research, once you have collected the initial observational data, analysis starts straight away. The collection and analysis of data interact and go in parallel. In this way, your observation becomes progressively focused on the emerging and interesting themes that relate to your research question.

As your study comes to an end, consider how you will withdraw from the field. Do this slowly, thanking participants for their involvement in the research and informing them of how you will use the data and their accessibility to it. It is polite to write a thank you letter to each participant after you have left the field.

Limitations and problems in observational research

Undertaking research by observational methods is time consuming. It takes time to negotiate access and time to spend in the field, familiarizing yourself with all the goings-on and making meticulous records at the same time. For this reason, observation in its most participative sense is rarely carried out by undergraduates whose availability for long research projects is often limited.

However, in some cases, the duration of observation may be shortened if you are already au fait with a setting. For example, previously you may have worked in an advertising agency and wish to return there to make a systematic observation of how they come up with new graphic designs for clients' corporate identities. You already understand the structure and culture of the company so would be likely to fit in very quickly. What you might overlook, however, are activities and situations that, while important to your topic, are taken for granted both by you and participants because they seem familiar. In this situation, there may be a trade off: a shorter introduction to the company but the potential to miss insights because you are already a cultural 'insider'. By suspending your prior assumptions, and looking at the company as a 'marginal native' your perspective will be fresher and more insightful.

The close relationships that develop between researcher and researched often result in researchers naturally acquiring the same worldview as those who live or work at the research setting. This is a common risk when you have much in common with participants. To overcome this, continue to remind yourself of your researcher role, and regularly discuss your findings with an outsider such as your supervisor.

As Deacon *et al.* (1999) note, participant observation can be fun – but managing to be involved (such as carrying out a job) while also playing the role of researcher requires good skills in time management and interpersonal communication. It is difficult to achieve a healthy balance between helping out your colleagues and carrying out the tasks related to your involvement, while also recording your observations and writing up your notes.

One of the advantages of using observational methods is that it gives you direct access to social processes as they happen. A corollary disadvantage is that you will only see what is in front of your nose (Deacon *et al.* 1999: 267) because you cannot be in several places at once and may miss crucial events because they occurred elsewhere.

A threat to the validity of your research arises during data collection. If participants are aware of being observed, there is the possibility that they may react to your presence and behave atypically or out of character. This is called 'the observer effect' and tends to disappear the longer you are able to spend in the research setting.

Earlier in the chapter, we wrote that observation techniques can be less disruptive and more unobtrusive than other methods. While this is true, we wonder just how feasible it is to enter and leave a scene without making some sort of ripple on its surface. Over the course of a period of participant observation, people get to know you, make friends with you, sometimes show off in front of you or even ignore you. These actions are all responses to your presence. No matter how careful you are not to disturb the setting, you will always make an impact, even if minimal, on those with whom you come into contact. Therefore, weigh carefully the consequences of your entry into the field. Will the people in your study be 'used' in an inequitable exchange relationship? If so, the research is likely to be unethical. Ideally, your aim as an observer is to treat people in your study as collaborators, that is, stakeholders who shape the inquiry itself (Angrosino and Perez 2000).

Summary

- Observational techniques, whether conducted online or conventionally, involve watching and recording contemporary events and activities as they occur in a particular setting.
- Usually observers closely engage with a setting although there are different degrees of involvement from covert observation to full participation as an 'insider'. Different types of involvement may be employed within the same study and even within the same period of observation.
- Observation often starts with a broad research question which is narrowed down and sculpted by the key issues at the scene.
- Fieldnotes translate observation into a written record. They prod your memory and provide data that can be used directly in the written report.
- Ethical issues are highly salient in observation because of the potential to do harm to participants.

Chapter 5 deals with some of the ethical issues we have touched on in this chapter. You may wish to peruse it before embarking on an observational study.

15 Additional qualitative methods

A number of techniques can be used to supplement interviews and focus groups. Others are capable of standing alone as a research technique. The following methods feature in this chapter:

- using documents as sources of data. These include written and visual records.
- using diaries as sources of data. These are often written expressly for research purposes, with informants recording their own thoughts about events that are personally meaningful.
- projective and enabling techniques require participants to project their own personality, beliefs and behaviours into another situation. They are very effective in cross-cultural research or research on sensitive topics.
- critical incident technique seeks to capture the frame of reference of informants with regard to one or a few highly salient events. It focuses on unpacking the connections between context, strategy and outcomes.

Documentary sources

Documents which have been produced by other people can be a rich source of supplementary or primary evidence in research, indicating the way an organization or industry views its past and present actions, achievements and people. They are important in qualitative research because, on the whole, access to them is low cost and often easy, the information provided in them may differ from or may not be available in spoken form, and because documents endure over time, therefore providing historical insights (Hodder 2000).

Key point
Documents consist of words and images that have been recorded without the intervention of a researcher. They are in written, printed, sound, visual and digital forms.

An example of documentary research is if you track the chronicling of marketing communications programmes through internal documents. These might include contact and status reports, timesheets, campaign plans, press cuttings folders, business television programmes and formal strategic policies.. The personal thoughts and feelings – as well as the power structures – of people as they communicate across all levels in organizations can be found in memos, emails, diaries and private correspondence between staff (and also between staff and researchers). The messages and corporate identity that companies wish to convey to key audiences are revealed in documents that are intended for external audiences, such as annual reports, press releases, briefing documents, newsletters, corporate videos, websites, advertisements and corporate mission statements.

Many documents are in existence before you start your work; others are initiated and organized by you. For example, historical documents, archives and products of the media exist independently of you, while personal diaries might be written at your instigation, or through your intervention (see the following section, p. 220, on Diaries). In many cases, these data are more comprehensive than the evidence you might acquire from interviews or questionnaires conducted over a short time period, especially if you are focusing on a case study organization or industry. This is because documents span time, allowing you to track historical processes or reconstruct past events and ongoing processes that are not available for direct observation. This helps you to better interpret the possible 'rewriting' of events by interviewees in later verbal accounts. It also enables you to identify the factors that over time have led to particular decisions or courses of action, such as why crisis communications may have been mismanaged, or how and why certain marketing alliances have developed. Using documents as sources, therefore, allows you to cover much longer time spans than are typically feasible through the application of other qualitative methods.

If you wish to gain information about individuals or companies where access is restricted or denied, then analysing documents is a useful method because of its unobtrusive, non-reactive nature. This means that you don't have to actively engage with individuals involved in your study. Instead, you can choose to examine documents such as company statements, press cuttings and reports that are freely available in the public domain. While there are limitations to this, as we discuss shortly, such indirect access can still be valuable as long as you don't take the data at face value but check, interpret and triangulate your evidence against other data sources.

The analysis of documents provides you with access to the evidence and thinking of other researchers. If you choose to base your study on data which have already been collected, and possibly also analysed, by someone else, then you are undertaking secondary analysis.

In secondary analysis, you re-analyse other researchers' data and/or research reports in the light of your own particular topic. Examples of documents which might form secondary data for research include reports produced by government departments and regulatory agencies (such as reports on viewer complaints about television advertising compiled by the Broadcasting Standards Commission),

---

Key point

Secondary analysis is any further analysis of an existing dataset which presents interpretations, conclusions, or knowledge additional to, or different from, those presented in the first report or the inquiry as a whole and its main results (Hakim 1982: 1).

---

reports produced by non-official agencies such as trade associations, consumer associations, professional bodies, market-research companies and pressure groups, reports produced by organizations, such as annual reports, programmes broadcast on television or radio, and articles and books generated by academics. Records and documents such as these can help to position your primary research within its broader context.

Example 15.1 Using documents as sources of data

Andrew D. Brown and Matthew Jones (2000) used document analysis for their study of impression management and sensemaking. Their research focused on the 'Arms to Iraq Affair', a trial and public inquiry into a British company's export of defence equipment to Iraq. Their data sources incorporated the following sorts of evidence:

1   archival records of documentary material submitted to the public inquiry by members of the government and their civil servants.
2   the personal experiences of those who were involved in the events.
3   a report produced by the head of the inquiry, based on all the evidence gathered for the inquiry.
4   the direct observations and analyses of the testimonies of witnesses to the inquiry made by journalists and political commentators.

Their documents were the government-sponsored report of the public inquiry, newspaper articles of the time, and books written by journalists and one written by the principal defendant in the trial.

Primary or supplementary purposes

Documentary materials are used either as the primary focus of research or as a supplement to the materials you have collected yourself. When you use documents for primary research purposes, they are the main or sometimes the only materials available. Research, therefore, centres mainly or wholly around the analysis of documents.

When documents are used for supplementary purposes, they allow you to 'flesh out, cross-check or question the picture' that has emerged from the evidence you have gathered yourself (Deacon *et al.* 1999: 14). This method enables you to counteract some of the possible biases of other methods such as interviews.

> **Example 15.2 Combining documents with interviews as data sources**
>
> Jacquie L'Etang's (1998) research into how the public relations occupation in Britain was established was based on interviews with public relations practitioners and supplemented with data derived from documents held in the archives of the Institute of Public Relations together with books and articles on British history.

Authenticity, credibility, meaning, representativeness

When using or quoting from documents in research, it is important to establish that they are authentic and credible, how they are interpreted, and the extent to which they represent the universe of relevant documents.

Authenticity: refers to a document that is genuine, complete, reliable and of unquestioned authorship (Macdonald and Tipton 1993). If it is not authentic, it may be a forgery or a deliberate misrepresentation. To establish authenticity, you need to consider the history of documents as well as the writers' motives and biases.

Credibility is concerned with whether a document is free from error or distortion. Accuracy might be affected by an author's proximity in time and place to the events described and also the conditions under which the information was acquired at the time. In order to be assured of the credibility of documents, you need to ask questions concerning who produced the document, why, when, for whom and in what context. It is also worth asking about what information the account is based on, and how accurate, honest, frank and comprehensive it is. Are there any signs in the account of partiality or axe-grinding? Consider, for example, the different motives that influence the messages contained in a sales brochure, a chief executive's speech to shareholders, a television investigation into a company's practices, a public relations consultant's contact report, and a document which presents the findings of a company's SWOT analysis.

Meaning concerns how documents are interpreted. Documents are socially situated products, produced and intended to be read, seen or heard within a particular social context; they are an integral part of other systems and structures. Therefore, they highlight understandings and interpretations of life within the organization, industry or culture where they were produced – which is likely to be a very different setting from the one in which you, as an analyst, are familiar. It is important, therefore, not to take documents at face value or to isolate them from their context (as content analysis does) or they will be deprived of their meaning. Try instead to interpret documents according to their setting, study the situation and conditions under which they were recorded and try to establish the writers' intentions. Remember, though, that as in other types of data analysis, the meaning is tentative and provisional and may need to be reappraised if new data present a challenge.

Representativeness is often difficult to prove because on many occasions you have no information or control about the numbers, variety or form of documents with regard to a particular event. Some documents may have been lost or destroyed, and others may exist but you may have no access to them. Therefore, whenever you undertake historical research (such as tracking a company's archived annual public relations plans or advertising strategies) you must take these gaps and limitations into account and make them clear when you present your results. Bear in mind, however, that qualitative document research is less concerned with representative samples than it is with purposive or theoretical samples (see Chapter 11 for more on sampling).

Limitations of documents

It is difficult to generalize about public relations and marketing communications from documents because documents are inevitably political and subjective. They are produced by people whose motives may be to persuade, to put a spin on information, or to represent only a particular viewpoint. Therefore they should be cross-checked and triangulated with other sources of data. You need to interpret them with a great deal of care, paying attention to authenticity, credibility, meaning and representativeness.

In archival studies, you have little control over what data are available and can end up having to make do with the material you have because little else exists. *Post hoc* analysis, therefore, may lead you to a variety of interpretations which cannot be validated from other sources. In this case, you need to make clear in your text the problems and issues facing you and note that your interpretation is not definitive but only tentative.

Hammersley and Atkinson (1995) warn that documents may generate biases as they are often produced by and for elites or people in power such as the senior management team. However, that in itself can be useful because not many sources exist that uncover the ideas of such informants.

Diaries

Diaries are used extensively in quantitative research where people are asked to answer closed questions or complete checklists in order that researchers might gather statistical data on topics such as television viewing habits or the time spent by consultants in agencies on client accounts. Unfortunately, in public relations and marketing communications, diaries are somewhat overlooked as a qualitative method even though they have the potential to offer invaluable insights from an insider's point of view.

> **Key point**
> Diaries used in qualitative research have an open format response style. They encourage informants to record an account of their personal feelings and experiences about events that are personally meaningful to them.

Diaries allow you to collect data about the responses of informants according to their interpretations and within the worlds in which they live or work. In effect, this means that diaries are useful for enabling you to:

- access situations and places that might otherwise be inaccessible for a participant observation study (such as the boardroom, or in customers' homes, or in a highly sensitive situation).
- study different events and organizations simultaneously, comparing the perspectives of several writers.
- come to an understanding of the attitudes, feelings, emotions and responses of those involved in particular situations.

Example 15.3 Using diaries in research

In Denmark, Poul Moller and Christian Alsted (1996) investigated consumer perceptions and behaviour towards cinema-going and cinema advertising. Their data collection methods were group interviews and diaries. Diaries enabled participants to record their media habits and make notes about the films they watched and where they saw them.

Diary-based research could be employed effectively in public relations and marketing communications to explore a variety of topics, including:

- the study of reactions and feelings over time. For example, consumer responses to advertising campaigns, employees' responses to management messages, consultants' attitudes to working in teams.
- the exploration of specific behaviours over time. For example, consumer patterns of shopping behaviour, experiences of consultants in managing client relationships, and the activities involved in preparing for a pitch or designing an advertising campaign.
- research into social interactions. For example, press officers' dealings with journalists, direct marketers' contacts with customers and customers' contacts with direct marketers.
- a comparison of the perspectives of different stakeholders over time. For example, the views of managers, publicists, customers and community members towards a company's emerging ethical stance.

The choice of participants depends on the aim of your study although a key question to ask yourself is, 'Who is relevant?' If, for example, you are interested in studying how press releases are used as a source for television news bulletins, your sample of diary recipients would be those involved in the process of media relations (public relations consultants, in-house press officers, television journalists, news editors, news agency journalists). Of course, such a study would need to have consideration for the busy lives of informants; diaries require time to complete and this is often a deterrent to participation. People who may be willing to spend an hour being interviewed are often unwilling (or unable) to take time out for periods of personal reflection and writing.

It is worth spending time at the start of the primary research to carefully set up the procedures for the study and explain them to your participants. Conducting a pilot study helps to iron out any problems with the general format of the diary and its feasibility. Because you will not be present when people are filling in their diaries, you should ensure that the method of completion is self-explanatory and any questions are clear. Participants will be motivated to complete the diaries on a regular basis if you explain the objectives of your study, and indicate how much time, and how often, they should spend on their diaries. Frequency will depend on the aim of the study but might be at the end of the day, after a particular event such as a visit to a client, or at defined intervals, say, every four hours.

You will need to decide how much structure is required in the diary. Some researchers argue that preset headings help to focus diaries. Such headings might indicate specific activities, events, attitudes or feelings. However, Mintsberg (1973) and Stewart (1968) note that this constrains diarists to writing only within pre-specified categories. Even if participants consider other information is pertinent, they are not able to record this. One way to overcome the problem is to allow participants to write about whatever they perceive to be of relevance to themselves at that point in time. Suggesting that writing takes up no more than a page at each session makes the task more manageable for writers. Alternatively, there may be particular issues or aspects of an event or experience that you want to see covered. In this case, you should draw participants' attention to these at the start of the diary completion process. Although paper and pen or computers are the usual diary tools, dictaphones are also useful.

Analysis takes place according to themes which emerge from the evidence. A point to note is that the confidential nature of the research material should be respected at all times. Not only will some of the information you receive be commercially sensitive, but it will also reveal the inner-most thoughts and feelings of your participants. Diary-based research involves high trust relationships between researchers and participants. For a well-illustrated example of the diary method, see Symon (1998).

Limitations of the diary method

The use of diaries in research will only be effective if participants are able to express themselves well in writing. People, therefore, need to be carefully selected with literacy a prime consideration.

A major concern is participant attrition, especially in the first week of the study. Maintaining a diary is a time-consuming, and often onerous task, especially if participants are busy communication practitioners. If diary-based research is to succeed, you need continually to offer encouragement and reassurance to participants to ensure they stay motivated and committed to completing their diaries.

Projective and enabling techniques

Although public relations researchers rarely use projective and enabling techniques, marketing researchers consider them invaluable for uncovering deep-seated beliefs and opinions such as consumers' basic motivations to buy or not to buy, and consumer reactions to colours, size and shape of packaging, or names of products. The insights gained from projective techniques are often used to inform the development of advertising campaigns.

Key point

Projective and enabling techniques are ways of uncovering and exploring the underlying characteristics of participants without making them feel threatened by direct questioning.

Because people's motives and attitudes are so deep-seated, they are often not able to articulate them. Therefore, by asking participants to interpret the behaviour of others, or to provide a response to ambiguous verbal or visual stimuli such as a picture or a story, you are inviting them to indirectly project their own personality, beliefs and feelings into the situation. This enables you to generate information about participants that they are not even conscious of themselves.

Projective and enabling techniques are useful when you are researching sensitive topics, such as if people are likely to avoid answering exactly what they think because it may be impolite or offensive, or because they are afraid to make themselves look silly or prejudiced. They are valuable in cross-cultural research because you do not impose a specific response format, or cultural referent, upon participants. A further benefit of using projective and enabling techniques is that they help to overcome the communication barrier of informants trying to say the right things to please the interviewer.

We will now consider commonly used projective and enabling techniques.

Word or picture association

Using this method, you ask participants to say the first thing that comes to mind when you show them a picture, or give them a particular word. For example, you might say, 'Tell me the first thing you think of when I say "X" Brand.' This provides clues about consumer vocabulary concerning a particular brand.

In cross-cultural research, it is important to develop stimuli that are equivalent in interpretation and meaning in all cultures. Line drawings and pictures are useful because they are not subject to problems of interpretation or culturally determined role models. They, therefore, help to avoid miscomprehension by participants.

Example 15.4 Using projective techniques in cross-cultural research

In a mixed method study conducted in New Zealand, Hester Cooper, Ann Holway and Michelle Arsan (1998) used line drawings to uncover attitudes towards various brands held by Asians, Polynesians and New Zealand Europeans. The line drawings consisted of highly stylized facial expressions which belonged to no particular gender or race. Their research highlighted the difficulty of finding stimuli which translate easily across cultures, that is, those that are culturally relevant. For example, certain expressions are inappropriate for some cultures. Some cues are even considered offensive.

Sentence completion

Like word and picture association, if you employ the technique of sentence completion, you are relying on spontaneity of response. Participants need to complete sentences, stories, arguments or conversations, such as, 'People who buy fast sports cars are . . .' or 'People who use the Internet to find information are . . .' Individuals are required to project themselves into the situation and indicate their perception of the sports car driver or the Internet user. If your participants are sports car drivers or Internet users, it is generally assumed that this description also applies to themselves.

If the area of inquiry is sensitive, you would begin your series with a few innocuous sentences, gradually 'funnelling' down to more difficult ones. The sentence completion test is particularly useful if people are unable to openly express anxieties and annoyance.

Brand mapping

This is also classed as a completion technique. You place a variety of brands or products in front of participants so they can see, handle and discuss them. This enables you to find out people's perceptions about the image of brands and their relationship to them.

Example 15.5 Using projective techniques for product research

Valerie Will, Douglas Eadie and Susan MacAskill (1996) used projective techniques to investigate people's knowledge about contraceptive products. They found that group discussion became more focused and animated when they introduced a tray displaying a range of contraceptives and asked people to examine and comment on the items. Interesting insights emerged that would have been difficult to gather from a more direct questioning approach.

Projective questioning

When you use projective questioning, you aim to discover participants' feelings by asking them to give their opinions about the actions or attitudes of other people. This allows them to respond freely because they are not stating explicitly how they would personally feel about or deal with the same situation.

Cartoons (or blank balloons)

Cartoons usually involve two characters where one character's words are in a speech balloon and the other's balloon is empty. You invite participants to give the reply that is suitable for the occasion. Responses are limited to a few words. The idea is that participants project their own opinions onto the words or thoughts of the cartoon character. A picture showing a consumer talking to a travel agent, for example, could be used to assess consumer attitudes towards travel agents in general or towards booking holidays through travel agencies.

The Thematic Apperception Test (TAT)

Here you ask individuals to graphically depict a story or scenario and then you look for the common themes in what they have said. An example from cross-cultural research is that in Arab countries, the meaning of dreams is very potent and therefore the use of the technique of a guided dream works well (Pawle 1999). Another way of applying the test is to present informants with a series of cartoons or pictures depicting a particular situation, say, a woman walking past an outdoor poster, then stopping to look at it. You then ask them to describe that person and her responses.

Limitations of projective and enabling techniques

Like other qualitative methods, the value of projective and enabling techniques depends to a large extent on your expertise as a researcher. It requires considerable skill to identify and code common themes in participants' answers. Also, as a moderator, you bring your own style to discussions and your subjective judgement to the interpretation of results. Interpretation of the data is highly subjective.

Projective and enabling techniques are time-consuming to apply – and therefore may be expensive to conduct. They are impossible to replicate identically over time.

Unless you are highly trained at interviewing or running focus groups, you are unlikely to be successful in employing projective and enabling techniques, which are always used in conjunction with interviews or focus groups. However, marketing researchers continue to use them because they break down many barriers to communication by enabling participants to associate a feeling or behaviour with another person or object rather than with themselves.

Critical incident technique

Critical incident technique is valuable for capturing the thought processes, the frame of reference and feelings about incidents from the point of view of participants.

Key point

Critical incident technique is a procedure which 'facilitates the investigation of significant occurrences (events, incidents, processes or issues) identified by the participant, the way they are managed, and the outcomes in terms of perceived effects. The objective is to gain an understanding of the incident from the perspective of the individual, taking into account cognitive, affective and behavioural elements' (Chell 1998: 56).

Say, for example, you are interested in exploring communication interactions in customer service departments between service managers and customers phoning in with complaints. In interviews with managers, you might ask them to give an account of their month's work, emphasizing any conversations and actions which, in their opinion, were critical, problematic or highly significant. Focusing on three of these incidents – including one which affects the business positively and one negatively – you would then encourage them to describe the incidents in depth, and explain their actions and motives. From these examples, you would be able to develop ideas about what is crucially important to those involved in customer service. Common themes across the interviews concerning repetitive patterns of communicating would enable you to build a picture of types of marketing communications tactics for handling difficult customer service situations.

The previous paragraph provides an example of an inductive method of data analysis based on grounded theory. To implement such a study, you would begin with a distinct research aim, but would be unlikely at the beginning to define

---

Example 15.6 Using the critical incident technique

The risk issue lifecycle (Regester and Larkin 1997) suggests that how information is managed during crises will determine whether crises escalate or diffuse. In order to assess the applicability of the Regester–Larkin model, the critical incident technique could be used together with purposive sampling. Consultants and in-house public relations practitioners could be asked about their recollections of communication during key crisis situations. Individuals' responses could then be coded according to predetermined categories of communication behaviours. Analysis of the data would indicate the public relations strategies used to manage crises, enabling you to evaluate the model and make recommendations for future crisis management planning.

specific critical incidents. This is because you are seeking to find out what incidents your participants identify as important *to them*. From the data, you would build up an explanatory framework that is particular to its context.

Alternatively, however, you may wish to test or develop further an extant conceptual framework. In this case, it is likely that you would specify types of incidents in advance, asking informants to give an account of their experiences in order to identify effective and ineffective behaviours in crucial situations.

An advantage of applying the critical incident technique is that you can more easily unpack the connections between context, strategy and outcomes. By focusing on one or more events, you explain them according to what happened, why it happened, how it was handled and what the consequences were. The method encourages you to develop case-based theory which is grounded in actual events. Depending on the aim of the research, you can build up case studies which individually consist of detailed investigation, and then draw comparisons across a number of studies. This leads to extended theoretical understanding and facilitates the development of policy and practice.

Limitations of the critical incident technique

Participants may not all understand the term 'critical' in the same way. This would inhibit you from comparing across both interviews and cases.

How do you know that you have captured all pertinent critical incidents when, in inductive research, this cannot be proved? One way around the problem is to consider conducting more than one interview with each participant, although time, budget and access issues may prevent this. Other data such as secondary sources may help to offset the problem. However, what you are after is not objective knowledge or a 'single truth' but an understanding of the viewpoint and actions of participants involved in critical incidents.

The technique relies on informant recall which has implications for selective retention of details about events. However, the significant nature of critical incidents suggests that what informants consider important will have been retained over time.

Issues concerning confidentiality need consideration because of the often sensitive nature of critical incidents. Employees may put themselves at risk by divulging company secrets, or offer information which may be deemed slanderous or even criminal. Strict codes of ethics and procedures for handling tape-recordings and transcripts need to be established and adhered to in order to protect all parties and the integrity of the research process.

Summary

- *Documents* are important in qualitative research because the information contained in them may differ from that which is obtainable from other methods of data collection.
- Documents endure over time, allowing you to gain historical insights.

- Document analysis can be undertaken without engaging with individuals involved in your study. This is helpful when access is restricted or denied.
- Documents should be cross-checked and triangulated with other sources of data.
- *Diaries* enable you to understand the attitudes, feelings, emotions and responses of people involved in specific situations.
- Because diary-based research involves high trust relationships between the researcher and the diary-writer, it is important to respect confidentiality at all times.
- *Projective techniques* allow participants to indirectly project their own personality, beliefs and feelings into situations. Therefore, they are valuable for sensitive or cross-cultural research.
- *Critical incident technique* enables you to gain an understanding about a specific, significant occurrence from the perspective of those involved in it. You explore what happened, why it happened, how it was handled and what the consequences were. This enables you to unpack the connections between context, strategy and outcomes.
- *Documents* and *diaries* are capable of standing alone as research sources. Other methods outlined in this chapter are used together with interviews or focus groups, and may also supplement observations.

Part IV

Analysing, interpreting and writing about the data

16 Analysing and interpreting the data

with Matt Holland

In most qualitative approaches, analysis of the data does not take place in a single stage after you have collected your data, but is a continuous, systematic process which runs simultaneously with data collection. This chapter outlines the process and suggests some techniques for analysing qualitative data. It considers:

- a general approach to qualitative data analysis that is initially inductive but which becomes deductive at a later stage.
- organizing the data prior to analysing them.
- coding and categorizing the evidence.
- finding patterns and working propositions.
- interpreting the data.
- evaluating your interpretation and demonstrating that it is reliable and valid.
- some specific analytical issues, including analysing multiple sources, documents, fieldnotes and secondary analysis.
- computer-aided data analysis software.

Introduction

When you have finished collecting your data, you may feel overwhelmed by the huge amount of evidence that you have accumulated from even a small-scale study. Over a short period of time, it is likely that you will have acquired an array of fieldnotes, company reports and records, emails, research diaries, transcripts of interviews, or perhaps even a collection of visual images such as photographs. Data analysis is the process of bringing order, structure and meaning to this mass of unstructured data.

Often researchers embarking for the first time on qualitative research do not fully appreciate what is in store for them when they come to analyse their material. Qualitative analysis is difficult, complex, lengthy and time-consuming. Morse highlights some of this when she writes that:

> It is a process that requires astute questioning, a relentless search for answers, active observation, and accurate recall. It is a process of piecing

together data, of making the invisible obvious, of recognizing the significant from the insignificant, of linking seemingly unrelated facts logically, of fitting categories one with another, and of attributing consequences to antecedents. It is a process of conjecture and verification, of correction and modification, of suggestion and defence. It is a creative process of organizing data so that the analytic scheme will appear obvious.

(1994: 25)

If you were undertaking quantitative research, it would be usual to begin both the data collection and analysis processes with a tightly structured collection and analysis scheme. This would not allow you to take account of anything unusual which might arise and which might cause you to rethink your overall research agenda. Qualitative research, on the other hand, allows you to be adaptable at all stages of the research process because it is both inductive and deductive. Initially it is inductive. This means that, to begin with, patterns, themes and categories emerge out of the data instead of being imposed on them prior to data collection and analysis. Later the process of qualitative research becomes deductive because, as your research progresses, you develop working propositions and ideas which you test out over the next stages of data collection and analysis. This may even involve searching for new data that confirm your propositions. There is a constant interplay, therefore, between analysis and data collection, which is why qualitative research is often described as iterative.

Key point
Qualitative data analysis is concerned with:

- data reduction: carving up the mass of unwieldy data into manageable chunks by coding, memoing and summarizing them into simplified patterns and configurations.
- interpretation: bringing meaning and insight to the words and acts of participants in your study by generating concepts and theories (or theory-based generalizations) which explain your findings. You then communicate the meaning of your findings to others through your written report.

Although data reduction and interpretation are common to most types of qualitative analysis, there are no rigid stages or rules for undertaking the process of qualitative analysis, unlike in quantitative research where there are well-established methods and procedures. Such flexibility and openness lie at the heart of qualitative research, suggesting that perhaps it is inappropriate to aim for homogeneous, classifiable types of qualitative analysis (Turner 1994). Instead you should follow the analytical approach which you consider best fits your overall research design and the nature of your data.

In this chapter, we present a general approach to qualitative data analysis, considering first the overall process of analysis and then some analytical techniques. We do not cover the specific requirements of data analysis for grounded theory or discourse analysis. These are found in Chapters 8 and 10.

The process of qualitative analysis

Analysis of the data does not start when data collection ends, but should be continuous throughout your entire study. Whenever you transcribe an interview, write up your fieldnotes, log and store any visual data, or reflect upon your research experiences, you are likely to be undertaking some form of preliminary analysis because new ideas will probably emerge which will lead you into a new area of exploration. As you undertake your fieldwork, you should be searching for common themes in your data, making a start on coding, and developing some early concepts.

Key point

Concepts are abstract or general ideas which you devise to describe a particular issue or subject.

The preliminary analysis is likely to be fairly simple although it will become more complex as your study evolves. From the start of your project then, it is best to get into the habit of listening to your tapes and reading your transcripts as soon as possible after interviewing. Similarly, it is worth immediately typing up any scribbled fieldnotes, notes of telephone conversations and visits, together with the systematic fieldnotes you make after observation periods. This is because it is easier to structure information while the details are still fresh in your mind.

As your research progresses, you should continue to search for themes, categories, clusters in the data gathered from all your sources, and then find interlinkages that will help you to explain them. Draw on the literature in order to relate your data to theoretical ideas. This will enable you to develop abstract concepts which explain your findings. Take care not to impose an external system on the data, such as a pre-determined theoretical framework, because this will not be open to adaptation as your research progresses. Qualitative research excels at finding points of entry into new areas of inquiry, and therefore it is important to remain open to new discoveries, allowing your patterns and concepts to grow naturally out of an interaction between what you discover in the field, your experience and your evolving knowledge.

Some suggestions for going about this process of analysis now follow.

Organizing the data

Before beginning to analyse your evidence, it is important to check that every-thing has been recorded and labelled in a systematic manner. This helps to keep your data intact, complete, organized and retrievable. Cross-reference dates, names, titles, attendance at events, descriptions of settings and situations (such as communications campaigns or events that relate to your study), chronologies, and so on. This is invaluable when you come to identify categories, piece together patterns, and plan for further data collection. In some cases, researchers like to keep a special project book or computer file in which they jot down all of their ideas and thoughts, cross-referencing to various data sources.

Ensure that all the data are to hand. Are your fieldnotes complete? Is there anything that you have put off to write later and didn't get around to finishing? Are all of the interview transcriptions complete and have they been accurately typed up? Check the quality of all the evidence you have collected before start-ing to analyse it.

Coding and categorizing

Coding provides a first step to developing your categories, patterns and con-cepts. Not only does it help to organize your mass of data, but it is also integral to the task of interpreting public relations and marketing communications phe-nomena. This is because your decision to create a particular code has a defining effect on what you find in your collated data. Coding informs the decisions you make about what is worth saving, how to divide up the material, and how inci-dents of, say, activities or talk relate to other coded items. This process is both intuitive and creative.

Key point

Codes serve as labels or shorthand devices which enable you to tag seg-ments of interest in the data. They help you to reduce and simplify the evidence in order to begin to make sense of it.

Coding starts after you have read through your evidence several times and con-sider that you are thoroughly immersed in it and have begun to get an overall idea of the big picture. Now begin to make notes in the margins about key words, themes, issues and remarks made by your participants. The idea of coding is to identify and constantly compare commonalities and differences in your material in order to formulate categories of interest. For the purposes of coding, you should treat written, broadcast and digital documents like transcrip-tions of interviews or detailed descriptions of observations. Where possible, time-code and log recordings according to minutes and hours. This enables you to more readily identify the content in each recording.

Even if you have conducted only a couple of preliminary interviews or observations, you will start to get a good idea of some of the key ideas and regular themes that are emerging. Look for indicators of these early concepts in other materials you have collected, such as documents and records, making a note in the margin against the relevant passages. When viewing visual data, categorize the data by writing your codes against the relevant logged details or in the white margins around photographs.

Write down each potential code, and then compare new evidence, as you collect it, against your original examples. Check to see that your new material fits with your code. If it does, it can be added to that code. For example, a theme that could conceivably develop out of a study of the consumption patterns of postmodern consumers could be 'experimentation'. Each time you find an indicator of this in your data, identify the relevant sentences with the code 'Experimentation', and write this in the margins of the document, transcript, your fieldnotes, your log of visual recordings or wherever you find the evidence.

A page of interview transcript may end up with many codes written in the margins. Some passages may be coded in more than one way because they relate to more than one theme or issue that you have identified. The same codes will also relate to relevant examples in other types of data you have collected. Don't worry at this early stage about having too many codes; you can refine them as you go along.

Example 16.1 Identifying initial categories

Karen Miller (1999) examined depictions of public relations and its practitioners in film and fiction from 1930 to 1995. Her reading of the texts drew out several categories related to the way public relations people were viewed. Her categories included: 'ditsy', 'obsequious', 'cynical', 'manipulative' and 'accomplished'.

In some cases, when you compare evidence against a code it might not fit. This may indicate that you need to consider developing another code – or perhaps your original codes may need modifying or refining. If you find that two codes describe the same phenomenon, condense them into one. As you continue collecting data, it is probable that some codes will no longer be relevant because you have found more suitable labels or because your research has taken a new direction. In this case, you will have to go back over all of your evidence, re-coding your earlier data-texts.

If you are analysing more than one type of data (documents and transcripts, for example), it is important to cross-reference between the different data sources, seeking similarities and differences within and between all your data-texts. As you identify codes, and material which fits with those codes, you need to transfer the evidence into files so all the examples for each code are collected together into one category. Remember to identify the extracts before adding them to the coded files. Traditionally, researchers used either pens of different colours to mark particular categories or themes, or they physically cut up their

Example 16.2 Coding an interview transcript

This extract of an interview transcript is labelled according to the following codes: extranet, up-to-date, client communications, relationships, global potential, integrated communications. The interview is with James Warren of Bullet PR and Donald Johnson of Text100.

(James) What we do is, you put the PR reporting system directly online on the extranet. The PR agency basically update all of their activity live so that the moment that they place an interview or they place a piece of coverage or a piece of coverage appears they just go onto the extranet and type the fact that they have done that in the relevant area on the report. The PR manager either gets sent an email or is alerted to that fact. He or she can go up and find out what's going on. You know it's hugely, hugely useful for the PR agency because they're keeping the client completely informed of what they are doing on a day to day basis, so the client is happier. And from the client point of view you know, if the PR manager gets a call from their chairman saying, 'Right, well you know, where are we with this' or 'There's a feature coming up in the Times I see next week on this particular thing. I hope we're in it'. The PR manager can access this and say immediately yes or no.

extranet

up-to-date

client com.
relationships

up-to-date

(Donald) It can be anywhere in the world.

global

(James) Exactly it can be anywhere in the world. It can be any time of night because the other thing with clients is that – I know a lot of clients work, a lot of PR people work strange hours. Core agency hours are generally nine to six. So trying to get hold of a PR agency representative out of hours can be very difficult. With this solution you know it can be . . .

up-to-date

(Interviewer) Could you, say, put the other types of agency into that as well?

integrated com.

(James) Yes, absolutely, I mean we have a number of clients who do use it, not only as a PR extranet but as a full marketing extranet, so, for instance, the advertising agency plug in, look at the forward features that are planned by the PR agency and they can then basically plan their advertising to coincide with features where they know . . .

integrated com.

(Donald) The PR coincides with advertising.

(James) Absolutely right, and you know direct mail people can go in there and say, 'Well, we're planning this direct mail on this particular product or service for this particular time frame' and the PR agency can then plan to support that activity through PR. So it's a really good way of pulling together all the marketing disciplines without having anybody step on anybody else's shoes. It's really just sharing information.

collaboration

data-texts, pasting sections into coded folders or ring-binders. Today, it is possible to do this more quickly by computer, opening an on-screen file for each code and pasting in sections of evidence. There are also several software programmes which have facilities to help you code and categorize your data. We discuss some of these towards the end of this chapter.

The limitations of coding

Although coding is a helpful way of narrowing down your data to something more manageable, it also deflects attention away from phenomena that are uncoded and therefore uncategorized. This points to the problem that every way of seeing is also a way of not seeing (Silverman 2000) and therefore potentially useful information may be ignored because it does not fit within a coding system.

One way to overcome this is to construct a coding system that allows for uncategorized ideas and activities to be accounted for, if appropriate (see also page 241 on Searching for Alternative Explanations and Negative Cases). Another strategy is to reject a coding system altogether and attempt to carefully tease out the subtle and various meanings of words, coupled with an informed understanding of the broader structures within the data. This takes account of other problems of coding. These include the loss of context of what is said when data are minutely fragmented through coding, and also the fact that some forms of data may be unsuitable for the coding method (Riessman 1993). Following a discourse analysis methodology allows you to overcome some of these difficulties (see Chapter 10 for a discussion on discourse analysis).

Looking for patterns and working propositions (or emergent hypotheses)

By now, your data will be fragmented into dozens, if not hundreds, of different categories. The next stage requires you to integrate these into something more stable, compact and coherent so that you can make sense of them all, and focus your subsequent fieldwork back onto your main research question.

Continue to work back and forth between the coded categories and their subcategories as you search deductively for relationships between them. These

---

Example 16.3 Identifying broad themes

When Karen Miller (1999, see Example 16.1) looked for patterns in the categories she had developed out of data, she was able to integrate the subcategories into the following major themes: the moral life of public relations practitioners, their effectiveness in their jobs, and the consequences of their professional choices. Overall, her findings indicated that public relations and its practitioners were viewed negatively.

relationships indicate patterns in your data. The patterns help you to identify some broader, central themes which are able to provide you with an overall understanding of all the disparate sub-themes. The patterns also enable you to relate your findings to concepts and categories in the existing literature. Indeed, in some cases it might be appropriate to derive new codes and concepts from the literature itself.

Patton (1990) notes that when you find themes and patterns in your data, you can classify these in two ways: according to the definitions used by participants themselves, or according to terms created by you to reflect categories for which participants do not have labels or terms. The first of these refers to the constructs that people in your study use to define the events, actions and behaviours with which they are involved. For example, in a study of the advertising agency–client relationship, you might discover that a common theme is 'them and us' because this is the way account executives, creatives and their clients describe and relate to each other. Alternatively, you yourself might create terms that reflect distinct categories that you are able to see in the data but which the people in your study are either not aware of themselves or are not able to express. It is important here to take a great deal of care in making this type of construction in order to avoid creating things that are not really in the data. One way to overcome this is to go back to your participants and ask them if they are able to recognize your constructions. When participants themselves say, 'Yes, that is there, I'd simply never noticed it before', then you can be reasonably confident that you have tapped into existing patterns of interaction (Lofland 1971: 34).

As patterns and central themes become apparent, you are likely to begin developing working propositions and testing their plausibility through the data. Prior to arriving at her final conclusion, it is likely, for instance, that Miller (see Examples 16.1 and 16.3) may have developed several propositions about the way in which public relations practitioners were depicted in film and fiction from 1930 to 1995. By continuing to search through your data, you challenge these emergent hypotheses, seek out negative instances of the patterns, and incorporate these into larger constructs, if necessary.

The compilation of interim summaries enables you to reflect on the work you have done, consider any changes you may need to make in your coding and further fieldwork, and focus on your main research question. If you are exploring multiple case studies, summaries provide you with an opportunity to develop some provisional cross-case analyses.

Helpful hint
Writing analytical memos to yourself enables you to explore connections between the data, and record your intuitive ideas as they relate to both the data and the literature. Store these in a separate folder or in a computer file.

Interpreting the data

Lindlof describes analysis as 'a matter of hearing the voices of the other and deciding which voices should be included and how those voices are to be stitched together' (1995: 243). We would add that it is also a matter of explaining those voices by putting your own meaning on the data you have collected and analysed, and comparing that with the conclusions of other researchers who have published relevant studies. This process of transcending the data – or interpreting – involves arriving at your own assessment of what your findings mean in relation to appropriate knowledge in public relations and marketing communication. In qualitative research, it also involves generating theory, new conceptual models or making theory-based generalizations that can be further developed in later comparative studies.

Key point
Theory is a supposition which explains or seeks to explain something.

So how do you go about generating theory? At the same time as you are concentrating on discovering relationships within the data, you are also seeking to explore relationships between your data and the relevant literature. This involves tacking back and forth between the evidence collected from your fieldwork and the literature. This helps you to find a coherent theoretical framework that is informed by and which fits with your interpretation of the data. True analysis involves giving your data wider significance by positioning your study within the body of knowledge that has been developed in public relations and marketing communications.

Not all qualitative research involves generating theory. For instance, some studies seek only to be descriptive, perhaps to illustrate or challenge a specific theory or model. Such studies, however, still endeavour to provide a link between data and theoretical knowledge in order to recontextualize a particular case or instance to a more universal sphere so that readers can identify more readily with it. In ethnographic studies, for instance, theorizing often involves identifying beliefs and values in the data and then comparing them with established theory. Through this process of analysing, new models or theories are developed.

As in grounded theory, the generalizability of theory that you develop is determined by its 'abstractedness'. If you have developed substantive theory, this will be context bound and applicable only to the setting in which your study took place. On the other hand, if you have developed formal theory, this will be more abstract and transferable to many contexts or experiences. Bear in mind, however, that much qualitative research involves single case studies or small samples and therefore your attempts at generalization will be tenuous (for more on generalization, see Chapter 6).

Example 16.4 Developing theoretical concepts

Andrew Brown and Matthew Jones investigated the 'Arms to Iraq Affair' by analysing a variety of documents (see also Example 15.1). They recorded the analytical process as follows:

1   the two researchers independently read the documentary sources.
2   they developed a baseline description of events.
3   they reviewed this description and developed theoretical concepts.
4   they elaborated these by referring to the established literature.

The process included several cycles of revision and refinement. At the same time as they analysed the documents, they also discovered that the literature on sensemaking and impression management was relevant to their study. When they found a coincidence of themes in both the 'Arms to Iraq' and scholarly literatures, they wrote analytical memos for these themes.

> In this way, we gradually came to focus on issues of self-deception, hypocrisy and scapegoating, and sought to place them in a coherent theoretical framework. Our incipient model was then subject to numerous revisions as we attempted to find an appropriate fit between it, our case study material, and our focusing concepts from the literature. Once we had satisfied ourselves that the explanatory framework we had developed was robust we then sought further critical commentary from colleagues and, latterly, reviewers for *Human Relations* [the journal which published the article]. This article is the result of these investigative, imaginative, critical, creative and reflexive processes.
>
> (Brown and Jones 2000: 659)

Evaluating your interpretation

Patton (1990) writes that qualitative analysis needs to be meaningful, useful and credible. If your conclusions relate directly to the questions that you have asked, your analysis will be meaningful. If your interpretation of the data is understandable to readers and is clearly presented, then your analysis is useful. Finally, to be credible, you must demonstrate that the perspective you have presented will stand up to rigorous scrutiny, with reference to reliability and validity. Although we discuss this in depth in Chapter 6, we note here three important aspects which you should consider when analysing your material. They concern:

* searching for alternative explanations and negative cases.
* carrying out a 'member check' or respondent validation.
* being reflexive about your interpretation.

Searching for negative cases and alternative explanations

Remember that you are seeking to develop an argument and make a case for your particular interpretation of the data. This means undertaking a *critical* analysis which you do by challenging the themes and patterns that initially seem so obvious, and also by considering instances that do not fit within the patterns. Sometimes deviant cases throw up useful new insights. It is important, therefore, to search for other, plausible explanations for the data, the connections between them, and their relationship to previous research. This involves identifying and describing rival or competing themes, negative cases, and explanations that might lead to different findings. It means thinking about other logical possibilities and then seeing if the data support those possibilities. Marshall and Rossman (1995) contend that if you are not able to find strong supporting evidence for alternative explanations, then you can feel confident that the explanation you offer is the most plausible of them all. This is discussed further in Chapter 6.

Helpful hint
When you come to write up your report, you should be able to demonstrate how you weighed the evidence and considered alternative cases and explanations.

Carrying out a 'member check'

To analyse the sense of your data in their context, consider carrying out what is known as a 'member check' or 'informant validation'. This can be done in a number of ways including asking respondents to read your written interpretation of the evidence you have collected, and comment back to you, or feeding back to respondents your impressions and findings about their organization, industry or activities. The aim is to seek confirmation that your interpretation of the data corroborates with the views of your research participants. Once again, a more detailed discussion of this topic is found in Chapter 6. For a clear, extended discussion of how data analysis was carried out in a research, see Elsbach and Sutton (1992).

Being reflexive about your interpretation

In Chapter 6, we noted that reflexivity was concerned with explicitly recognizing the role of the research process, including the researcher him- or herself, on the research situation. As a qualitative researcher, you are not an uninvolved bystander but a social being who has an impact on the behaviour of those around you (Cassell and Symon 1994). Therefore, when you come to evaluate your interpretation of the data, you should reflect upon the implications of your methods, values, biases and research choices for the public relations or marketing communications knowledge that you have generated. What, for example, might be the implications of a study into careers and equal opportunities practices in Australian advertising agencies if you, the researcher, were a woman of Aboriginal ethnic background? Would your ethnicity influence the theoretical perspective you chose to frame your topic? Would it influence the sample and research methods you selected? How might you, yourself, have influenced the data you collected, such as by being a black, female researcher interviewing predominantly white, male advertising executives about equal opportunities? Would your interpretation be biased by your ethnicity and any of your own previous career experiences? Issues such as these require critical self-reflection because of the notion that your role as a researcher is inherently tied up with how you have derived and interpreted your findings, that is, with how your have constructed knowledge in the field of public relations and marketing communications.

In some cases, you may also wish to reflect upon the view that language or text is socially, historically, politically and culturally located. In particular, if you are writing an account that is based on an ethnographic or discourse analysis study, you are likely to acknowledge that the documents or transcripts you read – and the research report which you produce – are versions of the social context in which they are situated. This entails recognizing the implications and significance of your decisions as both researcher and writer.

Some specific analytical issues

Analysing multiple sources

Many qualitative methodologies combine more than one method of data collection. In analysis it is important to cross-reference between the different data sources, looking for similarities and differences within and between all your data-texts. In the earlier part of this chapter we offer some universal suggestions for analysing and interpreting the data. Now we come to specific issues related to particular types of data-texts.

Analysing documents

Qualitative document analysis (also called qualitative content analysis) differs from quantitative content analysis which is where you endeavour to generate a statistical map of the basic contents of written and electronic documents by measuring the frequency and extent of messages. Quantitative content analysis involves establishing a set of categories and then counting the number of instances that fall into each category, such as the number of column inches devoted to a particular message or topic, the square inches of the photographs displayed, the number of times the message appears in the index, etc. The higher the number, the greater their significance.

In qualitative document analysis, on the other hand, narrative data are found (although sometimes you might also collect some numerical data to support your qualitative evidence). Whereas the major purpose of quantitative content analysis is to verify or confirm hypothesized relationships, the aim of qualitative document analysis is to discover new or emergent patterns, including overlooked categories which might be those used by participants themselves (for instance, consultants' own depictions of their client relationships). If you are dealing with statistical reports within a qualitative study, for instance, you should explore the ways that the statistics have been organized and presented, searching for the key messages and meanings that the authors wish to convey. For more on using documents as sources of data, turn to Chapter 15.

Analysing fieldnotes

When you are analysing interviews, codes can emerge from the words and concepts that are familiar to your informants. This does not happen when you are working with fieldnotes from your observation sessions. Instead, codes are likely to be the result of a 'brainstorming' session where you come up with a multitude of plausible accounts for the meaning of the activities you have observed. Each of these accounts forms possible codes which need to be compared with fieldnotes from other observations within the project. When you have refined your codes into more manageable patterns or themes, it is worth writing these up in formal, abstract terms. For example, if 'creativity' emerges as a code that is applicable to the data you have gathered for your research into the work roles of advertising copywriters and art directors, you should try to think of other situations where creativity is prevalent in marketing-related activities and interactions, as documented in the literature. This will help you to identify aspects of the process of creativity which you can then look for when you switch back into examining your own data on advertising.

Secondary analysis

Secondary analysis is when you analyse data that have been collected by someone else. We discussed this in Chapter 15 with regard to the analysis of documents. However, secondary analysis also refers to the reuse of 'raw' data such as transcripts and fieldnotes compiled by other researchers. A useful website which lists archive repositories holding qualitative data is http://www.essex.ac.uk/qualidata/. Its online catalogue is at http://www. essex.ac.uk/qualidata/data/catinput.html. One of the problems associated with reusing someone else's material is that you may not have an insider's understanding of the cultural and political context in which the data were produced because you were not there at the time of data collection (Hammersley 1997). Another research issue concerns the fact that you may have little control over what data are available; you are reliant on whatever exists in the archives. Analysing data *post hoc*, therefore, may lead you to a variety of interpretations which cannot be validated from other sources. Nevertheless, 'secondary analysis offers rich opportunities not least because the tendency for qualitative researchers to generate large and unwieldy sets of data means that much of the material remains under-explored' (Bryman 2001: 403).

Computer-aided qualitative data analysis software (CAQDAS)

By Matt Holland

Qualitative analysis software is good for mechanical research tasks, such as storing and organizing data, coding, searching and retrieving, annotating data, and displaying data in a variety of formats including graphical displays.

If you are skilled at using qualitative analysis software packages, you will find they can be relatively effective in supporting theory building although they cannot substitute for your own thinking, judging, deciding, and interpreting which are still best done by you, yourself (Tesch 1991). Neither can they be a substitute for learning the various data analysis methods. From the beginning, you need to know what needs to be done and how to do it before going on to employ software to do it for you (Weitzman 2000).

Therefore, before making the decision to use CAQDAS you need to reflect honestly on your own skills and resources. Begin with the question, 'What type of computer user am I?'

Level 1: I can use a computer for simple word processing tasks.
Level 2: I can use a variety of programs well and am comfortable with using new software.
Level 3: I am able to adapt programs to my own needs, for example, by using macros.

(Weitzman 2000)

If you have lower levels of computer skill, it will take longer to acquire the appropriate skills, and you may also require additional support. For instance, consider what resources are available to you. You may need training and expert advice depending on your own skill level. You will certainly need regular access to a computer and appropriate software. Higher education institutions usually provide facilities for students and researchers. However, if you don't have access to these resources, you need to cost them into your research budget.

Broadly, if you are using CAQDAS for analysis, you are likely to be doing some or all of these activities:

- coding: creating a coding system and applying it to your data.
- annotating: adding brief comments in your data.
- memoing: embedding reflections or summaries in the data.
- linking: creating links between data (codes, memos, files and printed materials, which comprise your project).

- searching and retrieving: for codes, memos and text (using Boolean search techniques).
- displaying: abstracting and collating text; creating graphical displays.

You need to find a fit between your methodology, the analytical techniques needed to implement the methodology you choose, and the software. Fielding and Lee (1998) provide an overview of commonly used qualitative methodologies and their accompanying analytical techniques. It is important to remember that the methodology drives the research. When you have a clear idea of what the methodology means in practice, you are not tempted to try to fit your research to the capabilities of whatever software you have access to.

Increasingly, qualitative researchers focus on a narrowing range of established products: ATLAS.ti, The Ethnograph, HyperRESEARCH, QSR NUD*IST, Nvivo, and, winMAX. All these products are marketed by SCOLARI Sage Publications Software (SCOLARI 2001). If your sponsoring institution supports one of these software packages, you may not have a choice about which one to use.

Consider as well the challenge of managing your data. The capabilities of software vary and it is important to ensure that CAQDAS fits appropriately with the data you generate. Take a view on where your project fits in terms of data complexity and predictability. Complexity is a function of the number of participants in your study and the number of sources of data. Lots of participants and many sources mean a large volume of data and more interaction between the data. This leads to complex coding and analysis. Predictability reflects the extent to which you can control things such as the length or number of interviews, the sources of your data (text, audio and video) and the extent of your coding system. If your project is complex, you might consider using the QSR NUD*IST package which handles complex projects very well, although it is more challenging to learn. On the other hand, ATLAS.ti handles simple projects easily and is easy to learn.

Finally, consider the extent to which you can realize the potential of using qualitative analysis software. For small amounts of data, it simply may not be worth the time it takes to learn a software package. Therefore, think carefully about, 'How much data do I have?'. It may not be possible for you as a new researcher to realize all the benefits of CAQDAS in one project. However, the skills you gain in learning a package are incremental and might be usefully applied to later projects, so consider if you are likely to use the software again.

If you are a postgraduate researcher embarking on an extended research project, CAQDAS is a potentially valuable analytical tool; for this type of project its benefits are likely to outweigh the difficulties of learning and using it. For further reading on the topic, we suggest you explore books which are aimed at novice researchers, such as Bryman (2001), which offer a more useful introduction to CAQDAS than those written by computer experts whose texts are often impenetrable unless you already have a working knowledge of the software. Case studies using CAQDAS (such as Buston 1997) are also useful for developing your knowledge of the techniques.

Summary

- Data analysis is concerned with reducing your data into manageable chunks and interpreting them.
- In most qualitative approaches, there is a constant interplay between data collection and analysis. Analysis begins when data collection begins.
- Qualitative analysis involves searching for categories and patterns in the data that will help you make sense of your evidence. Coding facilitates this.
- Finding patterns in the data enables you to relate your findings to concepts and themes in the existing literature. This helps to generate theory, new models or theory-based generalizations.
- A specialist software package can be a valuable tool for analysing the data but should not be a substitute for your own thinking, judging, deciding and interpreting.
- Your study should be able to stand up to rigorous scrutiny. Strategies for demonstrating that you have carefully weighed the evidence include searching for alternative explanations and negative cases, carrying out a 'member check', and being reflexive about your interpretation of the data.

It is often overlooked that report writing is intrinsic to analysis. In order to explain the findings of your study, you need to communicate them to a wider group of readers which you do by writing up your findings. The next chapter focuses on this aspect.

17 Writing the report

Writing is a crucial aspect of the research process where you develop your thinking, and communicate your ideas to a wider audience. This chapter deals with writing and structuring the research report. It notes that:

- the research report is a persuasive document which aims to persuade readers of the quality and importance of your work.
- the structure of the report conveys the process and outcomes of your work in a logical sequence. Some basic elements of structure are common to most research reports.

This chapter offers suggestions for:

- finding your own writing style and voice.
- structuring the report for an academic dissertation and a professional report.
- presenting the data and developing a storyline.

Introduction

After you have collected and analysed your data, you will be ready to complete the writing up of your research report. This may be in the form of a thesis, dissertation, professional report, conference paper or article. Writing is a crucial aspect of research because, in the process of putting your thoughts down onto the page, your ideas and arguments develop and solidify. Therefore, writing is not something you do only in the final weeks or months of your research project; writing starts early, right at the outset of your thinking about and reading around your topic. Writing is critical because this is the key way in which you communicate your ideas to a wider audience.

Helpful hint
Start to communicate from day one – in writing!

Doing qualitative research is an iterative or cyclical process whereby you write down your ideas, draft out a chapter or section, and then return later to redraft your written thoughts. As you go on reading discussing ideas with colleagues and your supervisor, undertaking your research, and writing up further chapters, so your thinking changes. Towards the end of your research project then, you may still be adding to or refining your literature review chapter in the light of your interpretation of the primary data.

When you first started thinking about your project, you may have come up with a rough outline for the structure of your research report. Don't worry if this changes as your research progresses. Initially a draft structure is helpful in organizing your thinking, ordering your information and encouraging you to get some words down onto paper. Start writing where you feel most comfortable. The introduction may not be the easiest place to begin so start elsewhere if you prefer and move on to the first chapter when you feel ready. As you write sections within chapters, you will revise and change the order along the route. A key advantage of qualitative research is its flexibility, and this applies also to the writing stage.

Most research reports share a basic structure which helps to convey the process and outcomes of your work in a logical sequence. There is nothing to prevent you organizing your work in a different way if you want to, as long as all the main elements (listed on page 25) are encompassed somewhere within your report.

> **Helpful hint**
> Write to persuade as well as to inform.

As you write and structure the report, it is worth reminding yourself that the presentation of research is essentially a rhetorical or persuasive activity (Golden-Biddle and Locke 1997). You are not just putting down onto paper your evidence and your interpretation; instead, you are seeking to convince readers that you have completed a piece of work of high quality that makes a significant contribution. If your report is an academic one, then your contribution will be in a particular area of public relations or marketing communications scholarship. Essentially, what you are attempting to achieve through your writing is an authoritative voice in the academic community. If you are writing a professional report, then it is likely that you will be making a contribution to the development of company or industry knowledge.

Your readers and your voice

Keep in mind the readers of your report and their expectations. There are differences in the style and structure of reports written for company settings, funding bodies or universities. Employers, for instance, are most interested in the results and implications for business. They are less concerned with philosophical and theoretical issues and will not wish to see references in the text or a long bibliography at the end. Academics, however, see these as vital.

To some extent, whether you write in the first or third person is a matter of personal preference, although the use of the first person singular indicates the integral role of the researcher in the study. Van Maanen (1988) has convincingly illustrated the difference between personal and impersonal writing styles, showing how each effects a different account of the same evidence (note the discussion about this in Chapter 9). He and others contend that the writer should not be excluded from his or her writing because there is an intrinsic connection between the researcher and the evidence.

Nevertheless, most of the academic and professional literature in public relations and marketing communications tends to be written in the third person ('the researcher concluded that . . .') or with a passive voice ('it was discovered that . . .'). Writers rarely use the 'I' word. Those who disembody themselves in this way imply that they have had nothing whatsoever to do with the knowledge they are presenting. It's as if the evidence and its interpretation arrived from out of the blue. This impersonal style of writing is essentially a quantitative research technique where objectivity is the name of the game, and distance and detachment are seen as important.

Qualitative research, however, is concerned with the researcher as the research instrument. Therefore, the use of the first person indicates the intrinsic connection between the writer and the evidence. Research reports which are written in the first person are 'more immediate, personal, committed and [do] not deny any inherent subjectivity' (Blaxter *et al.* 1996: 120). If you do decide to write in the first person, take care not to overdo the use of the word 'I' – otherwise you'll find yourself brought too obtrusively into the report.

Helpful hint
Learn to develop your own style and 'voice' – and enjoy using it – but check with the conventions of your institution about what is an appropriate style for submitted work.

However, your writing style may be dictated by the conventions of your academic institution, funding body or editor, forcing you to write in a formal, impersonal style. If this is the case, it is often a good idea to write your first draft in the first person because, in this way, you learn to develop your own style and tone of voice. Part of your voice is the rhythm of your natural writing, the words and phrases you use, and the way in which you structure your thoughts. The first person singular allows you to 'keep in touch with your ideas, your reactions, your beliefs and your understandings of what other people have written' (Rudestam and Newton 2001: 218). You can always remove the 'I' from your writing in the second or third drafts, although sometimes it is acceptable to leave it in for

---

Example 17.1 An original beginning to a research article

Chris Hackley's article about work life in a London advertising agency offers an original writing style and structure (see also Example 10.1). His opening lines start as follows:

I've been told I've got to talk to you.
To cut a long story short, I was sitting in one of the rabbit-hutch offices in the agency's open-plan 'planning' floor. Some agreeable advertising types had kindly let me come in and wander around and interview people. I had initially made contact with the agency in early 1997 and conducted three interviews with agency staff in my own office in November that year. I maintained informal contact, and by spring 1998 I had set up my main data-gathering session in the agency itself. For two consecutive days they rounded up anyone who could spare half an hour to come in to my little confessional and unburden themselves into my temperamental hand-held recording device. [...] I liked it there: it seemed an urbane, collegiate style of organization, very driven yet informal in terms of modes of dress, modes of address and non-essential time-keeping. My interviewees came across as advertising enthusiasts working at the top of an elite industry. Their regard for the privileged status of their agency in the industry was clear.

(2000: 239–40)

In this one paragraph, Hackley introduces the reader to his research context and briefly indicates how he went about collecting some of his data. He begins to develop a 'thick' description of the advertising agency and the social activities that take place there.

---

the introduction and methodology sections because here you are describing what you chose to do and why.

Structuring the report

A distinction between qualitative and quantitative research lies in the potentially flexible structure of the qualitative report. Despite this, most reports follow a basic structure similar to the one outlined in Example 17.2. However, this can vary depending on the aims of your research and your research design. If your methodological approach uses grounded theory, for instance, you might wish to begin your report with your methodology discussion. In qualitative research, the findings and discussion are the most important elements of the final write-up, and in consequence these sections contain more words than the others.

Professional reports follow a slightly different structure although the main elements are similar (see Example 17.3). Professional reports are often shorter in length than academic reports, with a style of writing that is detached, 'punchier' and more condensed. Sentences and paragraphs are shorter. The presentation

---

Example 17.2 A conventional structure for a qualitative, academic report

Title
Abstract
Acknowledgement and dedication
Table of contents
   including figures and tables
Introduction
   background and justification for the study (including the aim of the research)
Literature review
Methodology and research design
   description and justification of methods (including the type of theoretical framework)
   the sample and the setting
   data collection
   data analysis
   validity and reliability in qualitative terms
   ethical considerations
Findings/results and discussion
Conclusion
   including implications and reflections
   areas for future research
   recommendations
References
Appendices

---

involves more bullet points and diagrams than is usual in an academic report. There is usually less emphasis on the methodology and more on the recommendations.

Whether your report is an academic or professional one, each chapter should have an introduction and a summary with clear signals throughout to guide readers along the route. Your introduction should outline briefly the purpose of each chapter and provide an overview of its structure. It also may indicate to the reader how the chapter links to your research aim. The summary pulls together the main points you have made in the chapter, highlighting the key issues and showing how they connect to the following chapter. Through your discussion, the signals help readers to follow where they have just come from and where they are going to. For instance, helpful signalling techniques include sentences such as: 'Having presented the main debates concerning corporate identity and image, I now go on to discuss empirical research in this area.'

Example 17.3 A conventional structure for a qualitative, professional report

Title
Executive summary
Table of contents
   including figures and tables
Introduction and methodology
   background to the study
   purpose of the study
   description and justification of methods
   the sample and the setting
   data collection
   data analysis
   validity and reliability in qualitative terms
   limitations of the study
Findings
Discussion and conclusion
   implications for the organization or industry
   recommendations
Appendices

Helpful hint

Say what you're going to do (*in your chapter introduction*), say it (*in the body of the chapter*), say what you've done (*in your chapter summary*).

Title

When you began your research project, you will have made a stab at identifying a working title. This title is used mostly for administrative purposes initially and is only tentative, so can be changed easily as your ideas and focus sharpen (but don't forget to inform your supervisor and the research degrees committee of your university about this). The final title of a study is important because it is the first and most immediate contact the reader has with the research. We suggest a concise and informative title, one that captures attention but also gives an indication of the main focus of the report. It is quite common for writers to begin with a punchy main title followed by explanatory subtitles.

Novice researchers sometimes include unnecessary redundancies in the title such as, 'A Study of . . .', 'Aspects of . . .' or 'An Inquiry/Analysis/Investigation of . . .'. Although the title should reflect the aim of the research, it is rather clumsy to give the whole aim in the title. Make your title clear, succinct and informative.

The title page in a dissertation or thesis contains the title, the name of the

---

Example 17.4 Articles that have main and explanatory subtitles

- 'Why Media Matter: Toward a Richer Understanding of Consumers' Relationships with Advertising and Mass Media' (Hirschman and Thompson 1997)
- 'Defining a "Brand": Beyond the Literature with Experts' Interpretations' (de Chernatony and Dall'Olmo Riley 1998)
- 'Revisiting Publics: A Critical Archaeology of Publics in the Thai HIV/AIDS Issue' (Chay-Nemeth 2001)
- 'Exploring the Construct of Organization as Source: Consumers' Understandings of Organizational Sponsorship of Advocacy Advertising' (Haley 1996)
- 'Brands in Films: Young Moviegoers' Experiences and Interpretations' (DeLorme and Reid 1999)
- 'State Propaganda and Bureaucratic Intelligence: the Creation of Public Relations in 20th Century Britain' (L'Etang 1998)

---

researcher, the date of the dissertation, and the name of the educational institution where you are enrolled. There is generally a pro forma for the title page at most universities. Professional reports carry similar information on the title page.

Abstract

The abstract is a summary of the research and is written after the study has been completed. It appears on the page following the title but before the table of contents and the full report. Abstracts are important because, on the basis of these, readers often make a decision about whether or not to read the full report or article. In many cases, readers may discover your report by accessing a library abstract catalogue or online database of abstracts. Therefore, it is essential to use the abstract as a means of conveying as much information, as interestingly as possible, as concisely as possible.

Helpful hint

In your abstract, tell people what you did, why you did it, how you did it, what you found out, and why it's important.

The abstract should contain a brief overview of the following:

- the research question and aim.
- why the topic is important and worth studying.
- the methods you have adopted.
- the main findings of your study.
- the implications in the light of other research.

If you have space, you might also wish to emphasize the significance of the contribution made by your study. The abstract should contain between 150 and 300 words, usually no more than one sheet of A4 paper in single spacing and is usually written in the past tense, although not always, as Example 17.5 shows.

Example 17.5 An abstract

This is an abstract for a research article by Gillian Hogg, Sara Carter and Anne Dunne. The title of the paper is *Investing in People: Internal Marketing and Corporate Culture*. The abstract is 169 words long. In a student dissertation it could be a little longer and might also include the implications of the study in one or two succinct sentences.

The purpose of this paper is to explore the role of internal marketing in influencing corporate culture. The need for organizations to focus on human resources towards developing a marketing orientation is well recognized. The tactics for achieving this objective, however, have yet to be proven. This paper reports on the use of the Investors In People (IIP) initiative as a framework for internal marketing in changing the prevailing culture of an organization. Within this initiative enlightened employers must communicate the business aims, values and performance of their organizations, in order to encourage employees to participate actively in the success of the business. Using the example of a medium sized, family owned company operating in a declining market sector, this research reports the results of a longitudinal study designed to elicit employee attitudes towards, and understanding of, change in the organization. The results suggest that although there is a broad understanding amongst employees of the corporate objectives of the organization, there is resistance to the credibility of cultural change.

(1998: 877)

In a professional report, there is an *executive summary* rather than an abstract. The executive summary is usually one or two pages long, and provides an overview of the report, with the emphasis on the findings and implications. Key issues are often highlighted through the use of bullet points.

Acknowledgement and dedication

You might wish to give credit to those who supported, advised or supervised your research, or acknowledge the input of participants in the study. If you decide to dedicate the report itself to particular individuals such as family or friends, keep the dedication simple.

Table of contents

A table of contents acts as a guide to readers and also indicates the overall structure of your report. It is positioned before your first chapter and lists the chapters against their associated page numbers. Many studies (especially professional reports) choose to number not only chapters, but also subsections of chapters, e.g.

Chapter 5:   Findings and Discussion
5.1   Implementation of the Intranet
                 5.1.1 Just Another Technology
                 5.1.2 Replacing Other Communication Channels
5.2   Usage of the Intranet
                 5.2.1 Obstacles to Communication
                 5.2.2 Functions of Communication

Tables of contents include separate lists of figures or illustrations and tables contained in the report. In undergraduate student projects, the table of contents should be concise and need not be too long and detailed.

Introduction

The purpose of the introductory chapter is to orientate your readers and therefore this first chapter should explain what the study is all about. Do this by covering the following:

- the aim of the research.
- the research question or problem.
- the background or rationale for the research.
- the boundaries of the research.
- the importance and contribution of the study.

The above elements do not necessarily have to be written in this order; nor do they have to be written as separate sections. For instance, you may wish to integrate some of them. When you come to provide the background to your research, remember to justify why you have chosen this topic by explaining how you became interested in the research question. In an academic report, it is likely that you will indicate here how the project relates to scholarship (perhaps the topic has not been covered extensively or it has been neglected?). However, you might decide to point instead to an industry context in order to indicate the gap in knowledge that will be filled by your study. Edwards and Talbot suggest that if you are able to answer the following questions in your introduction, then you will have provided a good enough rationale or justification for your study: 'Why this (rather than another topic), why now, why there, why me?' (1994: 41).

In setting out the boundaries of your research, you are indicating the scope of your study. Is it an industry level study, or a multiple case study of a variety of settings, or a single case study of one organization, or a detailed examination of a communications process, for example? The scope of the study indicates to readers how far you will be able to make generalizations from your evidence. On the whole, research into a single organization, for example, would mean that your findings would apply only to that one organization and could not be transferred more widely (although it is possible to suggest 'tendencies' or to generalise to a theory – see Chapter 6).

Literature review

In Chapter 3 we discussed reviewing the literature and developing an argument that flows through your study. When you come to write up the report, the literature review either stands on its own as a separate chapter, or it becomes an integral part of the introduction. The literature in qualitative studies has a different place and purpose from that in quantitative research where an extensive review of all studies in the field is used to develop hypotheses that are tested through primary research. In qualitative research, however, an examination of the relevant literature is made in order, first, to identify gaps in knowledge that the study aims to fill, second, to inform the process of collecting and analysing the primary research, and third, to evaluate the implications of the study. By the end of the section, the reader should be in no doubt that your study is appropriate for meeting the research aim.

Of course, in all qualitative studies, you need to show some of the relevant research that has been done in the field. This involves summarizing the main methods and findings from previous research, and critically evaluating them. You also indicate how they relate to the project in hand. However, in qualitative studies, because some of the literature is integrated into the findings, only the most pertinent work needs be discussed in the literature review section.

Methodology and research design

The purpose of the methodology chapter or section is to tell your readers how you gathered your data, what you ended up with and how you analysed them (Silverman 2000). Silverman's idea of renaming the methodology chapter 'the natural history of my research' is a good one because this is more suggestive of a personal story which threads its way through the successes and false starts, the trials and the errors of your research progress.

In almost all cases, your discussion of the methodology is separate from your literature review and the presentation of your findings. However, if the primary aim of your study is to develop a particular approach (e.g. discourse analysis) or to compare and contrast the use of several different methods, then your whole thesis is devoted to methodological matters and a separate methodology chapter may be redundant. However, this is unlikely to be the case in most undergraduate or masters dissertations.

If you choose to write in the passive voice and do little to explain the issues that arose and the decisions that you made, then the methodology chapter can be the dullest section of the whole report. On the other hand, it can, and should be, one of the most lively sections because it is here that you introduce your personal involvement in the research, explaining:

- how you went about your research.
- what overall strategy you adopted and why.
- the design and techniques you used.
- why you chose these and not others.

(Silverman 2000)

Through the rest of the chapter, we provide extracts in the Example boxes of methodology discussions. We offer these not because we wish to promote them as lively, stimulating examples of writing (unfortunately some of them are not), but because they clearly illustrate some of the points we wish to make. For a fascinating, original and informative research report, which includes a lively documentation of the research process, we would point you instead to Hackley's (2000) account of work life in a London advertising agency, as introduced in Example 17.1.

In your methodology chapter, you are likely to include several subsections: the research design and methodology, the setting, the methods, including data collection, sampling, detailed data collection procedures, and a description of the data analysis. As a qualitative researcher, you are the main research tool and have to make explicit the path of the research so that the reader is able to follow your decision trail. In some cases it may be appropriate to write a section about yourself and your background if this is pertinent to the study, such as how your former work experiences allowed you to gain access to sensitive areas, or provided you with specialist insights. Therefore, write yourself into your methodology.

Methodology description and justification

It is usual to begin your methodology chapter with a description and justification of your chosen methodology, explaining the fit between the research question and the methodology.

The sample and the setting

Describe your sample, state how many participants were chosen and the reasons for your choice. Sometimes it is useful to provide a table indicating the relevance of your respondents' characteristics (such as their role and type of company). Your sampling strategies, whether they are theoretical or purposive, should be explained (see Chapter 11 on sampling).

If you are conducting case study research, you would usually begin by

---

Example 17.6 Explaining the methodological approach

An extract from an article by Ahmad Jamal and Malcolm Chapman illustrates how you might begin to explain your methodology:

> The study upon which this paper is based is an ethnographic study of acculturation of consumption experiences of an immigrant and a host community in Bradford in West Yorkshire, England. The major objective of the study was to investigate the relationship between the two communities, as lived and perceived by the two communities themselves. Our study was based on interpretive (Anderson 1986, 1989; Geertz 1973; Hirschman 1989; Spiggle 1994) and ethnographic (Atkinson 1990; Boyle 1994; Evans-Pritchard 1951; Malinowski 1922) approaches to the study of consumption. In keeping with the holistic ethos of ethnography, we studied many aspects of life . . .
>
> (2000: 372–3)

---

describing the setting (or settings) where your research took place before going on to discuss your sampling strategies. If your setting is a company, it is useful to provide a short history or some background information, also setting out details that are relevant to your study such as the number of people involved in the company, type of communications strategy, roles of employees involved in corporate communications, and so on. Jamal and Chapman (2000) provided details about the three suburbs of Bradford where they conducted their fieldwork and, in describing the ethnic background of people and businesses in Bradford, justified why they had chosen this city for their research (see Example 17.6).

Readers of your research report will be interested to hear how you gained access in order to undertake your investigation. Your access may be based on your work experiences in a particular setting which enabled you to gain entry for research. On the other hand, you might have experienced real difficulties in negotiating access to your targeted organization or informants that readers

---

Example 17.7 Explaining how the research setting was accessed

Gerard McCusker undertook research in Radio Scotland in order to study the role of sound in communicating organizational identity. He described his entry to the organization as follows:

> Gaining access to key informants followed a uniform pattern; an initial telephone call determined relevant potential informants, to whom a letter was subsequently faxed outlining the nature of the proposed research. A credentials-confirming letter, requesting a date and time at which to conduct and intention to tape record interviews, was mailed.
>
> (1997: 363–4)

would be interested to read about. State how participants were approached (in person, by email, or through an advertisement, for instance). Explain how you received permission from 'gatekeepers'. Note, however, that individuals should not be identified if you have guaranteed anonymity to them. The article by Buchanan, Boddy and McCalman (1988) is helpful in supporting your writing at this point.

Data collection procedures

In this section are the details of your data collection procedures such as interviewing, observation or other strategies you have used, together with any problems you encountered. This should not be an essay on general procedures but a step-by-step description of the work you carried out.

Example 17.8 Explaining data collection procedures

In a report on consumers' experiences of alcohol advertisements, Betty Parker described her interviewing procedures (see also Examples 10.2 and 10.3):

> The interviewing process lasted from 3.5 to 5.5 hours and was carried out in four phases over a two-week period. During phase 1 the informants responded to a series of questions taken from the work of Mick and Politi (1989) [*Author provides list of questions*]. After a break, each informant returned to the interviewing room for phase 2 of the research, the life story interview, which probed the informant's background, family history, interests, epiphanic life events and drinking behaviour. A questionnaire adapted from previous research (Csikszentmihalyi and Beattie 1979; McCracken 1988) was used to gather demographic and family background data and to uncover subjects' life themes and drinking behaviour. [. . .] The order of phases 1 and 2 was occasionally reversed to test for differences in either the quality or quantity of responses, but no differences were found.
>
> (1998: 101, 103)

Data analysis

You methods of analysing the data are explained here, including the way in which data were coded and categorized and how you generated your themes or theoretical constructs from the data. This section encompasses an explanation of analysis by computer, if relevant. In dissertations, a more detailed account of the analysis, with examples, is required.

If the above were a dissertation, more detail and examples of each step should have been given.

Example 17.9 Outlining the process of data analysis

Focus group research into moviegoers' experiences of brands in films by Denise De Lorme and Leonard Reid was analysed as follows:

> The analysis process involved listening to each audiotaped group discussion three times, transcribing each discussion verbatim, reviewing notes taken during the sessions, and talking with the research assistants about group dynamics. The investigation explored a range of concepts (e.g. conceptualization, knowledge, attitudes about brand placement), but first-person stories of everyday experiences seemed to be the richest, most meaningful information. Hence, a second analysis was conducted to search specifically for accounts of participants' everyday experiences. The transcripts were examined closely line by line to identify and code participant experiences. Comparisons and contrasts then were made between incidents in the experiences data. Last, the transcripts were reread carefully three more times and the remarks noted in context to verify the coding and analysis process.
>
> (1999: 74)

Ethics

At this point, ethical issues should be raised as they relate to your overall research design and also to specific instances (see Chapter 5).

Findings and discussion

In Chapter 3 we discussed how to develop an argument and a theoretical storyline which weaves its way through your writing. In the findings and discussion chapter, where the analysis of the data is presented, the theoretical storyline is now contextualized and extended with the addition of a field-based storyline. Golden-Biddle and Locke (1997) indicate how this works:

> Consisting of a field-based story nested within the structure of the theoretical story, the central purpose of the development is to take readers 'there' – to transport them into the field – and to bridge the worlds of the field and the readers. We take readers into the field by conveying the vitality of everyday life encountered in the field; we bridge the worlds of the [participants], authors, and readers by connecting the field life to our theoretical points. To transport the readers into the field, [reports] need to portray the researchers' firsthand experience with the [participants'] world.
>
> (pp. 50–1)

Note how Golden-Biddle and Locke draw attention to how the field-based storyline (or the way in which you present the story of your data) sits within a macro story, that is, the overarching theoretical framework that you develop through a review of the literature and from your fieldwork.

Although the writing of Golden-Biddle and Locke is oriented towards research in organizations, it is equally relevant to qualitative studies in public relations and marketing communications. Their ideas are useful for indicating how to incorporate data into your reports in a manner that shows everyday life and experiences in an authentic way, while also providing evidence for theoretical points. The data, they suggest, never stand on their own. No matter how 'detailed and accurate' the observations and quotations that you insert into your discussion, you should never leave the interpretation or implications to readers to work out for themselves. Instead, in conveying your data, you should look in two directions, backward to the research situation – to the points of view of consumers you have interviewed, for example – and forward to the theoretical points that you have identified in the literature and which you continue to develop from the data.

> **Helpful hint**
> Develop a storyline by telling, showing and telling.

There are different ways of developing a storyline, but a common form is by telling, showing and telling:

- *telling*: here you make a theoretical point. This might be a subheading which indicates what the subsequent paragraphs are about (such as 'conflict and communication') or it might be a discussion of an issue, such as the following: 'Conflict between team members was most apparent during rehearsals for client presentations. An account director's description of how some members disrupted preparations included the following . . .'
- *showing:* illustrate the point with a quotation or with an extract from fieldnotes, as appropriate. Use your data to bring your theoretical point to life.
- *telling:* now answer this question: 'What does this mean in the light of (a) my theoretical point, (b) my research aim, (c) wider theory?' Here you are explaining the data by shifting back to the theory. In some cases, you will respond only to (a) and (b). In other cases, as your discussion develops, you will go further and respond also to (c), building the discussion into a more general consideration of theory, that is, you endeavour to generalize.

By telling, showing and then telling again, you shift back and forth between theory and your data, using the data to contextualize the theory and also developing it at the same time. Your theoretical storyline and your fieldwork storyline become interwoven and grow together.

Direct quotations from interviews or excerpts from fieldnotes contextualize the theory, making the study more lively and dynamic. The content of the quotations also helps the reader to judge how the results were derived from the data, establish the credibility of the emerging categories and establish a means of auditing these. Avoid large chunks, continuous duplication or many short quotations which end up fragmenting your writing. 'Save the best and drop the rest' suggests Wolcott (1990: 67) and in this way your writing will be readable, interesting and compelling.

> **Helpful hint**
> Use quotations prudently (this applies also to quotations from the literature). Ensure they are not taken out of context but accurately reflect the meanings and feelings of participants. Only use those that make a significant point.

Structuring the findings and discussion chapter

There are several ways of presenting qualitative findings and your interpretation of them. The first is the traditional format where you separate your results from your discussion of them. Your discussion chapter or section is where you also introduce the appropriate literature. One follows the other. Applying this style, you would be unlikely to follow Golden-Biddle and Locke's advice; instead you would be 'showing' in one chapter and 'telling' in the next. More commonly in qualitative research, the findings and discussion are integrated for the sake of the storyline (but no rigid rule exists about this). At the start of a combined findings and discussion chapter, some writers present a brief summary of the results in a diagram, and then discuss each major theme in a few sentences before going on to discuss them more comprehensively, integrating the literature into the discussion where it fits best. In this way, the literature is allowed to serve as additional evidence for the particular category or as a problem for debate.

Keep in mind that you are telling a story which should be vivid and interesting as well as credible to your readers. The story also has an additional purpose, namely, to present a systematic analysis of the data and a discussion of the results.

Reflections on the research

At the end of your analysis (either in the discussion or conclusion sections), you might reflect on your project and take a critical stance to it. You can then demonstrate how the research could be improved or extended. You might point to its limitations and to your own bias which you might not have yet made explicit in your study. Although your methodology section will have described some of the problems which you encountered, it is appropriate here to provide a critical overview and suggest if there are other ways that your research could be carried out if it were to be done again. Not all studies contain this reflective section although this personal approach is seen as appropriate in qualitative research (Wolcott 1994).

Conclusion

Essential elements in the conclusion are:

- a review of what has been learnt.
- the implications of the study for theory or practice.
- the contribution of the study to knowledge.
- recommendations for future research.

In addition, the following are sometimes found in public relations and marketing communications reports:

- a critical reflection on the limitations of the study (we discussed this in the previous paragraph).
- recommendations to industry or organizations.

The conclusion reviews what has been learnt in relation to the aim and the theoretical ideas and propositions that emerged from the study. It must be directly related to the results of the specific study, and no new elements (or references) should be introduced here. The implications refer to how understanding of public relations or marketing communications has changed in the light of your study. In some cases, this is integrated into the section where you discuss the contribution your study makes to knowledge in the area. For example, your study might have challenged accepted thinking on a particular topic, or you may have pointed to a new technique that could be used in practice.

Areas for future research are suggestions that you are able to make to further your study. These may be ways of building on your study (say, by using different methods or sampling in a wider context) or they may be new directions that have been revealed through your findings. It is important to remember that the implications must be based directly on the results of the study.

Example 17.10 Making suggestions for future research

Denise DeLorme and Leonard Reid's findings of moviegoers' experiences of brands in films (in Example 17.8) suggest new areas for research such as the following:

> In addition to audience studies, research – be it qualitative or quantitative – is needed to examine other aspects of the practice of brand placement. One obvious research area should focus on groups involved with the production and placement of brand props – marketers, filmmakers, and advertising agencies in the United States and abroad.

(1999: 87)

References

A list of references includes all the texts you have cited in your report. Academic books and articles, professional texts, newspapers or videos, and online sources should all be included in the same list. A bibliography includes all of the above but also other texts which you may not have specifically referred to in your report but which you have drawn on for your study. It is usual to provide either a list of references or a bibliography but not both.

For academic studies the Harvard system of referencing is generally used (as in this book), although other formal systems of referencing are acceptable to outside agencies. It is best to find out about this before the start of the study. Compare the references in the text with the selected bibliography at the end of the report and make sure that every reference is included accurately. If you have made reference to one author who cites another, ensure that you have provided both references in full in your bibliography or reference list. For example, say you wrote the following in your text: 'Mann and Stewart (2000) refer to the work of Picardie (1998).' Now turn to the bibliography at the end of this book to find out how to reference both of these articles. Check out also the referencing sections in Chapters 3 and 4.

Appendices (plural of appendix)

Any material contained in your appendix is supplementary to your research. For clarification and interest, however, it is useful, to include some or all of the following:

- a list of participants (with pseudonyms if necessary) with their ages, experience or length of service if relevant – unless readers of the report are likely to be able to identify participants, in which case you should leave out the list.
- a list of organizations (perhaps with pseudonyms) involved in your research.
- an interview guide.
- a sample interview transcript in a study that uses interviewing. This helps readers to understand how your data collection developed.
- some fieldnotes from observations might be given to demonstrate their use.

Attach appendices in the order in which they appear in the chronology of the study. The words in appendices do not count as part of the study. Usually, appendices are placed at the very end of the report after the bibliography. However, custom and practice differ slightly in some institutions and therefore you should check the regulations of your own institution to find out whether you are required to insert them before or after the bibliography.

Summary

- The report tells readers what you did, why you did it, how you did it, what you found out, what it means, and why it's important.
- Two storylines flow through the report: the theoretical storyline and the field-based storyline. The field-based storyline brings theory to life and develops it.
- A useful way to discuss the data is by 'telling, showing, telling': make a theoretical point, illustrate it with the data, explain the data in the light of theory.
- The conclusion reviews what you have learnt, and considers the implications of the study and its contribution to knowledge.
- It is important to reflect critically on your study, considering how it might be improved or extended through further research.

18 Final thoughts

This chapter deals with some of the personal issues that are likely to confront you over the course of doing qualitative research. It provides:

- tips and techniques for working efficiently and staying motivated.
- the thoughts of former research students as they reflect on their experiences.

Introduction

If you have read this far, it is probable that you have already made a start on your research. No matter how enthusiastic you are when you start out, there are times when you start to flag or feel stressed out about the overwhelming amount of evidence that needs to be sifted and sorted. In some cases, you will feel that you are making little progress. Your study-time will feel disorganized and, despite your best efforts, you seem to be going nowhere. You might even start to doubt your own ability to deal with the intellectual discipline of carrying out and completing a research project. These feelings are quite natural. Most researchers experience them at some stage or another. The trick is to find coping strategies to minimize the frustrations and maximize the challenge, fulfilment and excitement that doing qualitative research is all about. The first half of this chapter sets out some of the techniques that have worked for us.

Staying motivated

- *Choose a topic that interests you.* It is essential to find a topic that fascinates you and which will sustain your interest over a long period. Undertaking research is often lonely, especially at PhD level where you may be working for many years in isolation. Even at undergraduate level, a dissertation can take up to nine months to complete. This is a long time if you have become bored with the area of investigation. Make sure, then, that your topic choice is an appropriate one for you. Turn back to Chapter 2 for more on this.
- *Plan the course of your research.* The course of research is never straightforward. Getting hold of books through inter-library loans takes time, interviewees cancel appointments, and analysis is achieved only slowly.

However, it is important to make a timetable of your *expected* progress because this provides a basis for your activities, even if you have to amend it along the way. It also means that you can tick off the various stages as you go along and chart your progress. Looking back over a whole series of ticks certainly helps to kick-start the momentum when it's flagging.

Make sure you talk through your plan with your supervisor who will be able to advise you on its feasibility. Ensure that you do not put the majority of your efforts into collecting the data and reading the literature because, although you analyse as you go along, the final interpretation and writing up *always* take much longer than expected. Build in plenty of time for this.

- *Get enough rest and relaxation and aim for a healthy lifestyle.* One of the reasons why stress and boredom set in is because you are too close to your work and too tired. Perhaps you've been studying every day without a break. Take some time off, go for a walk, meet friends for a coffee, get an early night! By setting your work aside for a day or so, you often return to it with much more creative energy.

- *Make a schedule for your day.* At some stage, the problem may not be that you are working too hard but that you cannot get round to starting at all. It's easy to waste a morning sleeping in or having a long lunch with friends. Try to schedule each day so that you work productively and in accordance with your own body rhythm. Some people work best in the morning, others late at night. Find out what's right for you and then concentrate your study periods into those times.

  Working in spurts of three-quarters of an hour is often helpful. Stop for a drink, spend five or ten minutes walking around a bit, then start back again for another three-quarters of an hour. In that way, the day doesn't seem to stretch endlessly ahead but can be dealt with in manageable chunks.

- *Talk to others about your research.* Even if you feel your progress is slow and there is little to discuss, continue to meet with your supervisor – don't go and hide in a hole! The mere act of talking through your ideas, or lack of them, with a supportive supervisor often triggers new thoughts because your supervisor will ask questions that bring a broader perspective to your work. Meet with friends, family and other research colleagues too. Discussions with those outside your field can lead to a fresh perspective on your work.

- *Start writing early and keep on writing.* Get into the habit of putting your thoughts down onto paper or the computer screen every day. We cannot stress highly enough the importance of starting to write as soon as you begin your project. One of the problems that cripples researchers is that they become overwhelmed by the volume of data they have collected. If you are able to write about it as you collect it, your analysis proceeds in a manageable way and your ideas and reflections develop coherently. This is good practice for your report writing skills too.

- *Remind yourself of the progress you've made already.* When things seem overwhelming, remind yourself how far you have travelled on your intellectual journey. Think back to when you first began the project and consider what you know now that you didn't then. You will surprise yourself at the knowledge you have gained and the skills you have acquired.

- *Take one step at a time.* Carrying out a research project is a daunting task. Think about it as a series of stages and consider them one at a time, only looking as far ahead as you need to. Before you realize it, the stages are behind you and you've successfully reached the end. Now congratulate yourself and book that holiday!

Student reflections on doing research

We end this book with the voices of former students as they offer their thoughts on doing qualitative research.

Sarah Woodhouse (British)
I wish I had done some more background reading before starting the final year. I wish I had had better computer skills so the whole formatting and amending process was easier. I wish I had believed in myself that I could do it. I really thought I was going to fail!

Kristin Goa (Norwegian. See also Example 5.8)
I think it worked out quite well because together with my supervisor we focused on one stage at a time. I made progress slowly – but at the same time I could see that I *was* making progress. This meant that the thesis didn't seem like a great big mountain that I couldn't see over. The high point was that I got to introduce the thesis to the case study company after-wards – and they showed interest and satisfaction. And then I got to publish an article about it as well. For me, it was important that I wasn't doing research just for my own curiosity but that I could also relate it to industry and to my job.

Saori Asakawa (Japanese)
If I was to do it differently, I think the research design would be more or less the same. But what I would change is the timing. I should have allowed more time to analyse the data and draw conclusions from it. It took more time than I thought and I'm not satisfied with my discussion chapter at all. But I got tired after working under all the dissertation pressure and I didn't take a rest and that made me more and more tired. Therefore, if I did it again I would make sure I left more time for the last two or three chapters. And I'd take a rest!

Deliah Cavalli (German)
My dissertation went pretty smoothly. I wrote one chapter after the other, met all the deadlines and never changed track completely as far as I can remember. However, some passing comments developed into major arguments and some initial major points developed into passing comments.

Rather than changing track along the way, I think I *lost* track sometimes and discussed some minor arguments over several pages which I then had to cut out completely afterwards. One of the highs of doing the research was the interaction with so many different people. That was personally enriching.

Joana Machado (Portuguese. See also Examples 1.1 and 8.2)
Until this day my feelings about the whole process remain very contra-dictory. It was very exciting, very interesting and I really enjoyed being able to dedicate all my time and effort to one piece of work. I had never before stretched my brain like I did during that time. The intellectual and personal challenge is enormous and that is good but painful too. And at the end, I don't know exactly what I have achieved, what does my dissertation mean? I feel the research could go on and on. It is never complete, which is extremely frustrating.

Glossary

Abstract   A synopsis or summary of the research which appears at the beginning of the research report stating the aim, nature and scope of the study and its findings and contributions.

Aide mémoire (*or* aide memoir)   Key words or questions on a sheet of paper which are used in in-depth interviews and which prompt the researcher.

Appendix (appendices)   Additional material at the end of the report. It is not included in the word limit.

Assumption   A belief or assertion which is taken for granted.

Audit trail (*or* decision trail)   A detailed explanation of the thought and action processes of the researcher to help the reader understand the logic and development of the research path.

Authenticity   A term which indicates that the research strategies used are appropriate for the 'true' reporting of participants' ideas, when the study is fair, and when it helps participants and similar groups to understand their world and improve it.

Bias   A distortion or error in the data collection or analysis which has its origin in strongly held values and orientations of the researcher.

Bracketing (in phenomenology)   When researchers hold their assumptions and presuppositions in abeyance in order to view the world as their participants do.

Case study   A case study is an intensive examination, using multiple sources of evidence (which may be qualitative, quantitative or both), of a single entity which is bounded by time and place.

Category   A group of concepts and ideas which have similar characteristics.

Code   A name or label given to specific data.

Coding (used in analysis)   Examining and breaking down the data and labelling particular expressions.

Concept   An abstract or generalized idea that describes a phenomenon.

Confidentiality   When researchers do not disclose issues or ideas which participants wish to keep off the record.

Confirmability   The data are linked to their sources so that a reader can establish that the conclusions and interpretations arise directly from them.

Constant comparison (in grounded theory)   Qualitative data analysis where each datum is compared with every other piece of the data.

Construct   A construct encompasses a number of concepts or categories and has a high level of abstraction. The term is often used for a major category which has evolved from the reduction of a number of smaller categories.

Contextualization   Researchers relate and locate the data to their context.

Core category (in grounded theory)   A concept which links with all other categories in the project and integrates the data.

Credibility   A study has credibility if the people in it recognize the truth of the findings in their own social context.

Criterion (pl. criteria)   A standard by which something is evaluated.

Critical incident technique   A data collection and analysis technique focusing on critical situations, events and incidents in the research setting.

Data (pl.)   The information collected through research.

Data analysis   The process of bringing order, structure and meaning to a mass of unstructured data. It involves reducing, interpreting and writing about the data.

Deduction   The procedure of testing a general principle or theoretical assumption in order to explain specific phenomena or cases.

Dependability   If the findings of the study are to be dependable, they must be consistent and accurate.

Description   An account of significant phenomena in their setting as seen by participants in the study.

Design   The overall framework for a research study which includes the research approach and the strategies for data collection, analysis and writing of the report.

Dross rate   The information gained from research participants that is irrelevant for the outcome of a particular study.

Emic perspective   The 'insider's' point of view (an anthropological term).

Epistemology   The theory of knowledge concerned with the ways in which we know the world. In research, it is the discipline of knowing what does and does not constitute knowledge. In qualitative research, this is usually associated with interpretivism.

Ethnography   Both a research methodology and the product of that research. It is concerned with a description of a culture or group and the members' experiences and interpretations.

Etic perspective   The 'outsider's' view. The perspective of the researcher.

Exhaustive description   Writing which aims to capture and describe the intensity and depth of the participants' experience (in phenomenology).

External validity   See generalizability.

Fieldnotes   A record of the observations of researchers 'in the field' who have collected data through interviews or observation.

Fieldwork (initially a term from anthropology)   Fieldwork is the collection of data 'in the field' in natural settings.

Focus group   A group of people – often with common experiences or characteristics – who are interviewed by a researcher for the purpose of eliciting ideas, thoughts and perceptions about a specific topic or certain issues linked to an area of interest.

Funnelling   When interviewing starts with a broad basis and becomes progressively more specific during the interview process.

Gatekeepers   Those individuals who have the power to permit or deny access to an organization, a setting or people in the setting.

Generalizability   The extent to which the findings of the study can be applied to other events, settings or populations. In qualitative research, generalizability usually relates to theory-based generalization.

Grounded theory   A research method which generates theory from the data through constant comparison.

Idiographic methods   These focus on the unique and individual rather than seeking generalizability. They differ from nomothetic methods which search for law-like generalities subsuming individual cases.

Induction   A reasoning process in which researchers proceed from the specific and concrete statements to general and abstract principles.

Informant (in qualitative research)   A person who takes part in a research study.

Informed consent   A voluntary agreement made by participants after having been appraised of the nature and aim of the study.

Interview guide   Loosely formed questions which are used flexibly by the interviewer in qualitative in-depth interviews. This differs from a structured interview schedule used in quantitative research (and often applied inappropriately in qualitative research).

Interviewer effect (*see also* observer effect)   The effect the presence of the interviewer has on the research.

Iteration   Continuous movement between parts of the research text and the whole, between raw data and analysed data.

Key informant   A representative of the group under study who has been in the culture long enough to have expert knowledge about its rules, customs and language.

Limitations   Weaknesses in the research.

Member check   The data and interpretations are checked and verified by the informants themselves.

Memoing   Writing memos or notes of varying degrees of abstraction when carrying out fieldwork.

Method   Strategy, technique and procedure for collecting, analysing and interpreting data.

Methodology   A framework of concepts, theories and strategies on which the research is based.

Narrative   The description or story of experiences and events.

Objectivity   A neutral and unbiased stance.

Observer effect   The effect the presence of the observer has on the setting and situation, and therefore on the research.

Ontology   A branch of philosophy concerning the nature of existence. In research, it relates to assumptions about the nature of reality, whether it is real or illusory. In qualitative research, this is usually associated with social constructivism, or subjectivism.

Paradigm   The worldview which is held by a community of scholars. It consists of shared beliefs, values and techniques.

Phenomenology   Both a philosophy and a research approach based on that philosophy which explores the meaning of individuals' lived experience through their own description.

Pilot study   A small-scale trial run of a research interview or observation.

Population   The totality (or total number) of sampling units from which the sample is chosen.

Positivism   A direction in the philosophy of social science which aims to find general laws and regularities based on observations and experiments which parallel the methods of the natural sciences.

Progressive focusing   See funnelling.

Proposition   A working hypothesis or informed hunch which, in speculating about the relationship between concepts, establishes some regularities.

Pseudonym   Fictitious names given to informants to protect their anonymity.

Purposive (or purposeful) sample   A judgemental sample of individuals chosen by certain pre-determined criteria relevant to the research question (sometimes called criterion-based sample).

Reactivity   Participants react to the presence of the researcher. The researcher also reacts to the responses of the participants.

Realism   An epistemological stance that assumes that reality is an objective, observable entity which is independent of those observing it.

Reflexivity   Reflecting on and critically examining the research process by considering the researcher's subjectivity and experiences brought to the research, and then using these reflections to interact with the rest of the research process.

Reliability   The ability of a research tool to achieve consistent results. In qualitative research, this relates to the thoroughness with which researchers have recorded their decision making regarding the data, methods and analysis.

Research question   The problem, puzzle or statement that guides a study and establishes the baseline for other questions.

Saturation   Sampling until no new categories emerge and the elements of all categories are accounted for.

Serendipity   A chance and unexpected discovery during data collection which is useful for the research.

Social constructivism (*or* social constructionism)   An ontological stance which is often linked with interpretivism. It asserts that reality is that which is perceived, taken for granted and continually accomplished by those who hold a shared history and shared meanings.

Storyline   An analytic description and overview of the story.

Subjectivity   A personal view influenced by personal background and traits. This differs from objectivity which is a neutral and distant stance.

Symbolic interactionism   An interpretive approach in sociology which focuses on meaning in interaction.

Tacit knowledge   Implicit knowledge that is shared but not openly articulated.

Theoretical sampling (in grounded theory)   Sampling which proceeds on the basis of emerging, relevant concepts and is guided by developing theory.

Theoretical sensitivity (concept developed by Glaser)   Sensitivity and awareness by the researcher to detect meaning in the data.

Theory   A set of interrelated concepts and propositions which explain social phenomena. Theory is a supposition which explains or seeks to explain something.

Thick description (concept developed by Geertz)   Dense, detailed and conceptual description which gives a picture of events and actions within the social context.

Transferability   The specific knowledge gained from the research findings of one study can be transferred to other settings.

Triangulation   The combination of different methods of research, data collection approaches, investigators or theoretical perspectives in the study of one phenomenon (e.g. qualitative and quantitative methods, interviews and observation).

Trustworthiness   The research is methodologically sound. The criteria for evaluating it are credibility, transferability, dependability and confirmability.

Validity   The extent to which the researcher's findings are accurate, reflect the purpose of the study and represent reality (validity in qualitative research differs from that in quantitative research).

Verification   Empirical validation after testing a hypothesis. In qualitative research: testing a proposition or a working hypothesis.

Working hypothesis   See proposition.

Bibliography

Adler, P.A. and Adler, P. (1994) 'Observational Techniques', in N.K. Denzin and Y.S. Lincoln (eds) *Handbook of Qualitative Research*. Thousand Oaks, CA: Sage, pp. 377–92.

Aldoory, L. (1998) 'The Language of Leadership for Female Public Relations Professionals'. *Journal of Public Relations Research*, 10(2), 73–101.

Alvesson, M. (1994) 'Talking in Organizations: Managing Identity and Impressions in an Advertising Agency'. *Organization Studies*, 15(4), 535–63.

Alvesson, M. and Sköldberg, K. (2000) *Reflexive Methodology: New Vistas for Qualitative Research*. London: Sage.

Angrosino, M.V. and Mays de Perez, K.A. (2000) 'Rethinking Observation. From Method to Context', in N.K. Denzin and Y.S. Lincoln (eds) *Handbook of Qualitative Research*. 2nd edn. Thousand Oaks, CA: Sage, pp. 673–702.

Arnould, E. (1998) 'Daring Consumer-Oriented Ethnography', in B.B. Stern (ed.) *Representing Consumers. Voices, Views and Visions*. London: Routledge, pp. 85–126.

Atkinson, J.M. (1984) *Our Masters' Voices: The Language and Body Language of Politics*. London: Methuen.

Atkinson, P. (1992) *Understanding Ethnographic Texts*. Newbury Park, CA: Sage.

Atkinson, P. and Silverman, D. (1997) 'Kundera's Immortality: The Interview Society and the Invention of the Self'. *Qualitative Inquiry*, 3(3), 304–25.

Barritt, L. (1986) 'Human Sciences and the Human Image'. *Phenomenology and Pedagogy*, 4(3), 14–22.

Becker, C.S. (1992) *Living and Relating. An Introduction to Phenomenology*. London: Sage.

Berger, J. and Pratt, C.B. (1998) 'Teaching Business-Communication Ethics with Controversial Films'. *Journal of Business Ethics*, 17, 1817–23.

Biernacki, P. and Waldorf, D. (1981) 'Snowball Sampling: Problems and Techniques of Chain Referral Sampling'. *Sociological Methods and Research*, 10(2), 141–16.

Billig, M. (1992) *Talking of the Royal Family*. London: Routledge.

Bingham, W.V.D. and Moore, B.V. (1959) *How to Interview*, 4th edn. New York: Harper and Row.

Blaxter, L., Hughes, C. and Tight, M. (1996) *How to Research*. Buckingham: Open University Press.

Boas, F. (1928) *Anthropology and Modern Life*. New York: Norton.

British Psychological Society (2000) *Code of Conduct, Ethical Principles and Guidelines*. Leicester: British Psychological Society. Accessed at http://www.bps.org.uk/about/rules5.cfm

Brown, A.D. and Jones, M. (2000) 'Honourable Members and Dishonourable Deeds: Sensemaking, Impression Management and Legitimation in the "Arms to Iraq Affair" '. *Human Relations*, 53(5), 655–89.

Bryman, A. (1989) *Research Methods and Organization Studies.* London: Unwin Hyman.

Bryman, A. (2001) *Social Research Methods.* Oxford: Oxford University Press.

Buchanan, D., Boddy, D. and McCalman, J. (1988) 'Getting In, Getting On, Getting Out, and Getting Back', in A. Bryman (ed.) *Doing Research in Organizations.* London: Routledge, pp. 53–68.

Buston, K. (1997) 'NUD*IST in Action: Its Usefulness in a Study of Chronic Illness in Young People'. *Sociological Research Online* 2, 3. Accessed at http://www. socresonline.org.uk/socresonline/2/3/6.html (5 March 2001).

Button, W.J. and Roberts, G. (1997) 'Communication, Clinical Directorates, and the Corporate NHS'. *Journal of Public Relations Research*, 9(2), 141–62.

Carey, M.A. and Smith, M.W. (1994) 'Capturing the Group Effect in Focus Groups'. *Qualitative Health Research,* 4(1), 123–7.

Cassell, C. and Symon, G. (1994) 'Qualitative Research in Work Contexts', in C. Cassell and G. Symon (eds) *Qualitative Methods in Organisational Research: A Practical Guide.* London: Sage, pp. 1–14.

Chay-Nemeth, C. (2001) 'Revisiting Publics: A Critical Archaeology of Publics in the Thai HIV/AIDS Issue'. *Journal of Public Relations Research*, 13(2), 127–61.

Chell, E. (1998) 'Critical Incident Technique', in G. Symon and C. Cassell (eds) *Qualitative Methods and Analysis in Organisational Research. A Practice Guide.* London: Sage, pp. 51–72.

Chen, V. and Pearce, W.B. (1995) 'Even If a Thing of Beauty, Can a Case Study Be a Joy Forever? A Social Constructionist Approach to Theory and Research', in W. Leeds-Hurwitz (ed.) *Social Approaches to Communication.* New York: The Guilford Press, pp. 135–54.

Cieurzo, C. and Keitel, M.A. (1999) 'Ethics in Qualitative Research', in M. Kopala and L. Suzuki (eds) *Using Qualitative Methods in Psychology.* Thousand Oaks, CA: Sage, pp. 63–76.

Colaizzi, P.F. (1978) 'Psychological Research as the Phenomenologist Views It', in R. Vallé and M. King (eds) *Existential Phenomenological Alternatives for Psychology.* New York: Oxford University Press.

Cooper, H.R., Holway, A. and Arsan, M. (1998) 'Cross-cultural Research – Should Stimuli be Psychologically Pure or Culturally Relevant?' *Marketing and Research Today*, February, 1–72.

Corbin, J. and Strauss, A.L. (1990) 'Grounded Theory Research: Procedures, Canons and Evaluative Criteria'. *Qualitative Sociology*, 13(1), 3–21.

Crane, A. (1998) 'Exploring Green Alliances'. *Journal of Marketing Management*, 14, 559–79.

Crème, P. and Lea, M.R. (1997) *Writing at University: A Guide for Students.* Buckingham: Open University Press.

Creswell, J.W. (1998) *Qualitative Inquiry: Choosing among Five Traditions.* Thousand Oaks, CA: Sage.

Cryer, P. (1996) *The Research Student's Guide to Success.* Buckingham: Open University Press.

Dall'Olmo Riley, P. and de Chernatony, L. (2000) 'The Service Brand as Relationships Builder'. *British Journal of Management*, 11(2), 137–50.

Davis, J.J. (1997) *Advertising Research: Theory and Practice.* Upper Saddle River, NJ: Simon and Schuster.

Daymon, C. (2000) 'Cultivating Creativity in Public Relations Consultancies: The Management and Organisation of Creative Work'. *Journal of Communication Management*, 5(1), 17–30.

Daymon, C. (2002) 'Making Money, Making Meaning: The Role of Communication in the Construction of a Television Station Culture', in A. Schorr, W. Campbell and M. Schenk (eds) *Communication Research in Europe and Abroad: Challenges of the First Decade.* Berlin: De Gruyter, in press.

De Chernatony, L. and Dall'Olmo Riley, F. (1998) 'Defining a "Brand": Beyond the Literature with Experts' Interpretations'. *Journal of Marketing Management,* 14(5), 417–44.

De Chernatony, L., Dall'Olmo Riley, F. and Harris, F. (1998) 'Criteria to Assess Brand Success'. *Journal of Marketing Management,* 14, 765–81.

De Pelsmacker, P. and Geuens, M. (1996). 'The Communication Effects of Warmth, Eroticism and Humour in Alcohol Advertisements'. *Journal of Marketing Communications*, 2(4), 247–62.

De Pelsmacker, P. and Geuens, M. (1998) 'Reactions to Different Types of Ads in Belgium and Poland'. *International Marketing Review*, 15(4), 277–90.

Deacon, D., Pickering, M., Golding, P. and Murdock, G. (1999) *Researching Communications: A Practical Guide to Methods in Media and Cultural Analysis.* London: Arnold.

DeLorme, D.E. and Reid, L.N. (1999) 'Moviegoers' Experiences and Interpretations of Brands in Films Revisited'. *Journal of Advertising*, XXXVIII(2), 71–95.

DeLorme, D.E., Reid, L.N. and Zimmer, M.R. (1994) 'Brands in Films: Young Moviegoers' Experiences and Interpretations', in K.W. King (ed.) *Proceedings of the 1994 Conference of the American Academy of Advertising,* Athens, GA: American Academy of Advertising, 60. Cited in D.E. DeLorme and L.N. Reid (1999).

Denzin, N.K. (1989) *The Research Act: A Theoretical Introduction to Sociological Methods.* 3rd edn. Englewood Cliffs, NJ: Prentice-Hall.

Dozier, D.M. (1984) 'Program Evaluation and the Roles of Practitioners'. *Public Relations Review,* 10, 13–21.

Dozier, D.M. (1992) 'The Organizational Roles of Communication and Public Relations Practitioners', in J.E. Grunig (ed.) *Excellence in Public Relations and Communication Management.* Hillsdale: Lawrence Erlbaum, pp. 327–256.

Drumwright, M. (1996) 'Company Advertising with a Social Dimension: The Role of Noneconomic Criteria'. *Journal of Marketing*, 60, 61–87.

Easterby-Smith, M., Thorpe, R. and Lowe, A. (1991) *Management Research.* London: Sage.

Edley, N. and Wetherell, M. (1997) 'Jockeying for Position: The Construction of Masculine Identities'. *Discourse and Society*, 8, 203–17.

Edwards, A. and Talbot, R. (1994) *The Hard-Pressed Researcher.* London: Longman.

Elsbach, K.D. and Sutton, R. (1992) 'Acquiring Organizational Legitimacy Through Illegitimate Actions: A Marriage of Institutional and Impression Management Theories'. *Academy of Management Journal*, 35(4), 699–738.

Emerson, R.M., Fretz, R.I. and Shaw, L.L. (2001) 'Participant Observation and Fieldnotes', in P. Atkinson, A. Coffey, S. Delamont, J. Lofland and L. Lofland (eds) *Handbook of Ethnography.* London: Sage, pp. 352–67.

Erlandson, D.A., Harris, E.L., Skipper, B.L. and Allen, S.D. (1993) *Doing Naturalistic Inquiry.* Newbury Park, CA: Sage.

Evans, M., Nairn, A. and Maltby, A. (2000) 'The Hidden Sex Life of the Male (and Female) Shot'. *International Journal of Advertising*, 19(1), 43–65.

Fairclough, N. (1995) *Critical Discourse Analysis*. New York: Longman.

Fetterman, D.M. (1998) *Ethnography: Step by Step*, 2nd edn. Newbury Park, CA: Sage.

Fielding, N.G. and Lee, R.M. (1998) *Computer Analysis and Qualitative Research*, 2nd edn. Thousand Oaks, CA: Sage.

Fill, C. (1999) *Marketing Communications*, 2nd edn. Hemel Hempstead: Prentice-Hall.

Fine, M. (1998) 'Working the Hyphens: Reinventing Self and Other in Qualitative Research', in N.K. Denzin and Y.S. Lincoln (eds) *The Landscape of Qualitative Research, Theories and Issues*. Thousand Oaks, CA: Sage, pp. 130–55.

Fogg, R. (2001) Personal correspondence, 13 April.

Fombrun, C.J., Gardberg, N.A. and Sever, J.M. (2000) 'The Reputation Quotient: A Multi-Stakeholder Measure of Corporate Reputation'. *The Journal of Brand Management*, 7(4), 241–55.

Forster, N. (1994) 'The Analysis of Company Documentation', in C. Cassell and G. Symon (eds) *Qualitative Methods in Organisational Research*. London: Sage, pp. 147–66.

Gabbott, M. and Hogg, G. (1996) 'Purchasing Public Relations: The Case of the Public Relations Industry in Scotland'. *Journal of Marketing Management*, 12, 437–53.

Gaddis, S.E. (2001) 'On-Line Research Techniques for the Public Relations Practitioner', in R.L. Heath (ed.) *Handbook of Public Relations*. Thousand Oaks, CA: Sage.

Geertz, C. (1973) *The Interpretation of Cultures*. New York: Basic Books.

Geertz, C. (1988) *Works and Lives: The Anthropologist as Author*. Stanford, CA: Stanford University Press.

Gilbert, G.N. and Mulkay, M.J. (1984) *Opening Pandora's Box: A Sociological Analysis of Scientists' Discourse*. Cambridge: Cambridge University Press.

Gilly, M.C. and Wolfinbarger, M. (1998) 'Advertising's Internal Audience'. *Journal of Marketing*, 62(January), 69–88.

Glaser, B. and Strauss, A. (1967) *The Discovery of Grounded Theory*. Chicago, IL: Aldine Press.

Glaser, B.G. (1978) *Theoretical Sensitivity*. Mill Hill, CA: The Sociology Press.

Glaser, B.G. (1992) *Basics of Grounded Theory Analysis*. Mill Valley, CA: Sociology Press.

Goa, K. (1999) *Intranet – Its Usage and Implications for Communication in an Organisation: A Case Study*. Unpublished masters dissertation, Bournemouth University.

Goa, K. (2001) Personal correspondence, 23 March.

Gold, R.L. (1958) 'Roles in Sociological Field Observations'. *Social Forces*, 36, 217–23.

Golden-Biddle, K. and Locke, K. (1997) *Composing Qualitative Research*. Thousand Oaks, CA: Sage.

Goodlad, N., Eadie, D.R., Kinnin, H. and Raymond, M. (1997) 'Advertorial: Creative Solution or Last Resort?' *International Journal of Advertising*, 16, 73–84.

Greenbaum, T.L. (2000) 'Focus Groups vs. Online'. *Advertising Age*, 71(7), 34.

Grunig, J.E. (1989) 'Symmetrical Presuppositions as a Framework for Public Relations Theory', in C.H. Botan and V. Hazleton, Jnr (eds) *Public Relations Theory*. Hillsdale, NJ: Lawrence Erlbaum Associates.

Grunig, J.E. and Hunt, T. (1984) *Managing Public Relations*. New York: Holt, Rinehart and Winston.

Guba, E.G. and Lincoln, Y.S. (1989) *Fourth Generation Evaluation*. New York: Sage.

Guba, E.G. and Lincoln, Y.S. (1998) 'Competing Paradigms in Qualitative Research', in

N.K. Denzin and Y.S. Lincoln (eds) *The Landscape of Qualitative Research: Theories and Issues.* Thousand Oaks, CA: Sage, pp. 195–220.

Gwilliam, J. (1997) 'Baby Boomers – the Same the World Over?' *Admap*, October, 33–6.

Hackley, C. (2000) 'Silent Running: Tacit, Discursive and Psychological Aspects of Management in a Top UK Advertising Agency'. *British Journal of Management*, 11(3), 239–54.

Hakim, C. (1982) *Secondary Analysis in Social Research: A Guide to Data Sources and Methods with Examples.* London: George Allen and Unwin.

Haley, E. (1996) 'Exploring the Construct of Organization as Source: Consumers' Understandings of Organizational Sponsorship of Advocacy Advertising'. *Journal of Advertising,* XXV(2), 20–35.

Hamilton, K. (2000) 'Project Galore: Qualitative Research and Leveraging Scotland's Brand Equity'. *Journal of Advertising Research*, January–April, 107–11.

Hammersley, M. (1997) 'Qualitative Data Archiving: Some Reflections on its Prospects and Problems'. *Sociology*, 31, 131–42.

Hammersley, M. (1998) *Reading Ethnographic Research*, 2nd edn. London: Longman.

Hammersley, M. and Atkinson, P.A. (1995) *Ethnography: Principles in Practice*, 2nd edn. London: Tavistock.

Hart, C. (1998) *Doing a Literature Review.* London: Sage.

Heath, R.L. (ed.) (2000) *Handbook of Public Relations.* Thousand Oaks, CA: Sage.

Heath, R.L. (2000) 'Shifting Foundations. Public Relations as Relationship Building', in R.L. Heath (ed.) *Handbook of Public Relations*, 2nd edn. Thousand Oaks, CA: Sage.

Heckman, J. (2000) 'Turning the Focus Online'. *Marketing News*, 34(5), 15.

Hirschman, E.C. and Thompson, C.J. (1997) 'Why Media Matter: Toward a Richer Understanding of Consumers' Relationships with Advertising and Mass Media'. *Journal of Advertising*, 26 (Spring), 43–60.

Hodder, I. (2000) 'The Interpretation of Documents and Material Culture', in N.K. Denzin and Y.S. Lincoln (eds) *Handbook of Qualitative Research*, 2nd edn. Thousand Oaks, CA: Sage, pp. 703–16.

Hogg, G., Carter, S. and Dunne, A. (1998) 'Investing in People: Internal Marketing and Corporate Culture'. *Journal of Marketing Management*, 14(8), 879–96.

Holloway, I. (1997) *Basic Concepts for Qualitative Research.* Oxford: Blackwell Science.

Holloway, I. and Walker, J. (2000) *Getting a PhD in Health and Social Care.* Oxford: Blackwell Science.

Holstein, J.A. and Gubrium, J.F. (1997) 'Active interviewing', in D. Silverman (ed.) *Qualitative Research: Theory, Method and Practice.* London: Sage, pp. 113–19.

Humphreys, L. (1970) *Tearoom Trade: Impersonal Sex in Public Places.* Chicago, IL: Aldine.

Hycner, R.H. (1985) 'Some Guidelines for the Phenomenological Analysis of Interview Data'. *Human Studies*, 8, 279–303.

ISI ResearchSoft (2000) Personal Bibliographic Software, Berkley: ISI ResearchSoft. Available at: http://www.risinc.com/ (11 Jan 2001).

Jacklin, K. (2001) Personal correspondence, 24 March.

Jamal, A. and Chapman, M. (2000) 'Acculturation and Inter-Ethnic Consumer Perceptions: Can You Feel What We Feel?' *Journal of Marketing Management*, 16(4), 365–92.

Jarratt, D.G. (1996) 'A Comparison of Two Alternative Interviewing Techniques Used Within an Integrated Research Design: A Case Study in Outshopping Using

Semi-structured and Non-Directed Interviewing Techniques'. *Marketing Intelligence and Planning,* 14(6), 6–15.

Johnson, M.A. (1997) 'Public Relations and Technology: Practitioner Perspectives'. *Journal of Public Relations Research,* 9, 213–36.

Kates, S.M. and Shaw-Garlock, G. (1999) 'The Ever Entangling Web: A Study of Ideologies and Discourses in Advertising to Women'. *Journal of Advertising,* XXVIII(2), 33–49.

Kimmel, A.J. (1996) *Ethical Issues in Behavioural Research.* Cambridge, MA: Blackwell.

Kitzinger, J. and Barbour, R.S. (1999) 'Introduction: the Challenge and Promise of Focus Groups', in R.S. Barbour and J. Kitzinger (eds) *Developing Focus Group Research: Politics, Theory and Practice.* London: Sage, pp. 1–20.

Kuzel, A.J. (1999) 'Sampling in Qualitative Inquiry', in B.F. Crabtree and W.L. Miller (eds) *Doing Qualitative Research,* 2nd edn. Thousand Oaks, CA: Sage, pp. 33–45.

Kvale, S. (1996) *InterViews: An Introduction to Qualitative Research Interviewing.* Thousand Oaks, CA: Sage.

LeCompte, M.D. and Preissle, J., with Tesch, R. (1997*) Ethnography and Qualitative Design in Educational Research.* 3rd edn. Chicago, IL.: Academic Press.

LeCompte, M.D. and Schensul, J.J. (1999a) *Designing and Conducting Ethnographic Research.* Walnut Creek, CA: Altamira Press.

LeCompte, M.D. and Schensul, J.J. (1999b) *Analyzing & Interpreting Ethnographic Data.* Walnut Creek, CA: Altamira Press.

Lee, R. (1993) *Doing Research on Sensitive Topics.* London: Sage.

L'Etang, J. (1998) 'State Propaganda and Bureaucratic Intelligence: The Creation of Public Relations in 20th Century Britain'. *Public Relations Review,* 24, 413–41.

Lincoln, Y.S. and Guba, E.G. (1985) *Naturalistic Inquiry.* Beverly Hills, CA: Sage.

Lindlof, T.R. (1995) *Qualitative Communication Research Methods.* Thousand Oaks, CA: Sage.

Locke, K. (2001). *Grounded Theory in Management Research.* London: Sage.

Locke, L.F., Spirduso, W.W. and Silverman, S.J. (2000) *Proposals That Work: A Guide for Planning Dissertations and Grant Proposals,* 4th edn. Thousand Oaks, CA: Sage.

Lofland, J. (1971) *Analyzing Social Settings.* Belmont, CA: Wadsworth.

McAlexander, J.H., Fushimi, K. and Schouten, J.W. (2000) 'A Cross-Cultural Examination of a Subculture of Consumption: Judo in Japan and in the United States', in R.W. Belk, J. Costa and J. Schouten (eds) *Research in Consumer Behavior.* Stamford, CO: JAI Press, Vol. 9, pp. 47–69.

McCusker, G. (1997) 'The Audio Logo: A Case Study of Radio Scotland's On-air Identity'. *Journal of Communication Management,* 1(4), 362–73.

McDaniel, C. Jnr and Gates, R. (1995) *Marketing Research Essentials.* St Paul, MN: West Publishing.

Macdonald, K. and Tipton, C. (1993) 'Using Documents', in N. Gilbert (ed.) *Researching Social Life.* London: Sage, pp. 187–200.

Machado, J. (2000) *Multiple Identity Traits and Multiple Identifications in a Geographically Dispersed Organisation: A Case Study Investigation of the British Council.* Unpublished masters dissertation in corporate communication. Bournemouth University.

Malinowski, B. (1922) *Argonauts of the Western Pacific: An Account of Native Enterprise and Adventure in the Archipelagoes of Melanesian New Guinea.* New York: Dutton.

Mann, C. and Stewart, F. (2000) *Internet Communication and Qualitative Research: A Handbook for Researching Online.* London: Sage.

Marshall, C. and Rossman, G.B. (1995) *Designing Qualitative Research*, 2nd edn. Thousand Oaks, CA: Sage.

Marshall C. and Rossman G.B. (1999) *Designing Qualitative Research*, 3rd edn. Thousand Oaks, CA: Sage.

Maxwell, J.A. (1996) *Qualitative Research Design: An Interactive Approach.* Thousand Oaks, CA: Sage.

Mead, M. (1935) *Sex and Temperament in Three Primitive Societies.* New York: Morrow.

Meenaghan, T. (1991) 'The Role of Sponsorship in the Marketing Communications Mix'. *International Journal of Advertising*, 10(1), 35–47.

Merton, R.K. and Kendall, P.L. (1946) 'The Focused Interview'. *American Journal of Sociology,* 51, 541–57.

Merton, R.K. and King, R. (1990) *The Focused Interview: A Manual of Problems and Procedures,* 2nd edn. New York: Free Press.

Miglani, R. (1996) 'Diagnostic and Predictive Advertising Pre-Testing'. *Marketing and Research Today*, August, 190–6.

Miles, M.B. and Huberman, A.M. (1994) *Qualitative Data Analysis*, 2nd edn. Thousand Oaks, CA: Sage.

Miller, K.S. (1999) 'Public Relations in Film and Fiction: 1930 to 1995'. *Journal of Public Relations Research,* 11(1), 3–28.

Mintsberg, H. (1973) *The Nature of Managerial Work.* New York: Harper and Row.

Moller, P. and Alsted, C. (1996) 'A Pioneer Media Survey – Based on Qualitative Research and New Consumer'. *Marketing and Research Today*, 107–15.

Moloney, K. (1996) *Lobbyists for Hire.* Aldershot: Dartmouth.

Morgan, D.L. (1997) *Focus Groups as Qualitative Research.* Thousand Oaks, CA: Sage.

Morgan, D.L. (1998) *The Focus Group Guidebook.* Vol. 1 of D.L. Morgan and R.A. Krueger (eds) *The Focus Group Kit.* Thousand Oaks, CA: Sage.

Morse, J.M. (1994) 'Designing Funded Qualitative Research', in Denzin, N.K. and Lincoln, Y.S. (eds) *Handbook of Qualitative Research.* Thousand Oaks, CA: Sage, pp. 220–35.

Motion, J. (2000) 'Personal Public Relations: The Interdisciplinary Pitfalls and Innovative Possibilities of Identity Work'. *Journal of Communication Management*, 5(1), 31–40.

Motion, J. and Leitch, S. (1996) 'A Discursive Perspective from New Zealand: Another World View'. *Public Relations Review*, 22(3), 297–309.

Motion, J. and Leitch, S. (2001) 'New Zealand Perspectives on Public Relations', in R.L. Heath (ed.) *Handbook of Public Relations.* Thousand Oaks, CA: Sage, pp. 659–64.

Mulvaney, T. (2000) *UKOLUG Quick Guide to Personal Bibliographic Software.* London: UKOLUG.

Muylle, S. (2001) Personal correspondence, 5 January.

Muylle, S., Moenaert, R. and Despontin, M. (1999) 'A Grounded Theory of World Wide Web Search Behaviour'. *Journal of Marketing Communications*, 5, 143–55.

Newland Hill, L. and White, C. (2000) 'Public Relations Practitioners' Perception of the World Wide Web as a Communications Tool'. *Public Relations Review,* 26(1), 31–51.

Parker, B.J. (1998) 'Exploring Life Themes and Myths in Alcohol Advertisements through a Meaning-Based Model of Advertising Experiences'. *Journal of Advertising*, XXVII(1), 97–112.

Partington, D. (2000) 'Building Grounded Theories of Management Action'. *British Journal of Management*, 11(2), 91–102.

Patton, M. (1990) *Qualitative Evaluation and Research Methods*. Newbury Park, CA: Sage.

Pawle, J. (1999) 'Mining the International Consumer'. *Journal of the Market Research Society*, 41(1), 19–31.

Peracchio, L.A. and Luna, D. (1998) 'The Development of an Advertising Campaign to Discourage Smoking Initiation among Children and Youth'. *Journal of Advertising*, XXVII(3), 49–56.

Pettigrew, A.M. (1997) 'What is Processual Analysis'. *Scandinavian Journal of Management*, 13, 337–48.

Philipsen, G. (1989) 'An Ethnographic Approach to Communication Studies', in B. Dervin, L. Grossberg, B.J. O'Keefe and E. Wartella (eds) *Rethinking Communication. Vol. 2. Paradigm Exemplars*. Newbury Park, CA: Sage.

Phillips, E.M. and Pugh, D.S. (2000) *How to Get a PhD*, 3rd edn. Buckingham: Open University Press.

Picardie, R. (1998) *Before I Say Goodbye*. London: Penguin, cited in C. Mann and F. Stewart (2000) *Internet Communication and Qualitative Research: A Handbook for Researching Online*. London: Sage.

Pike, K. (1967) *Language in Relation to a Unified Theory of the Structure of Human Behavior*, 2nd rev. edn. The Hague: Mouton.

Polkinghorne, D.E. (1989) 'Phenomenological Research Methods', in R.S. Vallé and S. Halling (eds) *Existential–phenomenological Perspectives in Psychology*. New York: Plenum, pp. 41–60.

Potter, J. and Wetherell, M. (1987) *Discourse and Social Psychology: Beyond Attitudes and Behaviour*. London: Sage.

Potter, J. and Wetherell, M. (1994) 'Analysing Discourse', in A. Bryman and R.G. Burgess (eds) *Analyzing Qualitative Data*. London: Routledge.

Punch, K.F. (2000) *Developing Effective Research Proposals*. London: Sage.

Reed, M. (1998) 'Organisational Analysis as Discourse Analysis: A Critique', in G. Grant, T. Keenoy and C. Oswick (eds) *Discourse and Organisation*. London: Sage, pp. 193–213.

Regester, M. and Larkin, J. (1997) 'Issue and Crisis Management: Fail-Safe Procedures', in P. Kitchen (ed.) *Public Relations: Principles and Practice*. London: International Thomson Business Press, pp. 212–22.

Richardson, K. and Corner, J. (1986) 'Reading Reception: Mediation and Transparency in Viewers' Accounts of a TV Programme'. *Media, Culture and Society*, 8(4), 485–512.

Riessman, C.K. (1993) *Narrative Analysis*. Newbury Park, CA: Sage.

Ritson, M. and Elliott, R. (1999) 'The Social Uses of Advertising: An Ethnographic Study of Adolescent Advertising Audiences'. *Journal of Consumer Research*, 26, 260–77.

Rudestam, K.E. and Newton, R.R. (2001) *Surviving Your Dissertation: A Comprehensive Guide to Content and Process*, 2nd edn. Thousand Oaks, CA: Sage.

Sarantakos, S. (1998) *Social Research*. Basingstoke: The Macmillan Press.

Schatzman, L. and Strauss, A. (1973) *Field Research*. Englewood Cliff, NJ: Prentice Hall.

SCOLARI (2001) *Scolari*. London: Sage. Available at: http://www.scolari.co.uk/ (5 March 2001).

Seale, C. (1998) *Researching Society and Culture.* London: Sage.

Seale, C. (1999) *The Quality of Qualitative Research.* London: Sage.

Seidman, I.E. (1998) *Interviewing as Qualitative Research,* 2nd edn. New York: Teachers College, Columbia University.

Serini, S.A., Toth, E.L., Wright, D.K. and Emig, A. (1998) 'Power, Gender, and Public Relations: Sexual Harassment as a Threat to the Practice'. *Journal of Public Relations Research,* 10(3), 193–218.

Shaffir, W. and Stebbin, R.A. (1991) *Experiencing Fieldwork: An Inside View of Qualitative Research.* Newbury Park, CA: Sage.

Sharp, J. and Howard, K. (1996) *The Management of a Student Research Project,* 2nd edn. Buckingham: Open University Press.

Sieber, J.E. (1992) *Planning Ethically Responsible Research.* Newbury Park, CA: Sage.

Silverman, D. (2000) *Doing Qualitative Research: A Practical Handbook.* London: Sage.

Silverman, D. (2001) *Interpreting Qualitative Data,* 2nd edn. London: Sage.

Spradley, J.P. (1979) *The Ethnographic Interview.* Fort Worth, TX: Harcourt Brace/Janovich College Publishers.

Spradley, J.P. (1980) *Participant Observation.* Fort Worth, TX: Harcourt Brace/Janovich College Publishers.

Sriramesh, K. (1996) 'Power Distance and Public Relations: An Ethnographic Study of Southern Indian Organizations', in H.M. Culbertson and N. Chen (eds) *International Public Relations: A Comparative Analysis.* Mahwah, NJ: Lawrence Erlbaum, pp. 171–90.

Stake, R. (1995) *The Art of Case Study Research.* Thousand Oaks, CA: Sage.

Stewart, D.W. and Shamdasani, P.N. (1990) *Focus Groups: Theory and Practice.* Newbury Park, CA: Sage.

Stewart, R. (1968) 'Diary Keeping as a Training Tool for Managers'. *The Journal of Management Studies,* 5, 295–303.

Strauss, A.L. (1987) *Qualitative Analysis for Social Scientists.* New York: Cambridge University Press.

Strauss, A.L. and Corbin, J.M. (1990) *Basics of Qualitative Research: Grounded Theory Procedures and Techniques.* Beverly Hills, CA: Sage.

Strauss, A.L. and Corbin, J.M. (1998) *Basics of Qualitative Research: Techniques and Procedures for Developing Grounded Theory.* Beverly Hills, CA: Sage.

Stuart, H. and Kerr, G. (1999) 'Marketing Communication and Corporate Identity: Are They Integrated?' *Journal of Marketing Communications,* 5, 169–79.

Symon, G. (1998) 'Qualitative Research Diaries', in G. Symon and C. Cassell (eds) *Qualitative Methods and Analysis in Organisational Research: A Practical Guide.* London: Sage, pp. 94–118.

Talmage, P. (1998) 'Isn't It Time We Stopped Treating Our Customers Like Numbers?' *Admap,* March, 16–18.

Taylor, M. (2000) 'Toward a Public Relations Approach to Nation Building'. *Journal of Public Relations Research,* 12(2), 179–210.

Tesch, R. (1991) 'Software for Qualitative Researchers: Analysis Needs and Program Capabilities', in N.G. Fielding and R.M. Lee (eds) *Using Computers in Qualitative Research.* Thousand Oaks, CA: Sage.

Thomas, A.O. (1998) 'Transnational Satellite Television and Advertising in South East Asia'. *Journal of Marketing Communications,* 4, 221–36.

Thomas, J. (1993) *Doing Critical Ethnography.* Newbury Park, CA: Sage.

Thwaites, D., Aguilar-Manjarrez, R. and Kidd, C. (1998) 'Sports Sponsorship Development in Leading Canadian Companies: Issues and Trends'. *International Journal of Advertising,* 17, 29–49.

Ting-Toomey, S. (1999) *Communicating Across Cultures.* New York: Guilford Press.

Turner, B.A. (1994) 'Patterns of Crisis Behaviour: A Qualitative Inquiry', in A. Bryman and R.G. Burgess (eds) *Analysing Qualitative Data.* London: Routledge.

Underwood, R.L. and Ozanne, J.L. (1998) 'Is Your Package an Effective Communicator? A Normative Framework for Increasing the Communicative Competence of Packaging'. *Journal of Marketing Communications,* 4, 207–20.

van Dijk, T.A. (1997) 'The Study of Discourse', in T.A. van Dijk (ed.) *Discourse as Structure and Process,* Vol. 1. London: Sage.

Van Maanen, J. (1988) *Tales of the Field: On Writing Ethnography.* Chicago, IL: University of Chicago Press.

Van Ruler, B. (1997) *Communication: Magical Mystery or Scientific Concept? Professional Views of Public Relations Practitioners in the Netherlands,* pp. 247–63.

Wade, N. (1999) 'The Impact of Digital Television: Will it Change Our Shopping Habits?' *Journal of Marketing Communications,* 5, 71–84.

Ward, K.J. (1999) 'Cyber-ethnography and the Emergence of the Virtually New Community'. *Journal of Information Technology,* 14, 95–105.

Weitzman, E.A. (2000) 'Software and Qualitative Research', in N.K. Denzin and Y.S. Lincoln (eds.) *Handbook of Qualitative Research,* 2nd edn. Thousand Oaks, CA: Sage.

Whitney, M.A. (1994) 'Analyzing Corporate Communications Policy Using Ethnographic Methods', in M. Goodman (ed.) *Corporate Communications.* Albany, NY: State University of New York Press.

Will, V., Eadie, D. and MacAskill, S. (1996) 'Projective and Enabling Techniques Explored'. *Marketing Intelligence and Planning,* 14(6), 38–43.

Wolcott, H.F. (1990) *Writing up Qualitative Research.* Newbury Park, CA: Sage.

Wolcott, H.F. (1994) *Transforming Qualitative Data: Description, Analysis, and Interpretation.* Thousand Oaks, CA: Sage.

Wooffitt, R. (1993) 'Analysing Accounts', in N. Gilbert (ed.) *Researching Social Life.* London: Sage, pp. 287–305.

Yin, R. (1994) *Case Study Research: Design and Methods,* 2nd edn. Newbury Park, CA: Sage.

Inquiries about ProQuest may be made to: Bell & Howell Information and Learning Company, 300 North Zeeb Road, Ann Arbor, MI 48106–1346, USA. Telephone. 734–761–4700. Email: info@bellhowell.infolearning.com. Web page: www.bellhowell.infolearning.com

Index